The Role of the Cyprus Attorney General's Office in Prosecutions: Rhetoric, Ideology and Practice

Despina Kyprianou

The Role of the Cyprus Attorney General's Office in Prosecutions: Rhetoric, Ideology and Practice

Springer

Dr Despina Kyprianou
Cyprus
dkyprianou@law.gov.cy
kyprianoud@yahoo.com

ISBN 978-3-642-01920-3 e-ISBN 978-3-642-01921-0
DOI 10.1007/978-3-642-01921-0
Springer Heidelberg Dordrecht London New York

Library of Congress Control Number: 2009928620

Cover design: WMXDesign GmbH, Heidelberg, Germany

Printed on acid-free paper

Springer is part of Springer Science+Business Media (www.springer.com)

To my family

Foreword

Attorney General, Republic of Cyprus

It is with great pleasure that I foreword the book of Dr Despina Kyprianou's for many reasons: The first one is that books on any area of Cyprus Law is particularly welcomed as there are limited studies which focus on this field and reveal the singularities and special features of Cyprus Law. The second one is that this book is about the Attorney General's Office, an office that I have served for almost thirty-five years and have personal knowledge of its crucial role not only regarding prosecutions but also regarding a wide variety of other legal issues. The third and most important reason is that this is an excellent work and a thought-provoking contribution to our understanding of the Role of the Cyprus Attorney General's Office in Prosecutions. The last reason that I am very happy to commend this study is the fact that, a few years ago, I was the one that granted access to the Law Office for Dr Kyprianou's research. The publication of this highly informative book is the best confirmation that I was right in doing so.

The Republic of Cyprus was established as an independent sovereign republic with a presidential regime on 16 August 1960, when its Constitution came into force and British sovereignty over Cyprus as a Crown Colony ceased. The post of the Attorney General, which existed throughout British rule, was retained by the Constitution and has been recognised as one of the great offices of the State. The Attorney General, as well as the Deputy Attorney General who serves on the same terms, is appointed by the President of the Republic from among persons who are qualified for appointment as Judges of the Supreme Court. He holds office under the same terms and conditions as a Judge of the Supreme Court and is not removed from office except on the like grounds and in the like manner as such Judge of the Supreme Court. He is the Head of the Law Office of the Republic, which is an independent office and is not under any Ministry.

Among the other roles that the Attorney General is entrusted with, the Constitution recognises him as the head of the prosecution system with '*power exercisable at his discretion in the public interest, to institute, conduct, take over, and continue or discontinue any criminal proceedings for an offence against any person in the Republic*' (Article 113.2 of the Constitution). It is true that the prosecutorial power and the discretion that is afforded to the Attorney General is wide and it is also correct, as Dr Kyprianou remarks, that as far as prosecutions are concerned, the Attorney General's role in the process appears broader and more multifarious than that of his counterpart in England and Wales. However, the constitutional position of the Attorney General and his independent status, unlike the political nature of the equivalent post in England and Wales and other Common Law Jurisdictions, as well as the terms of his appointment, constitute important safeguards for the right execution of his powers.

Dr Kyprianou's book, inter alia, makes a significant contribution to the discussion of this argument, since it provides a comprehensive account of the legal framework regarding the role of the Attorney General's Office in prosecutions, while highlighting the singularities of its status. Furthermore, based on unique and original data, it describes the developing functions and powers of the Office through time and the way these powers are executed in practice. The book places particular emphasis upon the workload of the Law Office and its relationship with the police, the role it acquires during investigations and its role in the formulation and application of prosecution policies and principles. Dr Kyprianou organises and analyses her data with skill, drawing conclusions which I am certain that they will be of interest not just to scholars, but to all lawyers and practitioners in the field. These are the reasons that I commend this book wholeheartedly.

February 2009

Mr Petros Clerides
Attorney General of the Republic

Foreword

Reader, Law School, University of Warwick

I first became aware of Despina Kyprianou's research on the prosecutorial function of the Attorney General of Cyprus, when invited to examine her thesis on this subject which had been presented to the University of London for the degree of PhD. I opened the thesis with some interest, since, like many English lawyers, I knew something of Cyprus's recent troubled history but little about its legal system. The research, based on an extensive ethnographic observation within the Attorney General's Office and detailed interview with former incumbents of that office, provides a fascinating insight into the operation of small legal system emerging from colonial roots and developing its own distinctive character.

The study will be consulted within Cyprus by lawyers and others wishing to understand the prosecution process and will no doubt be the first point of reference of future Attorney Generals. However, its impact will not be restricted to that jurisdiction. The work embodies a valuable addition to comparative socio-legal studies and will advance understanding of the manner in which historical, political and ideological factors shape the form and functions of prosecution systems.

I am delighted to hear that Dr Kyprianou's work is to be published as a monograph and I am greatly honoured to be associated with it in some modest way.

February 2009

Roger Leng
Reader
Law School
University of Warwick

Preface

In all criminal justice systems there is a public prosecuting authority which, on behalf of the society and in the public interest, is responsible for the prosecution of alleged offenders. As expected, the particular status and the exact functions and powers of these authorities are not identical in all countries, since they are rooted in the legal and political culture of the jurisdictions in which they are found. The Constitution in Cyprus, while recognising the right to private prosecutions, entrusts the Attorney General with the overall responsibility for all prosecutions and with very broad powers in the execution of his functions.

However, the exact parameters of the broad role of the Attorney General have not been specified in detail in respect of a series of issues including (a) the categories of cases that he is closely dealing with (in contrast to the rest of the cases where he only exerts an overall control); (b) the specific powers exercised regarding them (and specifically the extensive role the Attorney General acquires during investigations); (c) the criteria/policies applied and the formulation of policies for other prosecuting agencies.

Therefore, the central objective of this book has been to develop our knowledge and understanding of the role of the Cyprus Attorney General's Office in prosecutions, an undertaking lamentably neglected so far on both the theoretical and the empirical level. On a more general level, though, it is hoped that this study will also shed light on the choices of the Cyprus prosecution system in some of the most debatable issues regarding prosecutions in many jurisdictions. Questions concerning the desirability of prosecutors and police having a more clearly hierarchical constitutional relationship; the giving of direct investigatory functions to prosecutors; the retention by the police of the power to filter cases out of the system without any control from the prosecuting authorities; and the institution responsible for formulating the prosecution policy in the jurisdiction have constituted the most controversial topics of discussion among academics and practitioners and are still included in the reform agenda of various commissions. Cyprus prosecutorial arrangements make up a system which reflects the influence of the English legal model during its early development, but one which has been refined according to local needs and has also incorporated numerous characteristics associated with the inquisitorial rather than the adversarial tradition

This book is mainly based on my PhD thesis, submitted to the University of London (LSE) in December 2006. The completion of this research project needed the support and encouragement of many people and, therefore, there is a long list of people that I owe thanks to. First of all, I would like to thank my doctoral supervisor, Prof Jill Peay, not only for her constant support and valuable guidance but also for her patience and understanding when family emergencies delayed the progress of my research. I would also like to express my thanks and appreciation to Dr Roger Leng, of University of Warwick and Dr Mary Vogel, of University of London (King's College), my doctoral external examiners, for their constructive comments on my thesis and the fascinating discussion we had during my viva voce examination.

I also express my great gratitude to the Commonwealth Scholarship Commission and the British Council who generously funded my research and invested their money in a project mostly related to a foreign jurisdiction. Thanks are also owed to A.G. Leventis Foundation for their financial contribution to additional expenses of the project.

This study would not have been possible without the cooperation of the people I 'researched': Law Officers, and also the administrative staff at the Law Office, as well as police officers and defence lawyers who I interviewed, all have been very kind and helpful throughout the whole project, despite their lack of any previous experience with similar research studies. I am indebted to the serving – at the time of my fieldwork – Attorney General Mr Markides, as well as to the other two post-holders, Mr Triantafyllides and Mr Nikitas, who served office before and after Mr Markides, respectively. Mr Markides gave me permission to carry out research at his office and all of them agreed to be interviewed and share with me their knowledge and great experience. Very special thanks are owed to Mr Clerides, the Deputy Attorney General at the time of my main research, who is the present Attorney General of Cyprus. An empirical study – including observation and interviews - was something totally new not only for the Law Office but also for any branch of the Cyprus criminal justice system. Mr Clerides was the first person that opened the gates of the Law Office for my research, supported this project, and, certainly, made my time at the Law Office much easier.

The help of all my teachers and friends at LSE is greatly appreciated, as well as that of my teachers and friends at the Law School of the University of Thessaloniki and the Institute of Criminology of the University of Cambridge. I certainly owe a special mention, along with my gratitude, to Prof Nicola Lacey and Prof Angelika Pitsela.

In London, Nick Foundoukos, Siew Moh Wong, Olympia Mitaftsi, Jerry Liang, Miguel Castro, Spyros Messomeris, Michalis Foundoukos and Michalis Kritikos, have been valuable friends that supported me all the way. In Cyprus, Xenis Xenophontos, Katie Polycarpou, Maria Marda, Kleio Xatzigianni, Athina Papamichael, Despina Lambrou, Loukia Samata, Polina Efthivoulou, Neophytos Demosthenous and Angelos Kyratzis tolerated my nagging and offered their encouragement when I was desperate!

In turning my thesis into a book, the assistance of Mrs Anke Seyfried of Springer Publications, as well as the helpfulness and support of many new friends and colleagues, is greatly appreciated and the insightful comments of Mr Efstathios Efstathiou are, as always, valued.

Finally, my biggest debt is to all my family and, above all, my parents and my brother. Only they and I know how much they have sacrificed in order for me to realise my dreams. I dedicate this book to them, as a very small compensation for all that this research project took from them: most importantly, my ability to stand constantly by them when they really needed me.

May 2009 Dr Despina Kyprianou

Contents

Abbreviations

AG	Attorney General
CCP	Code of Criminal Procedure
CCPE	Consultative Council of European Prosecutors
CJA 2003	Criminal Justice Act 2003
CJU	Criminal Justice Units
C.L.R.	Cyprus Law Reports
CPS	Crown Prosecution Service
CPT	European Committee for the Prevention of Torture and Inhumane and Degrading Treatment or Punishment
CSS	Chief State Solicitor
DPP	Director of Public Prosecutions
ECHR	European Convention on Human Rights
EU	European Union
LAPS	"Lawyers at Police Stations" scheme
LO	Law Officer
PACE 1984	Police and Criminal Evidence Act 1984
PICA	Public Interest Case Assessment
PPD	Police Prosecution Department
PPS	Public Prosecution Service
PSNI	Police Service of Northern Ireland
RCCJ	Royal Commission on Criminal Justice
RCCP	Royal Commission on Criminal Procedure
RSCC	Reports of the Supreme Constitutional Court

List of Cases

Aeroporos v. The Police (1987) 2 C.L.R. 232
Attorney General v. Andrianou (1995) 1 C.L.R. 486
Attorney General v. Christodoulou (1990) 2 C.L.R. 133
Attorney General v. Ioannidi (1993) 2 C.L.R. 377
Attorney General v. KIRIX Publications LTD (CC 17393/63)
Attorney General v. Theodorou (2002) 2 C.L.R. 9
Azinas and Another v. The Police (1981) 2 C.L.R. 133
Bisaillon v. Keable and AG of Quebec (1980) 17 C.R. (3d) 193 (Q.C.A.)
Christodoulou v. The Republic (1967) 3 C.L.R. 691
Demetriades v. The Police (1997) 2 C.L.R. 312
Ex parte Blackburn (1968) 2 Q. B. 118
G. Pattiki and Another v. The Attorney General (2000) 1 C.L.R. 1669
Houris v. The Police (1989) 2 C.L.R. 56
In Re Koumougiouros (1995) 1 C.L.R. 805
In Re Polycarpou (1991) 1 C.L.R. 207
In Re Ttooulias (1984) 1 C.L.R. 885
Isaias v. The Police (1966) 2 C.L.R. 43
Ioannou v. The Police (1998) 2 C.L.R. 495
Kyriakides v. The Republic 1 RSCC 66
Lomjanidje v. The Police (2003) 2 C.L.R. 401
Louca and Another v. The Republic (1984) 2 C.L.R 141
Merthodja v. The Police (1987) 2 C.L.R. 227
Michalis Andrea Psillas v. The Republic (2003) 2 C.L.R. 353
Mouzouris v. Xylophagou Plantations Ltd (1977) 1 C.L.R. 287
Paikkos v. Kontemeniotis (1989) 1 C.L.R. 50
Parpas v. The Republic (1988) 2 C.L.R. 5
Parris v. The Republic (1999) 2 C.L.R. 186
Pitsillos v. The Police (1966) 2 C.L.R. 50
Practice Directions (Divisional Court of the Queen's Bench Division of the High Court of England) (1962) 1 All E R 448
Protopapas v. Gunther, (1974) 10 J.S.C. 981

Chapter 1
Introduction

> '(T)he constitutional powers of the Attorney General ... are due to the need for control, oversight and organisation of the prosecution system by an independent ... public prosecutor who will ensure the objective and fair functioning of the criminal justice system and will protect the public interest'. (Loucaides 1974, p. 44)

In all countries there is a state agency entrusted with the power and the responsibility for all, or a significant part, of criminal prosecutions; especially with the crucial decision as to whether criminal cases should be forwarded to the courts or not. Naturally, these agencies' particular structures, additional functions and powers differ from country to country, for they are rooted in the history and the legal culture of the jurisdictions in which they are found.[1] Nevertheless, the pivotal position that public prosecution services occupy in the criminal justice system is equally emphasised and appraised in every jurisdiction.

In Cyprus, the Constitution, although preserving the right to private prosecution, entrusts the Attorney General with a central role and wide powers as far as prosecutions are concerned. The Attorney General's Office (AG's Office), introduced in Cyprus for the first time during British rule, was retained by the Constitution after Cyprus gained independence (1960) and was granted an independent rather than a political status. In addition to functioning as the Legal Service of the Government, the AG's Office is also vested with the ultimate responsibility for, and control of, all prosecutions, and its role in this area appears far broader and more multifarious than that of its counterpart in England and Wales has ever been.

This research seeks to explore the role of the Attorney General's Office in prosecutions. The history of prosecutions in Cyprus after 1960 is characterised by the affirmation on any given opportunity of the supremacy of the Attorney General over the rest of the actors involved in prosecutions. However, this has never been combined with a detailed and thorough appraisal of the AG's exact role

[1] See Tak (2004a).

D. Kyprianou, *The Role of the Cyprus Attorney General's Office in Prosecutions: Rhetoric, Ideology and Practice*,
DOI 10.1007/978-3-642-01921-0_1, © Springer-Verlag Berlin Heidelberg 2010

in the process. Over the years, a number of important elements crucial to an understanding of the Law Office's[2] constitutional position, its workload and the functions that it is called upon to fulfil have been left out of discussions on the prosecutorial role of the Office.

This dearth of knowledge about the Law Office is not only confined to information about its workings in practice, but it firstly applies to matters of theory and rhetoric concerning its role within the prosecution system. This is partly attributable to the fact that legal provisions in this area have remained limited and vague, allowing the holders of the Office wide discretion. The way that this discretion has been interpreted by successive Attorney Generals also remains unexplored, as do the practices that have been developed concerning the role of the Law Office in prosecutions. The Law Office has managed to retain a certain mystique as far as the execution of its functions is concerned. Consequently, very little is known about the role that the AG is *supposed* to, is *expected* to and *actually* does play in the prosecution system.

This book is an exploratory study which attempts to shed light on the rhetoric, the ideology and the practice concerning the role of the Cyprus Attorney General's Office in prosecutions and aims to enhance understanding of its functions. More specifically, it has three main objectives:

Firstly, to give a comprehensive account of the legal framework regarding the role of the Attorney General's Office in prosecutions and to explore the *rhetoric* that has been developed over time in this area, as well as to reveal some contradictions and varying interpretations within this rhetoric. It is widely accepted that the "law in the books" or the official rhetoric about a certain area does not utterly correspond to the "law in action", but since the former "constrains, enables, and channels" (Johnson 2002, p. 13) the actual reality – even if this is done through the context of many other factors – it still merits careful scrutiny. Given the very broad legal provisions and the great discretion that is afforded to the Attorney General to specify his powers, it is also essential to examine historically how the successive office-holders themselves have interpreted their role.

Secondly, to uncover the *ideology* that characterises the Law Officers' approach to their role. As Lacey (1994, p. 7) advocates, a full picture about criminal justice agencies cannot be gained merely by learning their legal status: "To get a real sense of how their discretionary powers are exercised, we also need to know a great deal about the cultural context in which these agents are operating, and about how they themselves see their task". It is, therefore, important to gain an appreciation of the Law Officers' own understanding and attitudes towards their functions which, presumably, also infuse and influence their practices.

[2]The Attorney General's Office, as will be explained in Chap. 3, functions both as the Legal Service of the Government as well as the Office of Public Prosecutions. Therefore, "Law Office" is another name used for the Attorney General's Office, and "Law Officers" is the term used for the Counsel working at the Law Office.

Thirdly, to explore the *practices* developed in the Law Office when discharging its prosecutorial functions. This will provide a first insight into the actual day-to-day activity of the Office regarding prosecutions.[3]

The book is based on empirical data gathered during a five-month fieldwork period at the AG's Office which involved observation, semi-structured interviews with Law Officers and examination of criminal files. The findings are supplemented by the results of an examination of the internal circulars, press releases and documents of the successive Attorney Generals who have served since the establishment of the Cyprus Republic; and by interviews carried out with three of those office-holders.[4] The findings of this research are set out and discussed in the following chapters.

Before proceeding to the situation in Cyprus, in **Chap. 2** a comparative description of prosecution services in a number of other jurisdictions – including some of those traditionally associated with the common law tradition, as well as some associated with the continental one – will be attempted. The distinct choices and paths that different legal systems have followed will be explored. Emphasis will be given to the *organisation* of prosecution authorities and their *constitutional position* especially in relation to the other agencies involved in prosecutions, their *role in investigations*, and the way different prosecution systems approach the issues of *prosecutorial discretion*, diversion from prosecution and the formulation of prosecution criteria and policies.

The next chapter, **Chap. 3**, will serve as an introduction to Cyprus law and its prosecution system. It will commence with a brief *historical background* of the legal system in Cyprus, followed by an outline of the *criminal justice process* and an explanation of the Cyprus *pre-trial procedure*. This is useful in gaining an understanding of the origins and the general characteristics of Cyprus law and criminal process that, arguably, partly explain some of the choices adopted regarding prosecutions. Finally, the chapter will conclude with a study of the *evolution* and the *legal framework* of the prosecution system. This is essential in order to understand the inter-relationships of the various agencies that maintain an involvement in prosecutions and the extensive powers and key role of the AG's Office.

Chapters 4, 5 and 6 will present the results of my empirical study on the role of the AG's Office in prosecutions and the way in which the AG's broad and vague powers are interpreted and translated in practice. In **Chap. 4**, the *workload of the AG's Office*, and the various functions which it is called to fulfil regarding different categories of cases, will be explored. In the light of his overall control of prosecutions, and also the coexisting power of the police (as well as other agencies) to

[3]For the term "practice", the definition given by Lacey (1994, p. 31) is preferred "a relatively structured field of action of agents or groups of agents, which can only be understood in terms of the assumptions, values, goals, and interpretive frames which inform the agents' actions and infuse the surrounding context in which those actions take place".

[4]Mr Triantafyllides, Mr Markides and Mr Nikitas. The first Attorney General of the Cyprus Republic, Mr Tornaritis died in 1997 and, unfortunately, it was not possible to carry out an interview with Mrs Stella Soulioti, the second Attorney General of the Republic (1984–1988). See Footnote 39 in Chap. 4.

institute prosecutions, it is interesting to examine which cases the AG is expected to and actually does closely deal with and which others are left to the police to manage. In **Chap. 5** the role that the AG plays during *investigations* will be examined. In accordance with the wide powers that are delegated to him generally as far as prosecutions are concerned, the AG in Cyprus, in contrast to his common law background, is also entrusted with an important role in investigations. In **Chap. 6** his role in the formulation of *prosecution policies* will be described and an examination of the policies/criteria developed in the Law Office will be provided. Each of these three chapters will be divided into three main themes which reflect the objectives of my book: (1) the *rhetoric* that has been developed over time concerning these areas, combined with the manner in which successive AGs have approached their role; (2) the *ideology* developed in the Law Office and, in particular, the approach of the Law Officers towards these particular functions; and (3) the nature of the *practices* observed in the Law Office.

In **Chap. 7** all the findings of my research will be drawn together and further discussed so that the role of the Attorney General's Office in prosecutions can be elucidated and more profoundly understood. Implications for further research and reform proposals will also be considered.

In **Appendix 1** a chapter can be found which describes my research strategy and explain in detail the specific methodological choices I have made for this research. The lack of any prior scientific knowledge or research has dictated the choice of an *exploratory study*, instead of a theory-testing strategy, and a *flexible methodology*. This will be explained in the *first part* of the chapter, followed by an explanation of the necessity of two broad research strategies. In the *second part*, the first research strategy (fieldwork in the AG's Office) will be developed, starting from the description of the process of negotiating access to the AG's Office and followed by an account of the three different techniques of data collection (observation, documentary survey and semi-structured interviews). In the *third part*, the second research strategy, including a documentary analysis of internal circulars, press releases, memoranda, etc., issued by the successive AGs, as well as interviews with the AGs themselves, will be presented, followed by the development of an argument about the reliability and validity of the research and the approach to data analysis (*fourth part*).

The findings of this research are set out and discussed in the following chapters. Derived from data collected by a blend of methods, they are arguably more valid and reliable than they could have been if drawn from one source alone. These data, gathered by "watching, asking and examining" (Miles and Huberman 1994, p. 19), are used to build up a picture of the role of the Attorney General's Office in prosecutions: more particularly, their workload, their powers regarding investigations and their principles and policies on prosecutions. It can be argued that given the strategic position of the Office within the prosecution process, an – indirect and limited –insight into the whole prosecution system can be also achieved.

> 'If we are to make sense of this chaotic picture, we will have to look beyond official criminal justice rhetoric to the reality of criminal justice practice – whilst also recognising the sense in which the rhetoric is a part of the reality'. (Lacey 1994, p. 33)

Chapter 2
Comparative Analysis of Prosecution Systems

> 'Traditionally, European legal systems are described to include at least two cultures: (a) two cultures regarding the *organisation* of the criminal procedure (*adversarial and inquisitorial systems*), (b) two cultures regarding the requirements for deciding whether or not to engage prosecution (principle of *legality* and principle of *opportunity*), (c) two cultures regarding the role of the authorities entrusted with *investigating and prosecuting* alleged offenders. In reality, we can no longer establish such clear-cut distinctions. All our countries are taking from each other what they find suits better their own needs'. (Schwimmer 2000, p. 8) (Emphasis added)

Before focusing on my own research into the role of the Cyprus Attorney General's Office in prosecutions, in this chapter, a comparative description of prosecution systems in a number of other jurisdictions will be attempted, bearing in mind that "it is impossible to understand prosecution in one country or culture without seeing how it differs from prosecution elsewhere" (Johnson 2002, p. 89).

In the *first section*, the origins, constitutional position and organisation of prosecution services in three common law countries (England and Wales, Ireland and Northern Ireland), a mixed jurisdiction (Scotland), as well as a number of inquisitorial jurisdictions (mainly France, Germany and the Netherlands) will be described. The *second section* will deal with the role of the prosecuting authorities in investigations and the *third one* with the way different prosecution systems approach the issues of prosecutorial discretion, diversion from prosecution and the formulation of prosecution criteria and policies. This comparative analysis will not be constrained to a theoretical description of the systems; wherever empirical studies are available they will be cited, so that an insight into matters of practice, as well as principle, can be achieved. However, it has to be noted that, regrettably, empirical research studies in inquisitorial jurisdictions are significantly limited in comparison to the ones available in common law jurisdictions.[1]

This review is necessarily selective, as it is impossible for a single chapter to cover all the issues related to prosecutorial arrangements in a number of countries. The main focus will be on the aforementioned areas, for three reasons: firstly, these

[1] This is a common acknowledgment: see, e.g. Field and West (2003, p. 262), Hodgson (2001, pp. 2–5) and Jehle and Wade (2006).

D. Kyprianou, *The Role of the Cyprus Attorney General's Office in Prosecutions: Rhetoric, Ideology and Practice*,
DOI 10.1007/978-3-642-01921-0_2, © Springer-Verlag Berlin Heidelberg 2010

concern characteristics that distinguish one jurisdiction from another (usually deriving from the common law tradition or the civil law one) and, therefore, illuminate both the different choices adopted by various legal systems and also their implications; secondly, they have represented controversial topics of discussion among academics and practitioners, and at times have been included in the agenda of various Commissions vested with the duty to examine reforms in various jurisdictions; and finally, and most importantly, these very issues emerge from my own research as crucial areas for the understanding of the role of the Cyprus Attorney General's Office in prosecutions.

2.1 Origins, Constitutional Position and Organisation of Prosecution Services

> 'In the history of criminal law the institution of a prosecuting authority is a relatively new feature. It first appeared in the wake of the French revolution after which it, gradually, took up its position as a central institution in the legal systems of continental Europe. It is only in the past few decades that it has become established as a feature of common law systems'. (Jehle 2000, p. 27)

If we consider the development of the prosecution arrangements in various countries, it is evident that many jurisdictions have always been grappling with the question of the position of the prosecution service within the state structure and its relationship with the police. There is a long tradition in civil law systems of public prosecutors taking responsibility for prosecutions in the public interest, which pre-dates the creation of police forces. In the common law tradition, by contrast, as Stenning (1986, p. 17) describes, "the system of criminal prosecutions . . . relied heavily upon the initiative of private individuals, rather than being exclusively controlled by public authorities". In most common law countries the notion of a separate prosecution agency emerged after police forces had already been established, and is not so embedded within the common law culture. During the course of the last century, however, independent prosecution services established themselves and took responsibility for prosecutions.

2.1.1 England and Wales

The history of the prosecutorial arrangements in England and Wales[2] charts a progression from a clearly private activity to a half-hearted introduction of a public prosecution service in the mid 1980s, the Crown Prosecution Service (CPS) and then, after a series of piecemeal reforms, to the more recent changes (Criminal

[2]See Langbein (1973), Hay (1983) and Hetherington (1989) for a comprehensive account of the origins and the history of public prosecutions in common law.

Justice Act 2003) that at least appear to significantly alter the philosophy of public prosecutions in this country. However, as Lewis (2006, p. 179) remarks, "(t)he relative youthfulness of the CPS ... means that it powers are still developing and will continue to develop perhaps for the next 20 years, as they have for the first 20".

Until the nineteenth century, in England and Wales, there was no public official responsible for ensuring that crimes were prosecuted. Emphasis was placed upon the concept of individual responsibility in the administration of criminal justice and, thus, the responsibility for prosecuting the perpetrators of crimes lay predominantly with, and at the discretion of, private individuals. As Sanders (1996, p. xii) remarks, "(v)ictims who wished to prosecute did so by bringing an action which, in legal form, was similar to a civil action".[3] Since the early part of the nineteenth century, as the police developed and their powers increased, they progressively replaced the old system of law enforcement. As a result of evolution rather than of any deliberate decision, the police had become convenient substitutes for private prosecutors. However, no specific prosecution powers or responsibilities were conferred on the police and private prosecutions remained the model on which police prosecutions were based.[4] Sanders (2004, p. 100) points out that "(i)n the absence of specific laws to regulate their prosecutions, the police evolved their own systems. They prosecuted most of their own cases in the Magistrates' Courts ... and for Crown Court cases ... they instructed solicitors who then instructed barristers". Eventually, many police forces set up their own in-house departments of prosecuting solicitors or employed local firms of solicitors to act on their behalf.

Thus, throughout the nineteenth and twentieth centuries (until 1986), the police controlled the vast majority of prosecutions, with the exception of a small minority of the most complex and serious cases which were prosecuted by the Director of Public Prosecutions (DPP). The Office of the DPP was established in 1879 and was characterised as a "compromise between those who wanted to retain England's unsystematic approach to prosecution and those who wanted prosecutions in general to be structured and controlled as was believed to happen in most of Europe" (Sanders 1996, p. xii).[5] Previously, as a result of voices against the prosecution function of the police, there had been unsuccessful attempts to introduce a system of public prosecutions (with the Bills of 1872 and 1873). With the Prosecution of Offences Act 1879, the government avoided a radical change to the existing system and indeed gave retrospective legitimacy to the previous arrangements.[6]

---

[3]Langbein (1973, p. 318) refers to the inherent fallacies of such a system: "The obvious drawback to any system of gratuitous citizen prosecution is that it is unreliable. There will be cases where there are no aggrieved citizens who survive to prosecute, and others where the aggrieved citizens will decline to prosecute, or be inept at it".

[4]This legal form of police prosecutions with all its accompaniments survived the mid-1980s changes to the system. See Sanders (1996) and Bennion (1986, pp. 3–4).

[5]Sanders refers to Hay's (1983) analysis.

[6]See Edwards (1964).

During the 1980s, complaints and opposition to the system of police prosecutions increased. In 1970 the Committee of JUSTICE,[7] as a result of their inquiry into the problems relating to contemporary prosecution practices, published a report in which they highlighted the danger to public perception and the quality of justice when the same police officer decides on whether to charge a suspect, selects the charge, acts as prosecutor, and also takes the stand as his or her own chief witness. This report, as well as a report by Sir Henry Fisher in 1977 after the *Confait* Case[8] and growing public concern, led to the appointment of a Royal Commission on Criminal Procedure under the chairmanship of Sir Cyril Philips. They reported in 1981, recommending the establishment of a separate service responsible for the prosecution of all offences,[9] taking into account the following main considerations:

> '(a) concerns that combining the role of investigation and prosecution invests too much power and responsibility in one organisation; (b) the desirability, from a public confidence perspective and in order to secure a balanced criminal justice system, of separating the investigative and prosecutorial functions; (c) inconsistencies in prosecution policy across the country and concerns that too many cases were being prosecuted on the basis of insufficient evidence; and (d) a desire for greater accountability and openness and common standards on the part of prosecutors'. (Criminal Justice Review Group 2000, pp. 69–70)

The government, acting on the recommendation of the Commission, enacted the Prosecution of Offences Act 1985, which created the Crown Prosecution Service. The CPS became operational on 1 October 1986. It was a national service headed by the DPP and formally accountable to the Attorney General. It was organised into areas and branches, each branch serving the police area to which it corresponded.[10] Each area was headed by a Chief Crown Prosecutor who was responsible to the DPP for supervising the operation of the service in his area.[11]

The new service had a duty to take over the conduct of all criminal prosecutions[12] instituted by the police and advise the police forces on matters relating to criminal offences. It was also empowered to discontinue prosecutions or drop and amend specific charges when they disagreed with initial police decisions. The CPS was not given any role concerning prosecutions brought by a series of other organisations, such as the Serious Fraud Office, the Health and Safety Executive, the Environment Agency, etc. Neither was it given any powers to institute proceedings itself, nor a

[7] The British Section of the International Commission of Jurists.

[8] R v. Leighton, Lattimore and Salih (1975) 62 Crim. App. R. 53.

[9] But with considerably fewer powers than their Scottish counterpart, contrary to some of the suggestions heard in the Commission.

[10] The CPS was originally organised into 31 areas, which in most cases were built on existing prosecuting solicitors' departments for each police force. In 1993 it was reorganised into 13 regions with strong control from the London headquarters but this was criticised by the Glidewell Report (Glidewell 1998) as a mistake which led to over-centralisation. In 1999 42 separate CPS areas were created, coextensive with the police areas, to facilitate the suggestion in the report that more decisions be taken locally rather than centrally. For a further discussion, see Ashworth (2000).

[11] Prosecution of Offences Act 1985, s. 1 (1) (b) (as initially enacted).

[12] With the exception of the prosecutions concerning some minor offences.

role regarding the investigative stage of a case, contrary to some suggestions heard for the adoption of a public prosecution system similar to the Scottish one.

Even since its creation, the CPS has been the subject of considerable adverse publicity and criticism. As Belloni and Hodgson (2000, p. 106) report, the CPS was criticised "for the very weaknesses which it was set up to remedy: a lack of objectivity and legal scrutiny in the decision to prosecute; inconsistency in the decision to prosecute and in the choice of offence; and an inability or disinclination to weed out even obviously weak cases at an early stage in the process". Fionda (1995) reports that the CPS, in the early days of its creation, experienced criticism from various groups from all branches of the criminal justice process, such as the Association of Chief Police Officers, the General Council of the Bar and the Magistrates' Association. "The staff shortages, the incompetence of CPS staff and outside agents contracted to conduct prosecutions, poor administration and the civil service mentality of the service" (Fionda 1995, p. 19) were some of the criticisms leveled at the CPS which were partly adopted by the Commons House Affairs Committee in 1989[13] and the Audit Commission[14] in the same year.

A series of research studies revealed deficiencies in the CPS performance but at the same time commented on inherent structural problems of the system that could not be easily overcome, and also pointed at the conflicting expectations that the service was called to fulfil. Ashworth (2000, p. 274) pointed out "On the one hand there has been criticism of the CPS for discontinuing too many cases; on the other hand there has been criticism that too many Crown Court cases end in acquittal, suggesting that the CPS is not fulfilling its function of weeding out weak cases".

Research studies (e.g. Crisp and Moxon 1994), as well as the CPS's own surveys,[15] found that discontinuance rates have been rising in the years since the introduction of the CPS.[16] This could have been seen as a positive trend and as an indication that the CPS was actively screening cases but some commentators (e.g. Rose 1996) were critical that too many cases were dropped on efficiency grounds.[17] Closely related to these criticisms were accusations that too many cases used to be downgraded by the CPS, either by amending the charges preferred by the police or by accepting a plea of guilty to a lesser offence.[18]

[13] House of Commons, Crown Prosecution Service, Fourth Report of the Home Affairs Committee, HMSO (London 1989).

[14] National Audit Office (1989).

[15] See Crown Prosecution Service's Annual Reports and Discontinuance Surveys (Crown Prosecution Service 1993, 1994).

[16] However, in 2003–2004 the proportion of cases discontinued decreased to 13.8%, from 16.2% in 2001–2002. Ashworth and Redmayne (2005, pp. 193–196) argue that this is probably due to the changes brought by the Criminal Justice Act 2003 which transferred the authority to charge from the Police to the CPS.

[17] The Glidewell Report (1998) also expressed concern on this issue.

[18] See Ashworth (2000) commenting on the significant structural pressures exercised on the CPS to be flexible in adopting various forms of charge reduction and referring to research by Cretney and Davis (1995) and Hoyle (1998) confirming this practice.

Nevertheless, a decline in the number of convictions for indictable offences, as well as a rise in the number of non-jury acquittals, was observed since the introduction of the CPS, which suggested that prosecutors allowed too many weak cases to be forwarded to courts. A study by Block et al. in 1993 involved an examination of 100 case files in which there had been a non-jury acquittal and tried to identify the proportion of cases where this acquittal could have been foreseen. They found that in 55% of them, evidential deficiencies were sufficient to make acquittal either clearly foreseeable (27%) or possibly foreseeable (28%) and in 15% of the cases the evidential weakness was apparent before the committal. A similar study by Baldwin (1997) found that 80% of non-jury acquittals were foreseeable. Prosecutors failed to discontinue weak cases due to lack of experience or self-confidence and tended simply to endorse the initial police decision. Although in some cases it was very obvious that the chances of acquittal were very high, Baldwin reports that it appeared easier for the prosecutors "to pass the buck to the courts" (1997, p. 542) than to discontinue. As Ashworth (2000) points out, the most worrying finding of Baldwin's research was that some prosecutors shared a common value system with the police. Baldwin reports that "some prosecutors remain stubbornly of the view that the defendant may do the decent thing and plead guilty" (1997, p. 548) even in apparently weak cases – a view that reflects a classic police attitude – and they also believed that serious cases ought to be prosecuted "almost irrespective of considerations as to the evidential strength" (Baldwin 1997, p. 551).[19] Ashworth (2000, p. 277) concludes that "(t)his shows that the CPS has not been successful in inculcating an independent ethical approach, based on the model of the "Minister of Justice", in the minds and conduct of certain Crown Prosecutors".

Furthermore, research by McConville et al. (1991) found that prosecutors, constrained by police-generated information, most of the time, used to endorse the initial police view of a case. Cases were constructed by the police presenting evidence in a way which pointed to the disposal that they preferred. That research confirmed previous arguments by Sanders (1986c) that the CPS could not be independent of the police, partly because they relied on the police for information; the police had the power to construct cases for prosecutions and made weak cases appear strong.[20] Moreover, McConville et al. pointed out that prosecutors also lacked the incentive to weed out weak cases as, in an adversarial system, the goal of the CPS was to assist the police in achieving a maximum conviction rate; a half-hearted attempt to graft an inquisitorial element on to an adversarial system was destined to fail.

Many academics argued that the failure of the CPS to live up to their promises was inevitable precisely because deeper changes in the system were not introduced "In a system where the prosecutor becomes involved in a case at a stage when the

[19]See a similar finding of the research by Hoyano et al. (1997). They found that in some cases prosecutors felt under pressure to continue a prosecution in serious cases even when the case was weak, especially where a decision not to prosecute might have resulted in public or press criticism.

[20]This is more problematic due to the prosecutors' practice when reviewing the cases to rely mostly on police summaries, which proved to be very selective and sometimes misleading (Baldwin and Bedward 1991).

odds are already stacked in favour of prosecution, the objective and independent review of files which is expected of them is a difficult duty to carry out" (Fionda 1995, p. 59). Prosecution practices were not altered dramatically because the structural relationship between the CPS and the police remained problematic and ill defined.[21] The police retained their power to charge and make the initial decision of instituting a prosecution and the CPS was given only a reactive role, namely to review a police decision to prosecute based only on evidence collected by the police themselves. Sanders (2004, p. 105) argues that the fact that the CPS had been characterised as a police-dependent body was "not just a matter of, in many instances, over-identification with police goals and ideology, but also a structural problem: that, while the police made the initial decisions, the CPS were not decision makers, but decision-reversers".

Over the years, there has been a series of attempts to clarify the relationship between the CPS and the police, and efforts made to establish closer cooperation between the two services during the stage prior to charge.[22] With the Criminal Justice Act 2003, however, more radical changes have been introduced which "mark a significant reorientation of the English prosecution system" (Ashworth and Redmayne 2005, p. 173). The Criminal Justice Act 2003 implemented many of the changes suggested by Lord Justice Auld (2001) in order to improve the effectiveness and efficiency of the criminal justice system in England and Wales. As far as prosecutions were concerned, Auld (2001) concluded that one contributor to the high level of discontinuances was the "overcharging" by the police and the failure of the CPS to remedy it at an early stage. He identified one of the causes of this to be the fact that it was the police who initiated prosecutions, leaving the CPS to review the charge at a later stage and, in doing so, to apply a more stringent test than that of the police. To resolve these problems, Auld suggested that the CPS should become involved earlier in the process and be given the power to determine the charge and initiate the prosecution.

Therefore, with the Criminal Justice Act 2003 the responsibility for charging suspects and, thus, initiating criminal proceedings in all but very minor offences was transferred from the police to the CPS (Statutory Charging). The new legislation provided for new, extensive powers allocated to the CPS and the DPP[23] to enable them to discharge their new functions. It also emphasised and facilitated the early consultations between the police investigators and "duty prosecutors" before a charge is preferred.[24] As stated in Brownlee (2004, p. 897), the new system's

[21] See, *inter alia*, Ashworth (2000), Belloni and Hodgson (2000), Leng et al. (1996), Fionda (1995, Chap. 2).

[22] See the next section for a review of the gradual changes implemented as a result of recommendations of various commissions.

[23] E.g. the power of the DPP to issue guidance to custody officers as to how detained persons should be dealt with and as to what the police ought to do to facilitate the decisions on charge by prosecutors. The first edition of the DPP's guidance was issued in May 2004 and the second one in January 2005.

[24] For a detailed analysis of the new legislation, see Brownlee (2004).

objectives were "the elimination at the earliest opportunity of hopeless cases, the production of more robust prosecution cases, the elimination of unnecessary or unwarranted delays... and the reduction of the number of trials that "crack" through the ... acceptance of guilty pleas to reduced charges at a late stage in the process". Since the provisions of the CJA 2003 involved considerable resource and organisational implications, the new system came into being gradually,[25] but as early as in 2006 (almost one year ahead of schedule), the CPS has successfully introduced Statutory Charging in all its 42 Areas.[26] It remains to be seen whether in practice and in the long-term, the new system will achieve its objectives. Ashworth and Redmayne (2005, p. 178) argue that "the success of the new arrangements will inevitably turn on the commitment of the police and the CPS to implement the full spirit of the new division of responsibilities".

2.1.2 Ireland

Prosecutorial arrangements in Ireland are heavily shaped by their common law origins. Their development has evolved in an *ad hoc* manner rather than in a planned fashion since the last century and, as a result, currently, "the prosecutorial process in Ireland is governed by a mixture of common law and statute law which subjects it to a relatively loose form of regulation" (Walsh 2004, p. 283). Furthermore, most of the key relationships between the various agencies involved in prosecution "are regulated by custom, convention, informal liaison and a limited body of case law rather than statutory framework" (Osborne 1997, p. 23).

As in England and Wales, before the organisation of police forces, criminal prosecutions were brought by private individuals, mostly by the victims of a crime. However, while this model of implementation of the criminal law may have sufficed for England and Wales for a longer period of time, "in Ireland it began to reveal its deficiencies in the second half of the eighteenth century, as the consequences of a community polarised on religious and political grounds began to emerge" (Osborne 1997, p. 9). Bell (1989) reports that even the device of offering rewards to induce private prosecution failed and there was a growing concern over widespread abuses of the system. The same writer points out that, earlier than in other common law jurisdictions, "(i)n Ireland ... a deliberate policy was adopted to introduce a professional system of law enforcement, the main reason being that its impartial administration could not be otherwise guaranteed" (Bell 1989, p. 9).

---

[25] In advance of the passing of the CJA 2003, a pilot statutory charging scheme had operated in five CPS areas to test Auld's proposals. This scheme resulted in what was seen as a high level of success. The CPS reported that the benefits included a significant improvement in discontinuance rates and a reduction in the number of charges being dropped or changed (PA Consulting Group 2003).

[26] See Crown Prosecution Service's Annual Report, 2005–2006.

Police prosecutions in Ireland can be traced to the establishment of an Irish constabulary in 1836, replacing the county constabularies. It has to be noted, though, that although police officers quickly dominated the petty courts, they were not given a specific statutory responsibility for prosecutions and they prosecuted individual cases in their common law capacity as private citizens. Besides police prosecutions, as early as in 1801, Crown Solicitors responsible to the Attorney General were appointed for every circuit in the country. Initially, they were responsible for forwarding to the Attorney General information about cases which were listed for the next Assizes and which might be proper for prosecution by the Crown. As Osborne (1997) reports, during the years 1821–1825, the categories of cases which were prosecuted by the Crown were broadened from its previously narrowly-constructed criteria to include almost every serious felony and, thus, the role of the Crown Solicitors was significantly expanded. Again, these arrangements were not provided by a statute but they were based on the common law and existed side by side with the right of private prosecution.

With the Criminal Justice Act 1924 the Office of the Attorney General was placed on a statutory basis and was entrusted with a monopoly over prosecutions on indictment. However, the law did not interfere with the common law right of private individuals and police officers to conduct prosecutions in summary cases. While legislation governing the national police force (*Garda Síochána*) was introduced in 1924 and 1925, it did not provide for the issue of prosecutions and the role of the police in relation to the Attorney General's (and later the DPP's) role in prosecutions. The next major statutory intervention was in 1974,[27] when most of the Attorney General's prosecutorial functions were transferred to the Office of the DPP, again without attempting to regulate the conduct of prosecutions.

As a result of the retention of the basic historical structures regarding prosecutions, even today, no single service has the overall control of prosecutions in Ireland and "there is frequently no clear demarcation of function between the various agencies operating in this sphere" (Osborne 1997, p. 23). A number of agencies have concurrent responsibility for aspects of criminal prosecutions in Ireland. These include the *Garda Síochána*, the Office of the DPP, Local State Solicitors and, until recently, the Office of the Chief State Solicitor (CSS).

The *Garda Síochána* have assumed the role of public prosecutor in the lowest courts. As an organisation, they are responsible to the Minister for Justice and are totally independent of the DPP, the Attorney General and all other agencies. The decision to prosecute is most commonly exercised by the *Garda Síochána* alone, although, with increasing frequency, the police are referring some cases to the DPP prior to charge. Such referrals, however, remain a small minority of the total number of offences prosecuted, although they appear to account for a large proportion of the more serious offences. All offences which are to be prosecuted on indictment must be referred to the DPP, while some others are referred in any event as a matter of practice. Unfortunately, there has been no empirical research

[27] Prosecution of Offences Act (1974).

into this issue. Nevertheless, Bryett and Osborne (2000, p. 33–34), when conducting a comparative analysis of various prosecution systems, pointed out "We have been unable to determine the precise criteria applied by the *Garda Síochána* in deciding within their discretion whether to refer a matter to the DPP, although it seems to approximate to the category of indictable offences, a category which is much wider than the category of offences which are prosecuted on indictment". *Garda* prosecutions in the District Courts are generally conducted by members of the force, the investigating officer or a prosecuting inspector or superintendent, while more complex summary cases are sent to the State Solicitors.

As mentioned above, the Office of the DPP was established by the Prosecution of Offences Act 1974, which conferred on the Director "all functions capable of being performed in relation to criminal matters" by the Attorney General immediately before the passing of the Act. While he is a civil servant in the service of the State and is appointed by the Government, the DPP is required by statute and by constitutional convention to be independent in the performance of his duties. The Office of the DPP is located in Dublin and has no regional representation. Until recently, it used to have very few professional staff and the bulk of professional legal work in criminal prosecutions was handled by the Office of the Chief State Solicitor (CSS) or Local State Solicitors. The Director deals, in theory, with all indictable offences and those which are complex and sensitive. He has no right to undertake summary proceedings apart from those instituted in his name. He has no direct contact with the police and receives files from them via the State Solicitors. Thus the CSS fulfils the role of intermediary between the investigating *Garda* and the DPP in those files which are referred to the Director's Office. Furthermore, the CSS operates as the "solicitor" for the DPP in trials in the Dublin Circuit Criminal Court, the Special Criminal Court and the Central Criminal Court. Nevertheless, until 2001, the CSS was responsible to the Attorney General instead of the DPP and this was heavily criticised as leading to "abnormal consequences". The 1999 Report of the Public Prosecution System Study Group (Nally Report 1999) recommended that the staff of the CSS who perform functions on behalf of the DPP should be transferred to the staff of the DPP, and that the line of responsibility of Local State Solicitors should be altered to lead to the DPP and not to the Attorney General. In 2001, the first part of the Nally recommendations was implemented but it took more than eight years for the second part to be introduced.[28]

Summarizing, it can be said that in Ireland: (a) the decision to charge in virtually every case is made by the investigating *Garda*; (b) the vast majority of summary offences are prosecuted by the *Garda Síochána*; (c) summary offences of complexity are prosecuted by a State Solicitor on behalf of the *Garda Síochána*; (d) summary offences of sensitivity are passed from the police to the DPP via the State Solicitors and are prosecuted by a State Solicitor; (e) indictable offences are passed to the DPP's Office, and when they are to be tried summarily, such offences are prosecuted

[28]The transfer of responsibility for the Local State Solicitor Service from the Attorney General to the DPP's Office was completed in May 2007. See the Annual Report (2006) of the DPP's Office.

by the State Solicitors, whereas when they are to be tried on indictment such offences are prosecuted by an independent counsel briefed by a State Solicitor on behalf of the DPP; and (f) the DPP does not have the right to undertake the conduct of prosecutions instituted by private individuals or the police (Osborne 1997, p. 41).

These complex and inconsistent prosecutorial arrangements have been the subject of considerable criticism,[29] and have been scrutinised by the Public Prosecution System Study Group mentioned above (working under the auspices of the Office of the Attorney General and chaired by Mr Nally, former Secretary to the Government). Included, amongst other things, in the Group's terms of reference was the question of "whether there is a continuing role for the *Garda* to prosecute as well as to investigate crime". The report by Nally's Group concluded that, while there was scope for improvement in co-ordination and effectiveness, the existing system should not be replaced with a unified prosecution service. The Group reached this conclusion largely on grounds of financial considerations and general confidence in the current arrangements expressed during the course of its consultations.

However, a very important development in the area of new legislation took place in 2005 with the introduction of the Garda Síochána Act 2005. This Act represents the first major revision of the operation of the *Garda Síochána* since the foundation of the Irish State and contains a number of reforms regarding the management and administration of the force. In addition to this, it brings some changes in relation to prosecutions and the role of the DPP's Office. Section 8 of the Act confers on members of the *Garda Síochána* the power to institute and conduct criminal prosecutions in courts of summary jurisdiction in the name of the Director of Public Prosecutions. The Act also provides a statutory basis for the DPP to give both general and specific directions to the Gardav in respect of such prosecutions.

Section 8 of the Garda Síochána Act 2005 came into force in February 2007. A General Direction was issued by the DPP's Office to the *Garda Síochána* in January 2007 (which had effect from February 2007) containing instructions in relation to the institution and conduct of prosecutions by members of the *Garda Síochána*. It is reported in the Annual Report of the DPP's Office for the 2007 that the Office also published a revised edition of our Guidelines for Prosecutors taking account of the introduction of section 8 of the Act. Copies of the Guidelines were furnished to the *Garda Síochána* for distribution to sergeants, inspectors and superintendents with operational responsibility for the commencement and management of prosecutions under the Act. It is argued that "Section 8 of the Garda Síochána Act 2005 creates a new oversight role for the Office of the Director of Public Prosecutions with regard to prosecutions taken in the District Court by members of the *Garda Síochána*" (Office of the Director of Public Prosecutions 2007, p. 15).

[29] See Osborne (1997) and Bryett and Osborne (2000).

2.1.3 Northern Ireland

Northern Ireland shared a joint legal heritage with Ireland until the establishment of the Irish Free State in 1922 and, therefore, the historical development of criminal prosecutions until that time was common to these two jurisdictions. However, the introduction of the Prosecution of Offences Order (1972) and most importantly the recent introduction of the Justice (Northern Ireland) Act (2002) resulted in the adoption of a modern public prosecution system in Northern Ireland considerably different from its Irish counterpart.

Even after 1922, and until 1972, the structure of criminal prosecutions in Northern Ireland bore considerable resemblance to the system as it presently exists in Ireland and as described above. In a report of the Working Party on Public Prosecutions in 1971 a summary of the system, as it existed at that time, was given which confirmed the similar prosecutorial arrangements in force.[30] During the years 1969–1971, these arrangements received the attention of two government-appointed groups. The Hunt Committee, reporting in 1969,[31] was critical of the practice of the police in undertaking the majority of prosecutions. They expressed a concern that the impartiality of the police might be questioned if they were responsible for deciding who shall be prosecuted and thereafter acting in court as prosecutors. A concern was also expressed about the impression given of an over-close relationship between the police and the courts. The Hunt Report concluded that consideration should be given to the establishment of an independent prosecution service along the lines of the Scottish procurators fiscal. The MacDermott Committee, constituted to study this recommendation and give their advice, found "that it would be quite impractical to graft the Scottish system onto our system of criminal jurisprudence".[32] However, they did reach the conclusion that, as a matter of general principle, prosecutions should be conducted by public prosecutors, independent of the investigating process and of political influence. They recommended the establishment of a Department of Public Prosecutions staffed with full-time lawyers who would be responsible for prosecutions brought in all courts, other than minor summary cases.

In 1972 the Prosecution of Offences Order was introduced which established the Department of the Director of Public Prosecutions, adopting some of the suggestions of the MacDermott Committee. The Order, without precluding the right to private prosecution, gave primacy to the DPP, who had statutory power to control

---

[30]The Working Party on Public Prosecutions reported that: (a) the prosecution of 98% of cases heard at a Magistrates' Court were carried out by police officers; (b) police officers handled 93% of the cases in which the court committed an accused to a higher court of trial; (c) the remaining cases (mainly serious and particularly difficult cases, cases that have a political background and cases that involve a member of the Royal Ulster Constabulary) were dealt with by either a Crown Solicitor or a Crown Counsel; and (d) the ultimate responsibility for prosecutions rested with the Attorney General and in cases of a serious nature the relevant files had been referred to him for his directions and advice (Report of the Working Party on Public Prosecutions 1971).

[31]Report of the Advisory Committee on Police in Northern Ireland (1969).

[32]Report of the Working Party of Public Prosecutions (1971, para. 6).

all prosecutions in the jurisdiction.[33] Article 5(1)(c) of the Order provided that "the DPP shall, where he thinks proper, initiate and undertake on behalf of the Crown proceedings for indictable offences and for any summary offence or class of summary offence that he considers should be dealt with by him". Therefore, it was for the DPP to determine which type of case his Department would take on. In addition to indictable only offences, those requiring to be referred to the DPP had been selected for a variety of reasons including: seriousness; complexity both of substantive law and of evidential issues; political, racial or sectarian sensitivity; the fact that the accused is a police officer, etc.[34]

Article 6(3) placed a duty on the Chief Constable to inform the Director about indictable offences and any other offences specified by the Director as well as to respond to a request from the Director for information on "any matter which may appear to the Director to require investigation on the ground that it may involve an offence against the law of Northern Ireland". In practice, Article 6(3) was formally invoked on the rare occasions when the facts of an alleged crime were reported directly to the DPP but it also – together with Article 5(1)(b) – underpinned the routine requests for further information or enquiries frequently made of the police by the Director when considering whether to prosecute.[35] The Review of the Criminal Justice System in Northern Ireland (Criminal Justice Review Group, Northern Ireland 2000) reported that the DPP used to seek further information from the police before coming to a decision on whether to prosecute in about 30% of cases. They commented that "(w)hile this relatively proactive approach may add to the time taken to process cases at the earlier stages, it is the DPP's view that it improves the quality of decision making and is less likely to result in problems, such as discontinuance, at later stages".

On the basis of the above-mentioned statutory provisions (especially the mandatory reporting requirements), it was said that the Director was in a position to effectively discharge his supervisory role over all prosecutions apart from the particularly minor (Bell 1989). However, it was also remarked that his functions were principally regulatory rather than participatory since the DPP's office prosecuted in only a minority of cases – the cases in the Crown Court and the most serious cases in the Magistrates' Courts – while the police were still conducting the large majority of prosecutions.[36]

---

[33] And, thus, the right to take over prosecutions being conducted by any other individual or agency.

[34] See Bell (1989) and Osborne (1997).

[35] It should be noted that the DPP had no formal involvement in the conduct of police investigations, prior to charge or summons, or between the charge and the submission to him of the police investigation file. It was, however, open to the police to seek the advice of the DPP's staff in the course of their investigations, especially where it was apparent that complex issues of law or evidence were likely to be involved. The Director had also provided the police with detailed instructions on what should be included in an investigation file (Criminal Justice Review Group, Northern Ireland 2000).

[36] In the Review of the Criminal Justice System in Northern Ireland 2000 it is reported that in 1997 there were 1,128 prosecutions carried out by the DPP in the Crown Court, 7,262 by the DPP in magistrates' courts and 27,209 by the RUC in the Magistrates' Courts. Overall, 76% of cases were prosecuted by the police, including 79% of those in the magistrates' courts.

As a result of the Belfast Agreement in 1998, which provided for a "wide ranging review of criminal justice" in Northern Ireland, a Criminal Justice Review Group was established. Their terms of reference *inter alia* included the review of "the arrangements for the organisation and supervision of the prosecution process, and for safeguarding its independence" (Criminal Justice Review Group, Northern Ireland 2000, p. 2).

The Criminal Justice Review Group (2000, p. 83) "in line with international trends" and "founded largely on the desire to separate the prosecutorial function from the organisation responsible for carrying out investigations" recommended that:

> 'in all criminal cases, currently prosecuted by the DPP and the police, responsibility for determining whether to prosecute and for undertaking prosecutions should be vested in a single independent prosecuting authority. Thus the police would no longer have a role in prosecuting less serious cases before the magistrates' courts'. (Criminal Justice Review Group, Northern Ireland 2000, pp. 83–84)

As a result of these recommendations, the Justice (Northern Ireland) Act 2002 was enacted which established a Public Prosecution Service (PPS). Whilst the PPS came into effect as a statutory body in June 2005, the new PPS structures were fully in place throughout Northern Ireland during the last months of 2007.[37] The Prosecution Service is headed by the Director of Public Prosecutions for Northern Ireland who is appointed by the Attorney General for Northern Ireland. The new Service is regionally based. There are four regions in total, each coterminous with one or more court divisions. Each region is headed by a Regional Prosecutor who has overall responsibility for decision making on investigation files and for the conduct of prosecutions in that region, with the exception of certain files which will be dealt with centrally.

According to the law and the code published by the Service, the PPS are empowered to take prosecution decisions in all cases, offer prosecutorial and pre-charge advice to police, review all charges prior to their submission to court[38] and conduct prosecutions in the Magistrates', Youth and County Courts. Therefore, subject to the full implementation of the PPS, the Director is to assume responsibility for all criminal cases previously prosecuted by the Department of the Director of Public Prosecutions (DPP) and the Police Service of Northern Ireland (PSNI) and will be entrusted with particularly wide powers in the execution of his duties.

---

[37] See the Annual Report (2007–2008) of the Public Prosecution Service for Northern Ireland.

[38] Prosecutors retain the right (previously possessed by the DPP) to request further investigation into any particular matter where it is considered that additional information is required in order to take a fully-informed prosecution decision. In addition, the Prosecution Service may require the Police Service of Northern Ireland to investigate any matter that comes to its attention where it believes that a criminal offence may have been committed.

2.1.4 Scotland

The Scottish prosecution system has long been considered as a possible model to be adopted by various English and Irish committees when discussing the reform of their prosecution systems. Fionda (1995, p. 65) remarks that "(t)he Scottish criminal justice system has enjoyed the advantages of a public prosecution system, with independent prosecutors working in the public interest, for a good deal longer than England and Wales". The Scottish prosecution system has many characteristics which resemble those of its counterparts in continental jurisdictions and, therefore, it has been characterised as a quasi-inquisitorial prosecution system.

The Office of the *Procurator Fiscal* emerged during the late sixteenth to eighteenth centuries, when it took over the investigative and prosecutorial functions of the medieval sheriff who was left primarily with a judicial function. The police forces, on the other hand, came into being during the nineteenth century, being formed in a "piecemeal and largely unstructured way" (Gordon 1980, p. 21). The Fiscal in Scotland, therefore, pre-dates the police and has developed as an integral part of the Scottish system and culture over the centuries.[39]

The Lord Advocate, assisted in his functions by the Solicitor General, is the Government Minister responsible for the prosecution of crime in Scotland. Although a member of the Scottish Executive, as the head of the prosecution system, he is said by convention to be independent in making decisions concerning prosecution. Under the authority of the Lord Advocate, the Crown Office and the Procurator Fiscal Service provide the sole public prosecution service in Scotland. Officers known as Procurators Fiscal undertake prosecutions in the Sheriff or District Courts. These officers are based at six regional and 49 district locations throughout the jurisdiction. They have a commission to prosecute from the Lord Advocate. In addition, there is a number of Advocates Depute (collectively known as "Crown Counsel") who are practising members of the Bar and hold a commission to prosecute in the High Court, where the most serious cases are heard. The Crown Agent, who is the permanent civil service head of the fiscal service working from the Crown Office in Edinburgh, has responsibility for the management of the prosecution service but the Lord Advocate is politically accountable for acts and decisions taken by the prosecution service. Directions and guidance on policy and practice are issued to prosecutors on his authority and with his approval.

In Scotland all criminal prosecutions are conducted by a single service (the Fiscal Service). As Duff (1999, p. 117) reports, "(i)n Scotland, a few statutory offences may be prosecuted by a public body ... but, in practice, such proceedings are normally undertaken by the public prosecutor". Furthermore, the right of private prosecutions was abolished for summary cases with the Criminal Justice (Scotland) Act 1995 and in solemn cases such proceedings require the concurrence of the Lord Advocate or the High Court.

[39] See Moody and Tombs (1982, Chap. 2) for an historical account of the development of the office of Procurator Fiscal.

The police and other reporting agencies send reports of crimes to the Procurator Fiscal. The Procurator Fiscal then decides whether to begin criminal proceedings and, if he decides positively, he determines the forum and the procedure (summary or solemn) as well as the charges to be brought; otherwise, he decides whether to take alternative action or no action at all.[40] Depending on the nature of the offence, the decision to prosecute may be made by a more senior officer on behalf of the Lord Advocate, instead of the Procurator Fiscal. Thus, the decision to prosecute is not one for the police. In the Police (Scotland) Act 1967 it is specified that, when an offence is committed, the role of the police is confined "to take all such lawful measures, and make such reports to the appropriate prosecutor, as may be necessary for the purpose of bringing the offender with all due speed to justice".

What has been characterised as the most significant aspect of the Scottish system of Public Prosecutors is the hierarchical position of the Procurator Fiscal in relation to the police and his complete independence (Duff 1999). This hierarchical position of the Procurators Fiscals is also connected with their supervisory role over the investigation of crimes.[41] Fionda (1995, p. 66) points out that "since the office of fiscal was created early in the nineteenth century before permanent police forces were set up, the police remain in law subordinate to the prosecutor in the investigation of crime, a position now embedded in statute ... (s.17 Police (Scotland) Act 1967)".

However, although in theory Procurator Fiscals' decisions are entirely independent, in practice they are heavily and often exclusively based on information collected by the police. Research by Moody and Tombs (1982) concluded that the role of the police in the supply of information to fiscals was crucial.[42]

Nevertheless, Fionda (1995, p. 93) during her research observed a very good relationship between police officers and Procurator Fiscals: "There are close links between senior fiscals and Chief Constables who have regular meetings to discuss policy. Hostilities rarely arise, and the tensions that exist in England and Wales are not present in Scotland". Therefore, the same writer concludes, this good cooperation between the two services surely contributes to the dissemination of the information needed to make well-informed decisions.

2.1.5 Inquisitorial Jurisdictions

There is a long tradition in civil law systems, which pre-dates the creation of police forces, of public prosecutors taking responsibility for prosecutions in the public interest. Although the inquisitorial process originated in an inquiry by a judge,

---

[40] See Sect. 2.2 of this chapter.

[41] For further analysis, see Sect. 2.2.

[42] See also research by Stedward and Millar (1989), Duff and Burman (1994) and Duff (1997) confirming that fiscals are heavily influenced by the information contained in the police report when deciding whether to divert an offender to social work or psychiatric treatment.

specialised officials acting on behalf of the court later became charged with building the case against the defendant, long before police forces came into existence. In this section some of the broad characteristics of jurisdictions belonging to the continental tradition regarding the origins, constitutional position and organisation of their prosecution services will be examined, without concentrating exclusively on any specific country. More details about the specific characteristics (especially the role of the prosecutors regarding investigation and the legality principle which originally characterised their decision-making) that differentiate these systems from the traditional common law philosophy of prosecution systems will be analysed later on, in Sects. 2.2 and 2.3.

First, it has to be said that it would be wrong to assume that there is only one model of prosecution service in the civil law family of countries. Leigh and Hall Williams, after conducting their research on the prosecution systems of Denmark, Sweden and the Netherlands, concluded that "(i)t became clear that Continental institutions differ markedly from jurisdiction to jurisdiction ... There is no single Continental approach to this matter of the management of prosecutions" (Leigh and Hall Williams 1981, p. 1).[43] Naturally, the prosecuting authorities' specific structures and detailed functions differ from country to country. Nevertheless, there are still some characteristics in the prosecution system of these jurisdictions which are commonly associated with the inquisitorial model of criminal justice and prevail in the majority of these countries.

The origins of prosecutorial arrangements in most **civil law jurisdictions** can be traced back to the French *Code d'Instruction Criminelle* of 1808,[44] which created the *ministère public*, the French Public Prosecution Service. In the years following the creation of the *ministère public*, other European countries, which were under French rule at that time, saw the creation of their own equivalents of the *ministère public*. After regaining independence, the Public Prosecution Service was maintained in these countries; until quite recently, Belgian and Dutch Public Prosecution Services were still very similar to the French *ministère public*. In Germany,[45] the Office of the Public Prosecutor (*Staatsanwalthschaft*) was created in the middle of the nineteenth century by splitting the investigative and judicial functions of the inquisitorial judge.[46] Nevertheless, as Weigend (2004, p. 205) reports, "the separation between judge and prosecutor remained incomplete throughout the nineteenth and the greater part of the twentieth century. In that period, the public prosecutor

[43] See Ambos (2000) for a more detailed comparative overview of the prosecutorial arrangements of various civil law countries (as well as common law countries).

[44] As Verrest (2000, p. 211) reports, "similar institutions have existed since the fourteenth century, but it is difficult to place the debut of the *ministère public* earlier than the beginning of the nineteenth century. At that time, the current *ministère public* received its main characteristics".

[45] See, including others, Fionda (1995, Chap. 5), Albrecht (2000), Jehle (2003) and Weigend (2004) for information on the German prosecution system.

[46] Langbein (1974, p. 446) remarks that "(p)rior to that time, the prosecutorial function had been merged in the all-encompassing work of the inquisitorial judge, who both investigated alleged or suspected crime and then adjudicated on the basis of his own investigation".

shared dominance of the pre-trial process with the German version of the juge d'instruction". However, gradually the investigating judge lost his powers – the office was eventually abolished in 1975 – and the public prosecutor became the "undisputed master of the pre-trial process".

These days, prosecutors in civil law systems, as a rule, function in a *hierarchical structure* with strong internal guidelines controlling the use of discretionary prosecutorial powers.[47] For example, the organisation of the *ministère public* is based on French judicial organisation, and it is structured in two layers corresponding with the District Tribunals and the Courts of Appeal.[48] The *ministère public*'s office at each of the 181 District Tribunals constitutes its basic working level. It is directed by a public prosecutor, the *procureur de la République,* who assures the investigation and prosecution of criminal offences in the district of the tribunal. Other magistrates of the ministère public, called *substitutes*, assist the public prosecutor. At the 35 Courts of Appeal in France the *ministère public*'s office is directed by a *procureur général*, who has authority over the public prosecutors in the district of the Court of Appeal and is responsible for the application of the government's criminal policy. Article 5 of the French Judicial Organisation Act 1958 states that the members of the *ministère public* are subordinated to the Minister of Justice. The latter can give formal instructions to the procurators general and is politically accountable for the functioning of the Public Prosecution Service. A similar hierarchical structure of the prosecution system exists in Belgium,[49] the Netherlands[50] and Germany.[51]

As a rule, in the continental tradition the state *monopolises the right to prosecute* and vests it in the public prosecution services, which represent the public interest. This is in contrast to the common law tradition where originally the prosecution of crimes was largely the concern of private individuals and even these days the prosecutorial power is granted to both the state prosecution service and the individuals (e.g. in England and Wales). As Tak (2004a) reports, however, the general rule of state's monopoly in civil law countries has been somewhat compromised. In some countries there is a right to private prosecution restricted to certain crimes, mainly those which constitute a violation of private legal rights, and in others (e.g. Denmark, Finland and Sweden) this right can only be exercised when the public prosecutor decides not to prosecute. There are, however, a few countries

[47] For example, § 146 Law on the Constitution of the Judicial System in Germany states that prosecutors have to follow directives as issued by their superiors. According to this, the head of the public prosecution service, the Prosecutor-General, and also the Minister of Justice are authorised to direct and to supervise decisions made by individual prosecutors on criminal cases. Such directives can be issued as general guidelines but can also be related to individual cases.

[48] See Verrest (2000, pp. 212–213) for a more detailed description.

[49] See Parmentier et al. (2000), and Van Daele (2004) for a comprehensive review of the Belgian Prosecution Service.

[50] See Leigh and Hall Williams (1981), Fionda (1995, Chap. 4), de Doelder (2000) and Tak (2004b) for detailed descriptions of the Dutch Prosecution Service.

[51] However, in Germany the criminal justice system is organised on a federal basis and, thus, each of the 12 German States operates its own justice system headed by a different Minister of Justice.

(e.g. France and Belgium) where "the public and private rights to prosecute co-exist in a unique fashion" (Tak 2004a, p. 7).

Public prosecutors in continental jurisdictions normally belong to the *judicial branch* (e.g. in France and the Netherlands) or they are considered as quasi-judicial officers (e.g. in Germany). This is in accordance with the inquisitorial tradition in which the prosecutor is seen as a neutral and impartial party. Referring to the French Prosecution Service, Verrest (2000, p. 221) states "The impartiality of the Public Prosecution Service is contained in Article 66 of the Constitution. As part of the Judiciary, the mission of the Public Prosecution Service is to secure citizens' basic rights to freedom and liberty". Fionda (1995, p. 7) reports that "(i)n the Netherlands and Germany judges and prosecutors usually train together on the same postgraduate training course, with some law graduates opting to enter the judicial branch of the legal profession and others the prosecution and defence branches". The relationship between judges and prosecutors in France is even tighter.[52] The *procureur*, the *juge d'instruction* and the trial *juge*, after following the same education program at the *Ecole nationale de la Magistrature*, become members of the same body, the *magistrature*, and it is not uncommon for them to change from *ministère public* to the bench or vice versa during their career.

As a rule, in the continental tradition (and again contrary to the common law one), the police have never had a prosecutorial role.[53] This has always been the responsibility of prosecution services, which were created before the establishment of organised police forces. Furthermore (and, arguably, related to this), police are regarded as coming under the command of and being controlled by the public prosecution services[54] as far as all the functions related to prosecutions (in a broad sense, including also the investigative stage[55]) are concerned. The police must report to the prosecutors all offences known to them and the prosecutors take the decision on prosecuting criminal offences. Therefore, the responsibility for the decision to prosecute or not lies exclusively with the public prosecutors.[56] Thus, even in countries where the opportunity principle applies, the police, theoretically, are not allowed to end cases but instead are obliged to pass them on to prosecutors to decide. The Netherlands appears to be an exception to this rule: a clear legal framework is in place which allows the police to end cases by imposing a condition in accordance with general guidelines of the prosecutor-generals.[57] It has to be noted that in the other countries as well, in practice, police also enjoy some discretion

[52] See Hodgson (2001), (2002) and (2005) for a comprehensive account of the French prosecution system based on her extensive empirical work in that jurisdiction.

[53] See, however, an exception to this rule in the case of Norway, where in some particular minor cases the police have the responsibility for prosecutions (Jehle 2000).

[54] See, for example, Article 13 of the Dutch Police Act of 1993 which states that the police functions under the command of the public prosecution service and a prosecutor is entitled to give orders to the police in criminal matters that they are obliged to obey.

[55] See Sect. 2.2 of this chapter.

[56] Or the *juge d'instruction* in France.

[57] This is the so-called *transactie* system, which also applies to the prosecution level.

regarding their reporting requirements. Verrest (2000, p. 243) for example reports of the situation in France: "In a certain sense, the police do settle some criminal offences themselves. The police do not forward all the information they have on criminal offences to the *ministère public* – even though they are supposed to".[58]

2.1.6 Concluding Remarks

In all criminal justice systems, a state authority is entrusted with the power to prosecute alleged offenders. Nevertheless, as has been shown, "prosecution agencies do not have similar organisational structures and are not vested with identical prosecutorial powers and tasks. Moreover, the place of the prosecution services in the constitutional state organisation differs considerably" (Tak 2004a).

There is a long tradition in civil law systems of public authorities taking responsibility for prosecutions in the public interest. By contrast, in the common law tradition, prosecution services are a relatively new feature, the responsibility for prosecutions being left before to private individuals and mainly to the police. However, although in some common law countries (e.g. Ireland) police still retain significant prosecutorial functions the trend has been towards giving responsibility for prosecutions to a prosecution agency independent of the police. Despite some common trends observed, the varying structures, and the specific characteristics of the modern prosecution services, as well as their constitutional relationship with the police, can be traced back to their different roots and underlying principles.

2.2 The Role of Prosecution Services in Investigation

> 'While prosecutors may not play an investigative role in all or even most criminal cases, the majority of which are probably reactive as well as routine, the importance of the investigative role lies not in the number of cases it affects, but in the significance of the role in the matters where it arises'. (Little 1999, p. 728)[59]

While the decision as to whether a case should be brought before a court – whether to prosecute or not – is undoubtedly regarded as the central function of every prosecuting authority, the role and the powers that a prosecuting agency acquires during the investigation of a case is a matter of great variation across different prosecution systems. It is, furthermore, a controversial issue in the discussions about the relationship between police and prosecutors. In theory, it can be stated that in common law jurisdictions, investigations have been traditionally regarded as

[58] There are very few empirical studies in continental jurisdictions with which to draw a better picture of the situation that exists in practice. See, however, Hodgson (2005) for a valuable contribution.

[59] Quoted in Krone (2003, p. 1).

the preserve of the police, contrary to the pure continental tradition which places prosecutors in charge of the investigatory as well as the post-investigatory stage. In practice, and as time passed, there have been developments that have caused adjustments in this crude statement.

2.2.1 Common Law Tradition

As was shown earlier, in most common law countries there is not a direct line of authority between the police and the prosecution service and the police enjoy a considerable independence in the execution of their duties. Related to this, it has been declared that the responsibility for investigations lies exclusively in the hands of the police. After the creation of modern public prosecution services, the police may have been released from their responsibilities in prosecutions,[60] but they remained the institution responsible for the investigatory stage. Indeed, the main reason behind establishing the Crown Prosecution Service in England and Wales and the DPP Offices in Ireland and Northern Ireland was the desire to draw a clear line between functional responsibility for investigation and for prosecution.

The maintenance of an investigator–prosecutor divide was central to the report which led to the establishment of the Crown Prosecution Service. The Philips Royal Commission recommended that the CPS should not have a role in supervising police investigations apart from giving advice to the police, which the Royal Commission encouraged.[61] However, it also recommended that the CPS should not have the power to direct the police to undertake further inquiries. The Philips Commission saw the separation of the prosecutor from the charge decision as being essential to the maintenance of a proper relationship between prosecutor and investigator. The investigator–prosecutor divide was premised on the belief that if the prosecutor becomes involved in the investigation of a case, then the prosecutor may become committed to a particular line of inquiry and lose objectivity in assessing that case. Therefore, under the 1985 Act, the police retained the power to investigate and to decide what charge to bring without the interference of the CPS.[62]

In the early 1990s, a series of miscarriages of justice led to the appointment of another Royal Commission on Criminal Justice which examined once again the possibility of giving the CPS a role in investigations. The role of the *juge d'instruction* in France was particularly discussed as a possible model but in the end it was

[60]However, not entirely, as in many common law countries, including Ireland (and until very recently Northern Ireland) police still have a role in the prosecution of minor cases.

[61]Royal Commission on Criminal Procedure (1981, pp. 71–73).

[62]As Ashworth (1998, p. 173) remarks on the pre-Criminal Justice Act 2003 situation: "The English prosecutor has no power to order the police to interview different people, or to ask further questions of the defendant or other witnesses. The CPS may put a request to the police for further investigations, but it seems that in the past this has sometimes been a source of friction between the two organisations".

rejected along with any other proposal which went against the strict separation of the roles of investigator and prosecutor. The RCCJ stated:

> 'The relationship of the CPS with the police . . . is particularly relevant. We see as central to it the unambiguous separation of the roles of investigator and prosecutor. It was the need for a separate prosecution authority which led to the establishment of the CPS in the first place. In our view, just as the police should concentrate on discovering the acts relevant to an alleged or reported criminal offence, including those which may end to exonerate the suspect, so should the CPS concentrate on assessing both the strengths and weaknesses of the case which, if the decision is taken to proceed, will bring the defendant before the court'. (Royal Commission on Criminal Justice 1993, p. 69)

Field (1994, p. 121), as well as other commentators, criticised the Commission for not giving proper and creative thought to the possibility of introducing some inquisitorial elements in the pre-trial stage, adapting them to the English system of criminal justice. Instead, they were seeking to "take a pre-existing system and implant it in its entirety" and, naturally, this approach was destined to fail.[63]

A similar reasoning to that of the two Royal Commissions of Criminal Justice was followed in other common law countries when discussing the possible involvement of prosecutors in the investigative stage.[64] Thus in Ireland,[65] Australia, New Zealand, Canada[66] and other common law countries, prosecutors have no formal role in the pre-trial stage apart from that of advising the police whenever the latter wish to consult them.

2.2.2 *Problems and Inefficiencies*

The division between investigation and prosecution proved to be problematic in practice and researchers were critical of the absence of a prosecutor's power to exert a form of control in the investigative stage. They argued that the failure to give the prosecutor control over investigations meant that the control over prosecutions actually stayed with the police:[67]

> 'Independent decision-making, which is what is required of the prosecutor, is impossible so long as he remains dependent upon the police for the relevant information. In deciding whether to involve the prosecutor before a charge is made or in deciding what and how

[63] Field (1994, p. 121) comments on the Commission's approach: "The report complained that no foreign model existed in which the rights and interests of the various parties were so well balanced that it could simply be adopted. . . The idea that foreign experience might cast light on the kind of underlying principles needed for designing systems is not considered by the Commission".

[64] See Hunt Report (Advisory Committee on Police in Northern Ireland 1969) and Bryett and Osborne (2000) in Northern Ireland and Public Prosecution System Study Group (1999) in Ireland.

[65] In Northern Ireland, as shown earlier, the DPP had some indirect investigatory powers. See Articles 6(3) and 5(1)(b) of the Prosecution of Offences Order.

[66] See Law Reform Commission of Canada (1990) and Stenning (1986).

[67] See, *inter alia*, Lidstone (1987) and Fionda (1995, Chap. 2). See also the previous section of this chapter.

> much information the prosecutor should be given, the police will be guided by their law enforcement concerns which are not necessarily the same as those of the prosecutor'. (Lidstone 1987, p. 311)

Much research evidence concluded that prosecutors could not effectively monitor police investigations via police-constructed files,[68] that many police files contained insufficient and sometimes misleading evidence[69] with the result that weaknesses often came out only in or after the trial,[70] and that the police investigation focused prematurely upon a police suspect, sometimes overlooking other crucial evidence.

Furthermore, research studies revealed that there had been reluctance from the police to use the possibility available to them of seeking prosecutors' advice during investigations. McConville et al. (1991), based on their research undertaken in the early days of the CPS, reported that police asked for prior advice in only 51 out of 711 cases. Later research by Moxon and Crisp (reported in RCCJ Report 1993) found that police asked for the CPS's prior advice in 4% of cases, mainly in order to resolve doubts about the sufficiency of the evidence.

2.2.3 *Change of Thinking and Practice*

All the problems mentioned above caused a gradual change of thinking regarding the prosecutors' involvement in investigations. Before reflecting on this, it should be mentioned that the police themselves were gradually forced to seek prosecutors' advice more often. The appearance of new forms of criminality (organised crime, especially money-laundering and drug-trafficking) and the ever-increasing complexities of substantive and procedural law made the police more dependent on the prosecutors for legal advice. In many common law jurisdictions this has evolved into forms of cooperation that provide the prosecutor with some influence in the investigation process itself. In most jurisdictions, though, this form of cooperation has remained on an informal and usually *ad hoc* level, without changing the constitutional relationship between the two institutions.[71]

In England and Wales more formal responses started to emerge in order to face the inefficiencies observed in practice as far as investigations were concerned.

---

[68] McConville et al. (1991).

[69] Ashworth (1998, Chap. 6), Sanders (1988a, b) and McConville et al. (1991). See also Baldwin and Bedward (1991) who found that the police summaries, on which most of the time prosecutors based their prosecution decisions, were even more selective.

[70] Leng (1993).

[71] However, in many countries special offices were created long ago who were dealing with economic crime; for example, the Serious Fraud Office was established under the Criminal Justice Act 1987 (UK) and combined in one office the roles of investigator and prosecutor. See also the Criminal Assets Bureau in the Republic of Ireland and the Integrated Proceeds of Crime (IPOC) Units in the Canadian Federal jurisdiction.

The thrust of the new thinking, evidenced in such reviews as the Narey Report in 1997 and the Glidewell Report in 1998, has been to place the emphasis on co-ordination, partnership and integrated working between the police and CPS, with the prosecutor being fully involved from the point of charge. The Narey Report (Narey 1997, p. 11), stating that they did "not consider that working with the police in this way would necessarily impinge on the proper independence of the prosecutor", recommended that prosecutors should be placed permanently in police stations as a means of ensuring that appropriate decisions are made for the prosecution of cases from the start. However, in reporting on a review of the "Lawyers at Police Stations" (LAPS) scheme which was introduced as a result of these recommendations, Baldwin and Hunt (1998) concluded that CPS lawyers were being used inefficiently to provide oversight and guidance to police officers. Moreover, the police were not being required to internalise the demands of the CPS for the preparation of cases for prosecution. The fact that the police retained control of the decision to charge was arguably a factor that prevented a change in the balance of powers between prosecutors and the police.

The Glidewell Committee (Glidewell 1998) recommended the creation of Criminal Justice Units (CJU) in each major police station where CPS case workers and police civilian staff were able to work together on some cases. It was believed that, through co-location, the relationship between the prosecutor and the police would improve and cases would be prepared earlier and more efficiently. A first review of the CJU scheme was generally positive.[72] However, again, this scheme was criticised as being based on police control of the charging process[73] and as creating a danger that the CPS officers would lose a degree of their independence and objectivity by being co-opted into the rubber-stamping of police decision-making.[74]

With the Criminal Justice Act 2003, however, as was shown above, the responsibility for deciding whether to lay a charge has been transferred from the police to the CPS. Once the prosecutor has charge responsibility, the prosecutor can require the police to investigate further before agreeing to the commencement of criminal proceedings. In the guidance issued by the DPP according to the Act, "custody officers are expressly required to direct investigating officers to consult a duty prosecutor as soon as practicable after a suspect is detained in custody. During these consultations the lawyer is expected to identify whether a case is likely to proceed and to advise on lines of inquiry and evidential requirements" (Brownlee 2004, pp. 902–903). It is, therefore, evident that with the new

---

[72]"All sites report that the co-location of Police and CPS staff is eliminating unnecessary work through improved communications. Enquiries by CPS and the Police which used to take weeks to clear can now be resolved satisfactorily in minutes. Speedier notification of proposed discontinuance, for example, has reduced the wasted effort on upgrading files unnecessarily" (Glidewell Working Group 2001, p. 7).

[73]Decisions about the cases were taken jointly only after the completion of the police investigation and, most of the time, after the charging decision.

[74]See Baldwin and Hunt (1998), Sanders and Young (2000, Chap. 6) and Sanders (2004).

Law prosecutors have been given a more powerful role regarding investigations. It remains now to be examined, using empirical research, how they have been discharging it in practice.

2.2.4 Continental Tradition

In the inquisitorial environment the distinction between investigation and prosecution is more blurred than in common law systems. As Ambos (2000, pp. 513–514) remarks, "(t)he French distinction between *poursuite* and *instruction* refers to different phases of the proceedings and thereby distinguishes between the competences of *procureur* and *juge d'instruction*". Generally, prosecutors are responsible for the whole pre-trial stage, including investigations. There are a number of variations among different inquisitorial systems as far as the extent of prosecutors' powers is concerned. Nevertheless, in most of them, the prosecuting authority is empowered "to instruct the instigation of investigations, to give instructions on the scope of investigations, personally to investigate criminal cases, to participate in investigations and to decide on the type of investigations" (Tak 2005b, p. 4).

In **France**, the Code of Criminal Procedure (CCP) states that the *procureur* has formal authority over the police services when they investigate criminal offences. In order to facilitate the execution of their duties, the Code provides that prosecutors can issue general instructions (apart from the specific instructions they give in individual cases) to investigators in which they explain the choices in the crime policy and the priorities in the detection of particular categories of crimes. The police must report to prosecutors all offences known to them and seek instructions as to the lines of investigations. They also have the formal obligation to inform the public prosecutors of all arrests they make and of the decision to put a suspect in police custody, as well as to seek their authorisation for the use of undercover investigation techniques. The prosecutors may, if they think proper, take over the investigation themselves.

In the case of serious offences and complex investigations the public prosecutors can request that a judicial inquiry be opened. The case is then brought to the *juge d'instruction*, who opens the judicial inquiry. As Verrest (2000, pp. 213–214) describes "If there is already a suspect in the case, the examining judge will inform him of the existing charges and declare him 'the subject of investigations.' The examining judge continues the investigations and directs police services. He can order phone taps and basically any other investigation technique, as long as it remains within the legal framework and is needed to solve the case. He can also decide to put a suspect in preliminary detention". It is estimated that only 7% of all cases are the subject of judicial inquiries despite "the image of an omnipresent examining judge, sometimes imagined by foreign academics" (Verrest 2000, p. 215).

The **German** Criminal Procedure Law provides that the prosecution service is legally and functionally responsible for the pre-trial stage and it is referred to as "the ruler of the investigative stage".[75] It authorises prosecutors to perform acts of investigation themselves or to request the police to do so. They can also give general instructions to the police regarding how particular cases are to be handled and can set areas of priority of investigation. The police are obliged to inform the prosecution service of their actions and to provide them with information in order to facilitate their decisions for further investigatory actions. In practice, there are only a few areas where the prosecutor's office is involved from the very beginning in investigations. Weigend (2004) refers to homicide cases, serious white-collar cases and cases where significant publicity is expected. Furthermore, when there is a need of search and seizure, pre-trial detention, telephone tapping, deploying an undercover agent or DNA-analysis,[76] in principle a court has to authorise these actions and, therefore, the public prosecutors must serve as an interface in terms of moving a corresponding motion. In the rest of the cases the police can complete the investigation on their own and pass on the complete file to the prosecution service. Nevertheless, as Weigend (2004, p. 208) remarks, "(n)otwithstanding the practical domination of the investigation process by the police, the prosecutor's office remains ultimately responsible... The prosecutor must eventually make the decision whether or not to charge the suspect with an offence".

In **Scotland**, Procurators Fiscal have similar powers to their counterparts in continental jurisdictions. They have a common law duty to investigate crime and section 17(3) of the Police (Scotland) Act 1967 places Chief Constables under a statutory duty to comply with the lawful instructions of the fiscals. In practice, it is only in the more serious or complex cases that the fiscals would become heavily involved at the investigative stage, for example through attendance at the scene of a murder to take charge of the evidential aspects of the investigation and autopsy arrangements.

Some limited empirical research in continental jurisdictions revealed a number of inefficiencies[77] which do not match up to the ideal picture of the system that some common law commentators have in their minds. During the RCCJ 1993 discussions, there were allegations by some researchers of a lack of cultural commitment to impartiality amongst some prosecutors and *juges d'instruction* in France but Field (1994, p. 128–129) claims that these general assessments were not empirically founded and that "there does seem to be an impressionistic case of thinking that processes of training do not seem to shape cultural attitudes in quite the same way in France as they do in Germany and the Netherlands" (where there

[75] See Elsner (2005).

[76] See, however, the Law on Control of Organised Crime of 1992 by which the police have been authorised to initiate deployment of undercover agents and have also been authorised to make independent decisions in emergency cases.

[77] Apart from the mentioned inefficiencies, see also criticisms of the limited defence rights during investigations (Hodgson 2004). However, in an attempt to demonstrate conformity with the ECHR and under the influence of the Recommendations of the Council of Europe (e.g. Rec 97(13)), there are a series of reforms in inquisitorial countries aiming to strengthen the defence's position. See Field and West (2003) and Hodgson (2005) for a review of relevant reforms introduced in France.

was evidence that prosecutors do appear neutral and impartial). Hodgson (2001, p. 357), however, based on her research, also expressed doubts about the neutral stand of the *magistrats* in France, stating that "in practice independence does not guarantee neutrality and in particular, the stance of the *procureur* in representing the public interest is predominantly one of crime control".

Related to this, concerns are expressed that the regular involvement of prosecutors with the police in investigations might compromise their ability to make dispassionate judgments.[78] However, there is evidence that prosecutors are only involved in investigations on an everyday basis in very serious cases and for the rest they only exercise overall control and supervision.[79] This evidence leads to a contrary argument that the involvement of prosecutors in the investigative stage is largely rhetorical and not effective[80] and "a dangerous disguise for untrammelled police control of investigations" (Field 1994, p. 126). This argument, though, does not take into consideration the fact that prosecution services in civil law countries make a great use of their power to issue guidelines and directives to the police on how to investigate particular cases and what kind of methods they can use. They also require the police to keep them informed of the most crucial investigative actions.[81] Furthermore, prosecutors in their relationship with the police place a great importance on trust and mutual understanding (Hodgson 2001). Leigh and Zedner (1992, p. 69) report:

> 'A striking feature of the French and German systems which we might further emulate is the readiness of the police to request advice from prosecution. The foreign observer cannot but be struck by the harmonious working relationships in Germany between prosecutors and police which exist notwithstanding the independence and superior status of the prosecutor in the procedure'.

This is in contrast to the tension that has always characterised the relationship between police and prosecutors in England and Wales.

Leigh and Zedner (1992) confirm that the prosecutors' monitoring generally starts after preliminary police investigations. But, as Field (1994, p. 127) points out, these authors "do not conclude from this that prosecutors always become prisoners of a police-constructed file and their supervision meaningless". This is prevented partly by the defence actions which provide the prosecutor with additional information that challenges the police view of the case. It is argued (Field et al. 1995) that when prosecutors are alerted to ambiguities or impropriety in investigations, they are often decisive in response. Field (1994, p. 127) claims that especially the German and the Dutch systems "seem to depend on the development of a particular kind of relationship between the defence lawyer, prosecutor and (in the Netherlands) investigative judge in the development of the dossier".

---

[78] See evidence presented in Bryett and Osborne (2000).

[79] See Elsner (2005), Weigend (2004), Falletti (2004), Hodgson (2001).

[80] See Goldstein and Marcus (1977) and the discussions in the RCCJ 1993.

[81] See Weigend (2004), Jehle (2000).

2.2.5 *Concluding Remarks*

Comparative analysis in relation to prosecution systems reveals that both adversarial and inquisitorial systems either in theory or in practice have moved away from their traditional models. In common law systems a steady movement away from an insistence on prosecutor detachment from the investigator is observed; this either takes the form of informal arrangements between police and prosecutors without changing the constitutional relationship between the two services or, as in the case of England and Wales, a statutory reform. In inquisitorial systems, in practice it was observed (Tak 2005b, p. 4) that "the public prosecutor ... does not exercise his function as head of the investigation except in more important cases" mainly because of resource issues but partly due "to the recognition that with regard to investigative techniques and tactics, the police possess more expertise than the prosecution service". However, he still retains the overall control and responsibility for the regulation of the investigative stage.

2.3 Prosecution Principles and Policies

The power to decide whether a particular case should be forwarded to courts or filtered out of the system is regarded as the central function – the *sine qua non* – of every prosecuting authority. In this section, a comparative analysis will be attempted of the way different prosecution systems approach the issues of prosecutorial discretion, diversion from prosecution and the formulation of prosecution criteria and policies.

2.3.1 *Theoretical Background: Mandatory v. Opportunity Principle*

> 'A rigid view of the law is that it should be fixed and certain: if it is broken it should be enforced. Mandatory prosecution ensures that all individuals against whom there is a *prima facie* evidence are tried by the courts ... A more flexible view of the law is that it provides guiding principles for the regulation of the behavior, which are highly developed but do not ... anticipate every eventuality and every variation in circumstances. Such an approach in turn requires significant discretion to be vested in those making the decisions about whether to set the law in motion'. (Mansfield and Peay 1987, p. 27)

Prosecution systems have traditionally been characterised as coming closer to either the legality or the opportunity principle. This depends on the extent of the discretion that the prosecuting authorities are allowed over the decision to prosecute and the permission to take into account factors other than evidence in making this decision.

The *legality principle* commands that every case in which there is enough evidence and in which no legal hindrances prohibit prosecution has to be brought to court. Adherence to the legality principle in the procedural sense means that the prosecution service cannot exercise any discretion over the prosecutorial decision.[82] Its role is limited to the legal assessment of the sufficiency of the evidence against the suspect. Other considerations – what are known as public interest factors in opportunity systems – are not considered as factors that prosecutors are allowed to deploy in their decisions. Rather, the public interest is regarded as a consideration for the court which might be reflected in the verdict or the penalty imposed.

The adoption of the legality principle is usually connected with the continental tradition in which enforcement agencies are, at least theoretically, denied any discretion and primacy is given to the legislative power of the state. In these systems (e.g. Germany, Italy and Spain) "(t)he Penal Code is the foundation of legal authority: judges and prosecutors have no "inherent" power to take positions that modify or nullify the Code's requirements" (Goldstein and Marcus 1977, pp. 246–247). Ashworth and Redmayne (2005, p. 147) remark that "(i)f the administration of the criminal law produces unjust results, it is for the legislature to amend it and not for prosecutors to make their own policies".

Tak (2004a) refers to two principal reasons usually given for the mandatory prosecution of all offences as prescribed by the law. The first is the safeguard of the principle of equality before the law and the second is the upholding of the concept of general deterrence: "The guarantee that all offenders will be tried and that no offence will remain unpunished would be an important means by which to uphold the trust of the population in law enforcement, and in the proper administration of justice" (Tak 2004a, p. 9). Furthermore, the dispensation of justice in open court is seen as essential in ensuring that the law is impartially upheld and that undue influences by the executive are prevented.[83]

Prosecution systems that adhere to the *opportunity principle* (e.g. England and Wales, Ireland, Northern Ireland and all the rest of the common law countries) "allow enforcement agencies almost unfettered discretion over whether or not to prosecute, which allows prosecutors to take account of factors other than evidence in making their decisions" (Sanders 1996, p. xi). Therefore, not every offence in respect of which there is evidence of guilt of an individual must be prosecuted, for there may be other significant reasons which suggest that inaction is better than prosecution. These reasons are normally classified as exigencies of the public interest and cover a wide range of issues that entail consideration of factors associated with the accused, the victim, the gravity of the offence, the availability of resources, etc.

This high level of discretion with which the enforcement agencies are entrusted is mostly associated with the common law tradition. Unlike codified systems that aspire to provide in advance for all eventualities, the common law tradition admits the impossibility of pre-determined answers to all future questions and recognises

[82] As Langbein (1974, p. 440) remarks: "(t)he prosecutor's power of non-prosecution becomes controversial when it extends beyond the power to discard hopeless cases. Prosecutorial discretion ... means the power to decline to prosecute in cases of provable criminal liability".

[83] See Ashworth and Redmayne (2005, p. 165).

the need for flexibility in the law, so that it can be adapted to every variation in circumstances.[84] Consequently, as Walther (2000, p. 293) remarks, "this type of legal culture... makes it necessary to entrust professionals in the ranks of the enforcers of the law with far-reaching power of interpretation and application of the law in the books".

Furthermore, the permission that is given to prosecutors to apply extra-legal considerations to prosecution decisions is a recognition that within a society there are competing interests and values which must be reconciled (Mansfield and Peay 1987) and a realisation that prosecutors are possibly in the best position to pursue a cost benefit analysis.

Finally, it is advocated that the adoption of the opportunity principle has three main advantages: (a) it prevents "the negative counter-effects of the strict application of the legality principle which, under circumstances, could lead to injustice" (Tak 2004a, p. 9); (b) it enables the individualisation of criminal justice; and (c) it prevents "delays and backlogs in the court and prison system, which may in turn jeopardise the overall aim of protecting the rights and interests of the accused" (Fionda 1995, p. 10).

2.3.2 Changes in Practice and Remaining Differences

Despite the doctrinal contrast between the principle of legality and the principle of opportunity, the differences between the systems that were originally used to adopt either principle are increasingly eroded in practice. Sanders and Young (1994, p. 209) comment that "(i)n Britain, where discretion is theoretically total, most cases are prosecuted,[85] and in a legality system, where there is theoretically no discretion available, a similar, or perhaps even greater, number of cases are not prosecuted".

These days, most of those traditionally regarded as legality systems,[86] especially due to rising caseloads and scarce resources,[87] allow the prosecutors to also take into account other reasons apart form the evidential ones when deciding to prosecute or drop a case. Wade (2005, p. 2) reports that "in systems which do not explicitly allow this, practices achieving the same effect can be found (indeed

[84] See McConville and Wilson (2002) and Mansfield and Peay (1987, pp. 26–29).

[85] Especially in relation to adult cases, as the same authors report.

[86] With the exception of Italy, which theoretically still adopts the principle of strict legality. See, however (Di Federico 1998, p. 378): "The first clear element that emerges from our research is that, in spite of the constitutional provisions that require our magistrates to prosecute all criminal violations, penal action in Italy is de facto just as discretionary as in other countries, and perhaps more".

[87] Ashworth and Redmayne (2005, p. 147) mention another important reason for this trend, naming the "increasing realisation that prosecution and sentence in court are stressful for all participants and are not necessarily more effective (in terms of reconviction rates) than forms of diversion".

legislation allowing such drops, e.g. in Germany, France and the Netherlands, was introduced in order to codify practice)".

In Germany, which used to be considered as one of the strong representatives of the mandatory prosecution philosophy, as early as the 1960s, a statutory basis for discretionary non-prosecution was introduced (§ 153 German Code of Criminal Procedure) in order to cope with the rising caseloads. Since then, a number of exceptions from the mandatory prosecution rule have been enacted. Therefore, currently, prosecutors can refrain from or dismiss a prosecution in the following cases: (a) for minor criminal offences with low guilt and no public interest in prosecuting and (b) for less important criminal offences where the penalty would be insignificant alongside the punishment for some other crime committed by the same offender. In these cases there can be a dismissal without consequences, but also a conditional dismissal by which prosecutors impose upon the offender certain obligations, e.g. to make a payment to the victim, the state or a charity, to perform a community service or to undergo victim/offender mediation.[88] It is worth noting that the court's consent is necessary for the dismissal of cases concerning certain kinds of offences.

For more serious offences (felonies) only the Federal Prosecutor General is empowered to refrain from prosecutions in very specific circumstances: (a) when proceedings could endanger the Federal Republic or if other substantial public interests weigh against prosecution and (b) with the consent of the court "if the offender has, after the deed, contributed to avert the danger for the state created by the offence" (153e CCP).[89]

In France the expediency principle also applies currently in a number of cases and there is also a number of options available for prosecutors when they decide to divert a case out of the courts (e.g. *mediation penale*, *composition penale*).

However, although there is a good deal of convergence between opportunity and legality-based systems in practice, commentators draw attention to some important differences that still exist: "Because diversion in a legality system is an exception to a general rule, non-prosecution decisions are relatively strictly controlled even if they are greater in number than in systems like that in England and Wales" (Sanders and Young 1994, p. 209). As the examples of Germany and France indicate, the conditions under which those exceptions can be made are stipulated and diversion decisions are usually reserved for the prosecutors to make. Furthermore, in order to encourage consistency and adherence to official policy, only a relatively small number of senior decision-makers are empowered to take the most serious diversionary decisions.[90]

On the contrary, in opportunity-based systems such as that in England and Wales, "neither the basis for the exercise of discretion nor the level of decision-

[88]There has been criticism by some scholars in Germany that conditional dismissals enable rich suspects to buy their way out of criminal prosecution. See *inter alia* Jehle (2003).

[89]See Weigend (2004) and Fionda (1995, Chap. 5) for more information on the diversionary options in Germany.

[90]See Sanders (1986b), Leigh and Zedner (1992), Sanders and Young (1994, Chap. 6).

maker is consistent throughout the system" (Sanders and Young 1994, p. 209).[91] Diversionary decisions are not the exclusive responsibility of prosecutors. Most non-prosecution decisions are still made by a relatively large number of police officers and, thus, are difficult to control. Police are empowered to take no further action, give an informal warning, or administer a caution without notifying the CPS. Furthermore, until recently, prosecutors had no power to impose any diversionary measures instead of prosecution. Their only option was to recommend to the police – but not require – the administration of a caution.[92]

Prosecutors could, of course, discontinue a case for public interest reasons but research revealed that they were not very successful in doing so. McConville et al. (1991) found that the CPS rarely dropped cases on public interest grounds alone and although later on discontinuances of this kind were increased, most of the time, these occurred in trivial cases and mainly on cost grounds (Sanders and Young 2002). It was argued that police control of information and case construction used to make it extremely difficult for prosecutors to identify cautionable cases:[93] "Factors which could point towards caution or other forms of diversion are downplayed in the file, or such facts are not brought out by the police because of failure to ask appropriate questions" (Sanders 2004, p. 118).[94] The experiment with "Public Interest Case Assessment" (PICA) schemes, where the CPS were provided with information from other than the police sources (e.g. Social Services), proved that far more cases could be diverted provided that the right information was available (Crisp et al. 1995).

The introduction of the Criminal Justice Act 2003 has conferred a greater role on the CPS in relation to diversion. It gives them the power to offer conditional cautions to offenders and requires them to propose the conditions. However, as Ashworth and Redmayne (2005, p. 171) point out, the police seem to retain the power to offer a police caution or otherwise to divert the case. Therefore, even after the introduction of the new legislation, it appears that in England and Wales diversionary decisions will still not be centrally controlled by a single agency acting on explicitly pronounced policies and common starting points for all cases.[95]

---

[91]This is not necessarily the same in all expedience-based systems. See, for example, the situation in the Netherlands where prosecution policy is "strikingly organised and determinate, implementing a carefully considered and coherent working philosophy" (Fionda 1995, p. 63).

[92]Contrary to the situation in Scotland, where for a long time now there has been a sophisticated diversionary package available to the procurators fiscal, including fiscal warnings, conditional offers of fixed penalties, fiscal fines and diversionary schemes (e.g. supervision by a social worker, referral to drug treatment, restorative interventions).

[93]McConville et al. (1991), Leng et al. (1996).

[94]However, McConville et al. (1991) and Gelsthorpe and Giller (1990) report that, even when cautionable cases could be identified, the CPS was reluctant to drop them, especially where police working rules pointed to prosecution.

[95]See Ashworth and Redmayne (2005, p. 148): "In the heavily pragmatic English system, fundamental values and principles have little explicit recognition, even as starting points. Instead, the alternatives to prosecution have developed one by one, often without statutory foundations, and hardly constitute a 'system' of diversion".

2.3.3 *Formulation of Prosecutorial Policy*

> 'Prosecutors must be given discretion, so that they can respond sensitively to the great diversity of factual situations and policy issues which arise. Equally, the public interest in fair, consistent and principled decision-making sustains the case for policy guidance and for accountability.' (Ashworth 1987, p. 606)

Once it is admitted that a certain amount of discretion should be allowed to prosecuting agencies over the decision to prosecute or divert a case from the courts, a number of issues arise to which different jurisdictions have not responded in a similar manner.

First, should prosecutors act on a predefined policy, publicly announced or does this negate the very need for individualised decision-making (which, supposedly, discretion promotes)? In England and Wales the CPS are obliged by law to issue a code setting out their policies and criteria according to which prosecution decisions should be made.[96] This is a public document formulated by the DPP and revised periodically. Moreover, recently, as Ashworth and Redmayne (2005, p. 176) remark, "there has been a welcome step towards openness, with the publication on the CPS website of considerable amounts of prosecutorial guidance previously confidential to Crown prosecutors". Prosecutors are, theoretically at least, obliged to follow all these guidelines, although practice showed that there has been a considerable degree of variation regarding their approaches and their understanding of the code (Hoyano et al. 1997).

Other jurisdictions have adopted a different approach to the one mentioned above, which allows prosecutors a broader discretion regarding the creation of predefined policies, while at the same time significantly limiting the number of decision-makers. For example, in Germany there are no published documents specifying the conditions under which a prosecution is dismissed or reflecting on the proper conduct of criminal prosecutions. There are some internal guidelines issued by the Federal Chief Prosecutor that are not published. It is argued that the strong hierarchical structure that exists, as well as the concentration of the most crucial decisions in the senior prosecutors, makes up for the lack of detailed and published guidelines.[97]

The *second issue* concerns the question of who should formulate prosecution policies. The most important issue in this context is the relationship between the Executive and the prosecution services. Ashworth (2000, p. 282) argues that the quasi-judicial role that prosecutors play suggests that they should enjoy a certain independence in matters of policy-making. In England and Wales the DPP formulates the CPS policies on prosecution and the Attorney General is constitutionally answerable for these policies to Parliament. In practice, Parliament never

[96] In Scotland there is also a Prosecution Code which sets out the criteria for decision-making and the range of options available to prosecutors dealing with reports of crime.

[97] Furthermore, the law on which prosecutors base the exercise of their discretion is also relatively detailed.

debates the principles or the contents of the code (Sanders 2004). The relationship between the Attorney General and the DPP is in practice primarily consultative in nature, enabling the Attorney General to retain a general overview of prosecution policy; also, the DPP is expected to provide sufficient information to the Attorney General to enable him to answer to Parliament for the performance of the CPS. In theory, both the Attorney General and the DPP are independent of the Executive. However, as Ashworth (2000, p. 262) remarks, the CPS in the past failed to act in an independent way from the Executive and his policies have been highly influenced by the Home Secretary's policies for prosecution and diversion.[98]

In other countries, such as France, Belgium, Germany, and the Netherlands, the prosecution services act under the supervision of the Minister of Justice who can issue directives to his subordinates concerning prosecutorial decisions to be made. The instructions of the minister can relate to a specific case or be of a general nature and thus concern general prosecution policies.

For example, Article 5 of the French Judicial Organisation Act 1958 states that the members of the *ministère public* are subordinated to the Minister of Justice. The Minister of Justice is politically accountable for the functioning of the Public Prosecution Service and thus can issue general instructions "so that criminal politics of the government can be put in practice". Verrest (2000, pp. 223–224) argues that:

> 'the more ideological ground behind the criminal policy entirely led by the government, is the deep fear in France of 'judicial corporatism'. The belief is high that if the Minister of Justice would cede any of his prerogatives in the field of criminal policy, the government would rapidly lose control over legal practice. ... The *ministère public* could abuse the expediency principle to prosecute whatever it chose and the Minister of Justice would lack the power to address his political responsibility for the administration of justice'.

In Germany there is a similar situation to the French one regarding the formulation of prosecutorial policies. Nevertheless, it has been argued that although general rules for the proper conduct of criminal prosecutions are defined by the Minister of Justice, more specific prosecution policies are not usually determined at the level of the Ministry of Justice but at that of the Federal Chief Prosecutor (Weigend 2004).

---

[98] Ashworth (1998) reports that, in 1994, the Home Secretary announced a new policy on police cautioning followed by a new circular directed to the police requiring them to change their cautioning policies. In the 1994 edition of the Code for Crown Prosecutors, the influence of this policy was more than obvious: "... this episode casts doubt on the CPS's claim to be independent and quasi-judicial, and raises questions about the role of the Attorney General, a member of the government and the minister to whom the Director of Public Prosecutions is accountable" (Ashworth 1998, p. 196). See also Ashworth and Fionda (1994) and a response to this criticism by Daw (1994).

2.4 Concluding Remarks

The description of prosecution systems in various jurisdictions used to be characterised by dichotomies: on the one hand there were adversarial prosecution systems and on the other inquisitorial ones; there were systems where prosecutors were also responsible for the investigative stage and others where there was a complete division of responsibility regarding the prosecution and the investigative stage; finally, there were systems which adhered to the opportunity principle and others which adhered to the mandatory one. However, Cappelletti (1984, p. 207) points out that "dichotomies provide only two-dimensional slices through reality: they give us black and white and – depending upon their degree of refinement – innumerable shades of grey ... But they do not give us the reds and greens and blues".

This is particularly true for the description of prosecution systems these days. Both adversarial and inquisitorial systems, either in theory or in practice, have been moved away from their traditional models and, at the present time, no prosecution system can be characterised as coming under one particular model. There are as many variations in prosecution systems as the number of countries involved. Nevertheless, some common trends have been observed – encouraged also by the guidance of supranational institutions such as the Council of Europe[99] and the European Court of Human Rights – that argue for the adoption of some common principles regarding prosecutions.

In the *first section* of this chapter, the origins, constitutional position and organisation of prosecution services in a number of jurisdictions were analysed. There is a long tradition in civil law systems of public authorities taking responsibility for prosecutions in the public interest, which pre-dates the creation of police forces. By contrast, in the common law tradition prosecution services are a relatively new feature, the responsibility for prosecutions having previously been left to private individuals and mainly to the police. Yet, although in some common law countries (e.g. Ireland) the police still retain significant prosecutorial functions, the trend has been towards giving responsibility for prosecutions to a prosecution agency independent of the police. Nevertheless, the varying structures and specific characteristics of the modern prosecution services, as well as their constitutional relationship with the police, can be traced back to their different origins. In common law countries, there is still a *right to private prosecution*, a number of other agencies apart for the main prosecution service carry out a significant number of prosecutions, and the *police enjoy a strong independence* not coming under the control of the prosecution service. In inquisitorial jurisdictions, as a rule, the state

[99] See a series of Recommendations issued by the Council of Europe relating to prosecutions: Rec (2000) 19, Rec (97) 13, Rec (92) 17, Rec (95) 12, etc. See also the recent Opinions of the Consultative Council of European Prosecutors (CCPE) "Alternatives to prosecution" – Opinion No 2 (2008) and "The Role of prosecution services outside the Criminal Law Field" – Opinion No 3 (2008).

monopolises the right to prosecute and prosecution services function in a *hierarchical structure* with strong internal guidelines. Public prosecutors normally belong to the *judicial branch* or they are considered as quasi-judicial officers. The police have never had a prosecutorial role and are regarded as coming under the command of, and being controlled by, the public prosecution services.

The *second section* dealt with the role of the prosecuting authorities in investigations. The classical divide between the prosecutor and the investigator, which is often seen as a distinguishing characteristic of common law systems, in some countries tends to dissolve. This either takes the form of informal arrangements between police and prosecutors without changing the constitutional relationship between the two services or, as in the case of England and Wales, a statutory reform. In inquisitorial systems, prosecutors have always been regarded as responsible for the investigatory as well as the prosecuting stage. Although, in practice, the police are left to investigate alone the majority of – especially less serious – crimes, prosecutors still retain overall control and responsibility for the regulation of the investigative stage.

The *third section* dealt with the way different prosecution systems approach the issues of prosecutorial discretion, diversion from prosecution and the formulation of prosecution criteria and policies. Prosecution systems have traditionally been characterised as adhering to either the *legality* or the *opportunity principle* depending on the extent of the discretion that prosecutors are allowed over the decision to prosecute and the permission to take into account factors other than evidence in making this decision. Most of those traditionally regarded as legality systems, due to rising caseloads, currently provide for exceptions in the legality principle. However, although in practice there is a good deal of convergence between opportunity and legality-based systems, commentators draw attention to some important differences that still exist. Because diversion in a legality system is an exception to a general rule, usually the conditions under which those exceptions can be made are stipulated and diversion decisions are usually reserved for the prosecutors to make. There are also relatively small numbers of senior decision-makers and a more centralised approach regarding diversion from prosecution. In opportunity-based systems, on the contrary, diversionary decisions are not the exclusive responsibility of prosecutors. Most non-prosecution decisions are still made by a relatively large number of police officers and, thus, are difficult to control.

As far as the formulation of prosecutorial policies is concerned, in some countries prosecutors are obliged to issue a code stating their policy and criteria according to which prosecution decisions should be made. Other jurisdictions, however, have adopted a different approach, which allows a broader discretion while at the same time significantly limiting the number of decision-makers. Furthermore, the formulation of prosecutorial policies, in some countries is the responsibility of the prosecution service itself, while in others it belongs to the control of the Executive (usually the Ministry of Justice) which also defines the government's criminal policy.

In this chapter, the distinct choices and paths that different legal systems have followed, their underlying philosophy, as well as the implications of these choices as documented by empirical studies, have been explored. This analysis was intended to serve as an additional context within which the particular choices of the Cyprus prosecution system can be understood. As stated in the Introduction, in Cyprus there is a dearth of theoretical as well as empirical research which sheds light on the issues discussed in this chapter for jurisdictions elsewhere. The objective of this book is exactly this: to attempt a first exploration of these issues, focusing on the pivotal role that the Attorney General's Office occupies in the Cyprus prosecution system.

> 'The value of comparative work is not simply to document differences and similarities between counties and systems, for the comparative perspective is also a valuable tool for analysing the distinctive character of one's own domestic and policy'. (Zimring and Johnson 2005, p. 794)

Chapter 3
Introduction to Cyprus Law and Prosecution System

> 'A system of administering criminal justice is a detailed tapestry woven of many varied threads. It is often difficult to understand the nature and the significance of any particular fibre without at least a general appreciation of the function of the other threads, and also the realisation of the impact on the whole'. (Pugh 1962, p. 1)[1]

By way of a background to the analysis in the more empirical chapters that follow, this chapter will commence with a brief historical background to the legal system in Cyprus, followed by an outline of the criminal justice process and a study of the evolution and the legal framework of the prosecution system.

The *first* task is useful in gaining an understanding of the origins and the general characteristics of Cyprus law. Although Cyprus is mostly characterised as a common law jurisdiction, it will become apparent that it has attracted influences from various legal systems and under those influences even original common law institutions have been modified. The *second* section discusses the law relating to the criminal justice process, highlighting again its particular characteristics and the way that a written Constitution has modified some rules and practices of the original English system. *Finally*, in the last section, the evolution of a private system of prosecutions to a unique prosecution system which concentrates extensive powers in the Attorney General's Office will be outlined and the present – limited and vague – legal provisions that regulate the prosecution process will be examined. This is essential in order to understand the inter-relationships of the various agencies that maintain an involvement in the prosecution of criminal offences and the key role of the Attorney General's Office. In some aspects there is a blurred division of responsibilities between criminal justice agencies that needs to be further explored. Overall, in this chapter, I will provide a discus\-sion of the *law* and describe how it serves as an additional context for the rhetoric and the operational practices regarding prosecutions, which I will investigate in the following chapters.

[1] Quoted in Johnson (2002, p. 268).

D. Kyprianou, *The Role of the Cyprus Attorney General's Office in Prosecutions: Rhetoric, Ideology and Practice*,
DOI 10.1007/978-3-642-01921-0_3, © Springer-Verlag Berlin Heidelberg 2010

3.1 Historical Evolution of Cyprus Law

> 'In contrast to its size and population Cyprus has an extensive legal history. Study of that legal evolution provides an exceptional example ... of the possibilities of harmonious co-existence and sometimes even the blending of legal systems'. (Markides 2000, p. vii)

This section will examine the historical evolution of the Cyprus legal system in order to demonstrate that it incorporates influences from different families of law but also that, like other "mixed systems", it "... has combined these influences with its own ethos to produce its distinct way of doing justice" (Gebbie and Bein 2002, p. 253).

Due to its geographical position at the crossroads of Europe, Asia and Africa, Cyprus throughout its history attracted the invasion of many foreign conquerors. Inevitably, its legal history was greatly influenced by the legal systems and legal traditions of those invaders, as well as by the legal systems of its neighbours. Markides (2000, p. vii) reports that:

> 'starting with the Hellenic system of city-kingdoms of the island,[2] Cyprus legal history was affected by neighbouring legal orders, such as those of Egypt, Babylonia and Assyria. More permanent influences came in the Roman and Byzantine periods with the introduction of Roman law, its codification and development by Justinian, the second codification and further development during the reign of Leon the Sixth, and the growth of ecclesiastical law. In later periods, first the French customary law and then the Turkish law and the concepts of *Sharia*[3] were brought to Cyprus, followed by English law from 1878'.

The Turkish rule in Cyprus lasted from 1571 to 1878. In 1878, with the Treaty of Constantinople, Turkey ceded Cyprus to Great Britain. Neocleous and Bevir (2000, p. 11) describe that when the British arrived in Cyprus, they found a legal system already in place. There was *inter alia* the Commercial Code (enacted in 1850), the Maritime Code (enacted in 1863), the Imperial Ottoman Penal Code, a comprehensive criminal code whose general arrangement and principles followed that of the French Penal Code, which had been enacted in 1858, the Sheri Courts (administering Islamic and Ottoman law) and the ecclesiastical courts of the Greek Orthodox Church had supreme authority in family matters, exercising jurisdiction over Muslims and Christians respectively. Meanwhile, land law was governed by the Ottoman Land Code and the Ottoman Civil Code, while a system of wide local government existed and was operating extensively.[4]

Regarding family matters, the British kept on the above division but transferred jurisdiction in all other matters to the civil courts. They also retained the Penal Code, which remained valid until 1928, when the Criminal Code still in force today

---

[2] For a detailed description of the legal institutions of the Ancient Kingdoms of Cyprus, see Colotas (1988).

[3] See Kemal Cicek (2002).

[4] See Tornaritis (1980, p. 17).

was introduced. As Neocleous and Bevir (2000, p. 11) report, "soon after their arrival, and probably in 1879, they established Assize Courts, District Courts and a Supreme Court. The Supreme Court had jurisdiction over all criminal or civil causes that did not come under the jurisdiction of the Ottoman Courts".

In 1882, the first major reorganisation of the judicial system took place by an Order in Council. The power of the Sheri Courts was further restricted by the transfer of their jurisdiction to the civil courts and a Supreme Court was set up. As Kapardis (2001) argues, the establishment of a decent court system in 1882, headed by legally qualified individuals instead of the *cadis* in Ottoman times, was one of the successes of the colonial administration, which managed to rid the courts of corruption and arbitrariness and establish a more equitable system of justice.[5] However, although the District and Assize Courts were composed by professional judges, English and Cypriots, "(t)his Order retained the element of judges belonging to each of the two communities of the Island, being represented on the Bench in the trial of criminal cases ..." (Loizou and Pikis 1975, p. 2).

On 5 November 1914 Great Britain annexed Cyprus and on 27 November 1917, Cypriots, who were Ottoman subjects and were in Cyprus on the date of the annexation, became British subjects. However, Ottoman law continued to be applied in some cases, because litigants were allowed to choose to have their rights determined either by Ottoman or by English law. Symeonides (2003, pp. 447–448) points out the peculiarity that the mixture of legal systems provoked: "Ottoman law was applied by English judges, trained in the common law and following the English procedure that had already been introduced in 1882. This was a very interesting phenomenon because all too often these judges resorted to English law to fill the real or imaginary gaps of Ottoman law".[6]

In 1935, the judicial system was revised again. With the Courts of Justice Law a modern judicial system was introduced, where, as Loizou and Pikis (1975, p. 3) remark the communal origin of the judge had no significance. Furthermore, in the same year British common law was fully introduced in Cyprus and applied to all cases. In addition to the common law, Cyprus was now subject to all of the special British colonial legislation, as well as those statutes of the British Parliament which were of "general" (as opposed to local) character.[7] However, according to Symeonides (2003, p. 448), this should not give the impression that the 1935 law "succeeded in, or even tried, eliminating the diversity of sources that comprised the law of Cyprus". As the same author argues, legal diversity was not eliminated because, *firstly*, Ottoman law was partly preserved: (a) by retaining in force the Ottoman Land Code and the Maritime Code, which was partly French; and (b) by recognising the jurisdiction of the Muslim Religious Courts to adjudicate pursuant to their law matters of personal status of the Muslim inhabitants of Cyprus; and,

[5] See also Katsiaounis (1996) and Georghallides (1979).

[6] For an overview of the justice system in Cyprus during British rule, see Limbourides (1983).

[7] The effects of the British common law on a culture different from that of Britain and the move away from local customs combined to create legal conflicts. See Demetriadou (1989).

secondly, because Byzantine law was preserved through the recognition of the jurisdiction of the Episcopal Courts and the law-making authority of the Orthodox Church for matters of personal status of the Greek inhabitants.[8]

The Republic of Cyprus was established as an independent sovereign republic with a presidential regime[9] on 16 August 1960, when its Constitution came into force and British sovereignty over Cyprus as a Crown Colony ceased. The Constitution provided that the Laws previously applicable should remain in force in the Republic, to the extent that they did not contravene the Constitution, until repealed or amended by any law enacted by the Cyprus Parliament.[10] In the meantime, the pre-1960 Laws were to be interpreted consistently with, and when necessary adapted to, the Constitution. In this way, as Symeonides (2003, pp. 449–450) points out, "the Constitution provided the necessary continuity of law without prejudging the future legal orientation of the Republic".

However, the Parliament of Cyprus, four months after the establishment of the Republic, enacted a law (Law 14/1960) by which the previous legal system was adopted without any temporal limitations or reservations, except the inevitable one that all laws should be compatible with the Constitution. This law provided that when not otherwise provided by applicable statutes, the courts of Cyprus would continue to apply the English "common law and the principles of equity". In this way, as Symeonides (2003) remarks, it authorised the application of not only the pre-independence common law, but also of the post-independence common law. According to one theory, this provision made the post-independence common law binding, not just persuasive, on the courts of Cyprus. Symeonides (2003, p. 450) explains that this meant that a post-1960 decision of the House of Lords would be binding on the courts of Cyprus, even if a subsequent statute of the British Parliament had superseded that decision. In contrast to some very enthusiastic supporters of this view who believed that English law had served the country

[8]Symeonides (2003, p. 449) also reports that "even some of the statutes that the colonial authorities enacted during this period increased rather than decreased the diversity of Cypriot law. For example, two statutes, one on contract law and the other on the sale of goods, were supposed to be codifications of the English common law in those respective areas. This was true to some extent. However, strangely – but not surprisingly – these statutes also contained elements of Indian, including Hindu, law. Why? Because they were copies of 'codifications' undertaken in India, another British colony, a few years earlier ... Similarly, the Law of Intestate Succession drew from provisions of the Italian Civil Code, while the Law of Horizontal Ownership of Buildings was based on a corresponding Greek statute".

[9]The structure of the new state was based on the separation of powers. The legislative power vests in the House of Representatives, the executive power is exercised by the President and the Council of Ministers and the judicial power is vested principally in the Supreme Court and its subordinate courts as established under Part X of the Constitution. It should be also pointed out that the Constitution of Cyprus is one of the most complicated constitutions of the world, due to the effort to construct a bi-communal state, the basic function of which were requiring the participation of the members of the Greek-Cypriot and Turkish-Cypriot communities. See, *inter alia*, Loucaides (1982), Tornaritis (1980) and De Smith (1964).

[10]Article 188 of the Constitution.

well and should continue to do so,[11] there were some others who expressed concern and criticised this provision in the Law.[12] Along these lines, Symeonides (2003, p. 450) fairly argues that this statute "went much further than the letter and spirit of the Constitution, and sought to tie the legal system of Cyprus surreptitiously and permanently to the English common law". Fortunately, as the same writer explains, this "danger" has not fully materialised, and the Cyprus legal system remained as – if not more – mixed as before for a series of reasons. Some important ones are the following:[13]

Firstly, two years after Independence, when the Supreme Court was asked to follow English case law issued after 1960, it adopted the position that this did not have binding authority. It accepted though, that as a general practice (for reasons of "judicial comity") it would be followed,[14] unless courts are convinced that it is false.

Secondly, "Cyprus courts have also asserted the right to subject the application of the English common law to the condition that it be 'suitable for Cyprus'. This is similar to the position that American courts took during the formative period of American law before importing the common law of England. The difference is that in Cyprus there is no statutory authorisation for imposing this condition, although, as in the United States, there is ample justification in logic" (Symeonides 2003, p. 451).[15]

Thirdly, Cyprus courts, in dealing with pre-1960 statutes, have not confined themselves to simply refusing to apply unconstitutional statutes (Courts of Justice Law 14/1960), but they have also applied their power provides by Article 188 of the Constitution to either abolishing the unconstitutional statutes or amending them so as to make it consistent with the Republic's Constitution.[16]

Fourthly, Article 146 of the Constitution introduced into Cyprus a new conception compatible to the continental systems and similar to the administrative jurisdiction exercised by the Greek and the French *Conseil d' État*. It provides that the Supreme Court has jurisdiction to review administrative acts and to annul them if it finds them unconstitutional, illegal or *ultra vires*. As a result, in applying this

[11] See Pikis (1981), who argued that the reason why common law was adopted in Cyprus *en masse* with the Law 14/1960 was the common belief of both Greek and Turkish Cypriots that it had been tested in the country for a while and provided security for people and effective protection of civil rights.

[12] Loucaides (1982) and Symeonides (1977).

[13] Most of the reasons mentioned here are analysed in Symeonides (2003, pp. 451–454).

[14] Stylianou v. The Police (1962) 2 C.L.R. 152. See also Mouzouris v. Xylophagou Plantations Ltd (1977) 1 C.L.R. 287, The Police v. Xidia (1992) 2 C.L.R. 26 and Parris v. The Republic (1999) 2 C. L.R. 126.

[15] "(T)he Common law must be planted here as a living growth which can be pruned by judicial decision to suit local conditions [because] ... the intention of the country's legislator was the service of people in this country". (Paikkos v. Kontemeniotis (1989) 1 C.L.R. 50 at 73). See also Protopapas v. Gunther, [1974] 10 J.S.C. 981.

[16] Christodoulou v. The Republic (1967) 3 C.L.R. 691.

power, the Supreme Court has drawn extensively on Greek and French academic and judicial authorities, including the decisions of the Greek and French *Conseil d' État*. This, as Symeonides (2003, p. 453) remarks "gave rise to the creation of a whole new corpus of Cyprus law derived from Greek and French sources". As the same writer continues:

> '(a) similar, but less pronounced, borrowing from non-English sources has also taken place in the area of constitutional law, particularly individual rights. Here, English law was not particularly helpful given the absence of a written constitution in England. This explains, at least in part, why in dealing with certain constitutional issues the Supreme Court of Cyprus has occasionally turned to the jurisprudence of the United States Supreme Court'. (Symeonides 2003, p. 453)

Lastly, although until 1988 the official language in courts was English, with the enactment of Law 67/1988 the use of Greek was finally established.

To sum up this brief discussion of the evolution of Cyprus law, it can be said that Cyprus history is marked by long periods of foreign conquest and, consequently, "its legal history is interwoven with the legal systems of its conquerors" (Loizou and Pikis 1975, p. 1). Given that Great Britain was its most recent foreign ruler, "Cyprus has received and retained most of the essential elements of the English common law tradition, especially in the areas of procedure and methodology" (Symeonides 2003, p. 441). However, as has been shown, in the Cyprus legal system elements or principles of, *inter alia*, Roman and Byzantine law, Ottoman land law, Greek and French administrative and public law and American constitutional law can be found.[17] Moreover, the Cyprus legal profession is no longer as tied to Britain as it was during the first years of Cyprus independence. Although many Cypriots continue to study Law in England, equally as many, if not more, do so in Greece (given the very close relations and national ties between Cyprus and Greece) and are inescapably influenced by the continental legal system of this country.[18] Therefore, although some still insist to characterise Cyprus as a common law country,[19] it becomes obvious that, especially in the course of the last five decades, the Cyprus legal system has gradually moved closer to being characterised as a "mixed legal system":[20]

> '... the above developments and borrowings contributed to turning the law of Cyprus into a fascinating legal mosaic where the English common law coexists with Greek and French administrative law, European and American constitutional principles, Roman-Byzantine law, and Ottoman law. The fact that this diverse law is applied and reshaped by Cypriot judges, some of whom have been trained in the common law tradition and increasingly

---

[17] As of 1 May 2004, Cyprus is a full member state of the European Union. Therefore, European Union law and principles are also applicable in Cyprus.

[18] See Symeonides (2003).

[19] "(A)lthough Cyprus legal system comprises various statutes not based solely on English law but also on various other continental legislation, nevertheless, the common law cardinal rules of legal construction continue to prevail and the Republic of Cyprus may still be considered as a common law country" (Tornaritis 1982, p. 40).

[20] For further discussion, see Symeonides (1977) and Neocleous (2000)

more of whom have been trained in the Greek and Continental tradition, makes the Cypriot amalgam one of the most interesting legal systems within the Western legal family'. (Symeonides 2003, p. 453)

3.2 The Criminal Justice System

It can be argued that criminal law and procedure represent areas where the common law tradition and principles have been preserved to a greater extent compared to other areas of Cyprus law. Having said that, even in this area the influence of other legal systems is not totally absent and often provisions originating from them are being advocated for proposed changes in Cyprus criminal procedure.[21] The variety of influences, although not objectionable *per se*, combined with the absence of a detailed and systematic review of the system, sometimes leads to confusion about the principles and aims of the criminal justice system. It is regrettable that criminal procedure has received only intermittent official attention since the foundation of the state and there has never been a designed strategy to update the system in a structured and comprehensive way.

3.2.1 Law in Force

The relevant law which presently regulates criminal justice is embodied in the Criminal Code (Cap. 154) and the Criminal Procedure Law (Cap. 155), while the structure and jurisdiction of the Courts are regulated by the Courts of Justice Law, No. 14/60. The courts involved in the administration of criminal justice are: (a) the District Courts (single Judge), (b) the Assize Courts (three Judges), and (c) the Supreme Court in its appellate jurisdiction.

The Criminal Code represents a codified version of all major offences which exist under common law. As was stated previously, though, prior to the British occupation the applicable criminal law was the Ottoman Penal Code, which was mainly based on the French Penal Code. Therefore, in the existing criminal code, certain resemblances to the Ottoman Penal Code can still be identified, such as in the area of premeditated murder, where no malice aforethought is required, in contrast to the common law.[22]

The system of criminal procedure currently in force in Cyprus emanates from the English system of criminal proceedings with the necessary adaptations in certain respects to Cyprus particular circumstances. The Criminal Procedure Law (Cap. 155) is based on English statutes regulating criminal procedure and clearly states

[21] See particularly the discussions about the reform of the Evidence Law in criminal cases (House of Representatives: Discussions on the Draft Bill on Evidence, 2001–2003).

[22] Clerides (1984).

that where no provision is made in the Law or in any other enactment in force for the time being in Cyprus, every court shall in criminal proceedings "apply the law and rules of practice relating to criminal procedure for the time being in force in England".[23] Three crucial points should be kept in mind at this point:

1. In interpreting the above Laws, the Cyprus judiciary is assisted by the precedents of English case law. Although, as was shown above, according to the Supreme Court, these have no binding authority, they nevertheless provide useful guidance on numerous points of law, and it is rarely that the courts will depart from them.[24] On the other hand, decisions of the Cyprus Supreme Court are binding on all inferior courts.
2. A very important difference between Cyprus and other common law judicial systems, which in some cases modifies the orthodox common law criminal procedure rules or the interpretation of them, is that the jury system is not and has never been applicable in Cyprus.[25] It has been asserted that the sitting of three Judges to deal with serious criminal cases in the Assize Court makes up for the jury's absence to a considerable extent,[26] but others claim that this absence takes away from the trial the democratic element of public participation in the administration of justice.[27]
3. Criminal law and procedure are also influenced by the fundamental rights and civil liberties entrenched in the Constitution (Part II). Article 11.5 of the Constitution partly reproduced the provisions of Article 5(3) of the European Convention on Human Rights, which was ratified by Law 39/1962, and it forms part of the legal order of Cyprus.[28] Artemis remarked that "the Constitution has moulded present day rules of criminal law and procedure in such a manner as to uphold in an effective way civil rights and liberties" (Artemis 1989, p. 4016).[29]

---

[23] Criminal Procedure Law Cap. 155 s.3.

[24] Especially in this area of law, Cyprus courts appear more reluctant to deviate from common law principles; see Loizou (1968) and Artemis (1989).

[25] The British did not introduce the jury system in all of their former colonies, as the public participation in the administration of criminal justice was not well suited to a colonial regime. See Kapardis (2001, p. 60). See also Vidmar (2002), who reports that the jury system was introduced in a number of British colonies, albeit with various modifications (e.g. in some African colonies only whites were eligible to serve on juries and in other instances property or other requirements effectively excluded non-whites).

[26] Loizou (1972).

[27] See, *inter alia*, Drakos (2005).

[28] See European Commission's Report (1999, p. 58): "The Constitution safeguards fundamental rights and liberties in a comprehensive way. The constitutional charter of human rights is modelled on the European Convention on Human Rights, even though it is more detailed and extensive".

[29] An example of this was the abolition of the mandatory or minimum sentence as it was judged contrary to the constitutional principle which states that "no law shall provide for a punishment disproportionate to an offence" (Article 12.3 of the Constitution). Another example would be the power of arrest and detention that has been formulated in such a way as to comply with the constitutional requirements contained in Article 11 and the right of liberty of an individual – see the discussion later in this chapter.

3.2.2 Arrest – Detention – Questioning

Article 11 of the Constitution provides that «every person has the right to liberty and security of person». Article 11.2 contains an exhaustive list[30] of the situations whereby interference with a person's right to liberty may be affected, including arrest on reasonable suspicion of having committed an offence. However, it is declared that, save in the case of flagrant offences punishable with imprisonment, a person may be arrested only under the authority of a reasoned judicial warrant.

Based on this section the Supreme Court has stated that sections 14 and 15 of the Criminal Procedure Law, which make it possible for a police officer or a private citizen to make an arrest without warrant in certain cases, are not fully applicable:[31] they must be read and applied subject to the provisions of Article 11 of the Constitution and must be construed as reading that there is a power to make an arrest without a warrant only where an offence is flagrantly committed before such a person.

Sections 18 and 19 of the Criminal Procedure Law regulate the procedure for the issue of a warrant of arrest. According to them, a judge may issue a warrant of arrest if he is satisfied that there is reasonable suspicion that the person in question has committed the offence or that the detention of the person is reasonably necessary for preventing the commission of offences or the escape of the suspect. These sections, as they are today, were introduced in 1996 after a decision of the Supreme Court (In Re Polycarpou (1991) 1 C.L.R. 207) which stated that the previous provisions of the Criminal Procedure Law (allowing a judge to issue a warrant for the arrest of a person "if he considered it to be necessary or desirable") were unsatisfactory, as they failed to address the real essence of the problem, which was the interference with the liberty of a person. Thoma (2000) remarks that under the previous provision it was very easy for the police to abuse their power and issue warrants against persons only on mere suspicion of having committed an offence and then release them due to lack of incriminating evidence. In the same decision, the Supreme Court also stated (a) that in deciding whether to issue a warrant of arrest the court must draw its own conclusions from the affidavits presented to it when deciding whether a reasonable suspicion exists or not, and (b) that the opinion of the police officers making the statements do not form the basis for issuing an arrest warrant.

It can be concluded from the above that the police in Cyprus have relatively narrow arrest powers, in comparison for instance with their counterparts in England and Wales. The necessity of a judicial warrant in the absolute majority of cases (apart from flagrant offences), at least in theory, provides a safeguard against the absolute discretion of the police to arrest people based on very little evidence.

---

[30]Pitsillos v. The Police (1966) 2 C.L.R. 50.

[31]Kyriakides v. The Republic 1 RSCC 66.

However, given the lack of any empirical studies, it is difficult to say how easily courts issue such warrants in practice and based on what type of evidence.[32]

The Constitution also stipulates that every person arrested must be informed of the reasons for his arrest, in a language that he understands, and must be allowed to have the services of a lawyer of his choice. The right to legal advice is guaranteed by Article 11.4 of the Constitution but, until recently, it had not been specified in detail with statutory legislation.[33] Law 163(I)/2005 (The Law on the Rights of Persons who are Arrested and Detained Law) specified this right and introduced a number of other provisions which regulate the rights and the treatment of suspects in a police station. Furthermore, it provides for criminal sanctions in cases where staff responsible for a place of detention obstruct the exercise of certain rights.

According to section 13.1 of Criminal Procedure Law, any person arrested by the police – whether or not under an arrest warrant – shall be taken with all reasonable dispatch to a police station or any other place authorised for the reception of arrested persons. As soon as is practicable after his arrest, and in any event not later than twenty-four hours, be brought before a judge (Article 11.5 of the Constitution). Not later than three days after the appearance of the person arrested, the judge must either release him (on bail or not), or remand him in custody.[34]

The principles on which the court will exercise its discretion in remanding an arrested person in custody have been considered in a number of cases.[35] The judge: (a) must be satisfied that there is a genuine and reasonable suspicion of involvement of the suspect in the crime under investigation; (b) must determine that the inquiries and investigations conducted by the police have not yet been completed; and (c) determine that the remand of the suspect is necessary because he is likely to interfere with the prosecution witnesses or destroy or hide any incriminating evidence, abscond or generally interfere with the investigation process.[36] The courts have repeatedly pronounced that in deciding on a remand order, the judge is interfering with the fundamental right of freedom (as enshrined in the Constitution) of the accused and therefore must exercise proper care in ensuring "a healthy balance between individual liberty on the one hand and public interest in the

[32]Nevertheless, as people (especially police officers and Law Officers) I interviewed argued, currently, it is considerably more difficult for the police to issue arrest warrants compared, for instance, to two decades ago. An example of the stricter approach of the courts has been the decision in Re Polycarpou (1991) 1 C.L.R. 207 mentioned above.

[33]See, however, section 13.2 of Criminal Procedure Law.

[34]An arrested person may be remanded in custody for renewable periods of up to eight days. And the total period of remand in custody must not exceed three months (Article 11.6 of the Constitution).

[35]Tsirides v. The Police (1973) 2 C.L.R. 204, Stamataris v. The Police (1983) 2 C.L.R. 107, Aeroporos v. The Police (1987) 2 C.L.R. 232, Shimitras and Another v. The Police (1990) 2 C.L.R. 397, Houris v. The Police (1989) 2 C.L.R. 56, Simillides v. The Police (1997) 2 C.L.R. 160, Demetriades v. The Police (1997) 2 C.L.R. 312, Ioannou v. The Police (1998) 2 C.L.R. 495, Lomjanidje v. The Police (2003) 2 C.L.R. 401, etc.

[36]An application for a remand must be made by a police officer not below the rank of inspector (Criminal Procedure Law s.24).

investigation and suppression of crime on the other" (Stamataris v. The Police (1983) 2 C.L.R. 107 at 113–4).

Furthermore, Article 11.7 of the Constitution recognises a right of appeal to the Supreme Court regarding remand orders of the courts. Loizou and Pikis (1975, p. 34) remark that "Article 11.7 of the Constitution should therefore be considered an additional safeguard for the protection of the liberty of the subject ... The principle of judicial control over arrest and detention, enshrined in the above article of the Constitution, connotes control by an authority possessing a judicial character with attributes of independence from the executive and the parties".

Regarding the procedures of the questioning of suspects in Cyprus, section 8 of the Criminal Procedure Law provides that they are governed by the Judges' Rules which are defined by the Queen's Bench Division in England. The courts decided that Judges' Rules do not constitute rules of law but they have the same status as in England: they are practice rules that offer guidance during the investigation[37] and, therefore, the breach of these rules does not automatically result in the exclusion of evidence in court. It is, however, taken into consideration by the court in order to decide whether a testimony was taken voluntarily or under oppression and conditions unfair for the suspect. Nickolatos (1993a) argues that the Supreme Court in Cyprus, although recognising this wide discretion of the courts, has taken a strong line against the breach of these rules:

> 'In Cyprus ... the Supreme Court in a series of cases has emphatically stressed that the courts should freely exclude testimonies that had been obtained as a result of a breach of the Judges' Rules; this should be done in their effort to promote the rule of law and deter any misconduct and unfair practice by the police'. (Nickolatos 1993a, pp. 19–20)

At this point, it is very important to stress that Cyprus courts have been following a strict exclusionary rule regarding evidence that has been obtained in breach of constitutionally protected rights.[38] As far as illegally or unfairly obtained evidence is concerned, the courts have also been strict, albeit recognising some exceptions to this rule.[39]

3.2.3 Commencement of Criminal Proceedings and Mode of Trial

According to section 37 of Criminal Procedure Law, a criminal prosecution is commenced by a charge preferred before a court of competent jurisdiction, unless

[37] Azinas v. The Police (1981) 2 C.L.R. 9.

[38] See *inter alia* Attorney General v. Aeroporos (1999) 2 C.L.R. 232, The Republic v. Kyprianides (1994) 2 C.L.R. 37, The Police v. Yiallouros (1992) 2 C.L.R. 147, Parpas v. The Republic (1988) 2 C.L.R. 5, Merthodja v. The Police (1987) 2 C.L.R. 227 and The Police v. Georghiades (1983) 2 C.L.R. 33. See also Pikis (2003, Chap. 6).

[39] See, e.g. Michalis Andrea Psillas v. The Republic (2003) 2 C.L.R. 353 and Parris v. The Republic (1999) 2 C.L.R. 186.

it is otherwise provided by law. A charge is an accusation in writing of an offence preferred against the accused in a summary trial or a preliminary inquiry.

There are two forms of criminal trial under Cyprus Law: summary trial and trial on information. A summary trial means any trial held before a judge in the exercise of his summary jurisdiction (section 2 of the Criminal Procedure Law). According to s.24.1 of the Courts of Justice Law 1960, every President, Senior District Judge and District Judge of a District Court has jurisdiction to try summarily all offences punishable with imprisonment not exceeding 5 years and/or a fine not exceeding CY£50,000.[40] They also have jurisdiction to try any offence beyond the above limits summarily, provided the consent of the Attorney General is obtained.[41] However, in this case, the sentence passed by the court could not exceed the sentence which could be passed by the court trying the case summarily, regardless of the maximum punishment provided by law for this offence.

Trial on information takes place before the Assize Courts. As provided by section 20.1 of the Courts of Justice Law 1960, Assize Courts have jurisdiction to try all types of offences with the exceptions of those where specific provisions are made in Article 156 of the Constitution of the Republic. A trial on information involves the filing of an accusation of an offence in writing exclusively by or on behalf of the Attorney General in the Assize Court.[42] Loizou and Pikis (1975, p. 66) point out that the filling of an information by the Attorney General is an indispensable prerequisite for a trial on information, irrespective of the presence of a committal order. Section 102 of Criminal Procedure Law provides that a person tried on information has the right to obtain a copy of the charge, the deposition and his statements and where practicable any documents which may have been put in evidence at the preliminary inquiry, on payment of the prescribed fee. According to section 109, an information, like a charge before a District Court,[43] must contain the name and the description of the accused and set out the offence preferred against him. However, unlike the charge, it must also contain (at the back of the information) the names of the witnesses who gave evidence at the preliminary inquiry.

If the Attorney General, after an accused is committed to the Assize Court for a trial on information, considers that a case is more appropriate for a summary trial,[44] he has the power to remit the accused to the District Court for a summary trial. Likewise, it is possible for a court dealing with a case in a summary trial to commit the case to the Assize Court and order a preliminary inquiry if before or during the

[40] Since 1 January 2008, this amount corresponds to 85,430 Euro.

[41] Courts of Justice Law 1960, s.24.2.

[42] This information must comply with all the formalities provided under the Criminal Procedure Law, s.39.

[43] See section 39 of Criminal Procedure Law.

[44] Criminal Procedure Law s.155(b).

summary trial, it appears to the court that this is a case which should have been committed for trial to the Assize Court.[45]

The holding of a *preliminary inquiry* is another condition precedent to trial on information.[46] Therefore, whenever any charge has been brought against any person for an offence not triable summarily, a preliminary inquiry must be held. The preliminary inquiry should not be regarded as the start of the trial of the case, since as Loizou and Pikis (1975, p. 159) argue, "it is a preparatory investigation, not a trial in any respect, meant to elicit the evidence forthcoming against the accused with a view to deciding whether there are grounds for committing him to trial".

The first task of the Judge at this stage is to acquaint the accused with the charges against him, without, however, allowing him to plead to the charge. Subsequently, the evidence of witnesses testifying at the preliminary inquiry is taken in the form of disposition and the Judge usually records the substance of the evidence in the form of a narrative and read it over to the witness in order to give him the opportunity to correct what he has said in case of error. When all prosecution witnesses give their disposition, it is the duty of the Judge to decide whether there are sufficient grounds for committing the accused for trial. In deciding this issue, the judge must be guided by section 94 of the Criminal Procedure Law, which provides that where there is a conflict of evidence, he shall consider the evidence to be sufficient to commit the accused for trial if the evidence against him is such that, if un-contradicted, it would raise a probable presumption of his guilt. The extent to which the available evidence raises a probable presumption of guilt is a matter of fact and degree. Loizou and Pikis (1975, p. 167) point out that "an interplay of logic and common sense should guide the Court in its task. Bearing in mind that the probability envisaged by the law must be a real and not a fanciful one, the guilt of the accused must be probable as a matter of logical inference". Therefore, if the judge is satisfied that there is enough evidence, the accused must be committed for trial at the Assize Court's next sitting in the district in which the offence is alleged to have been committed. Otherwise, the accused must be discharged. However, this discharge does not bar any further prosecutions of the accused based on the same facts.

After the Turkish invasion of 1974 and dealing with the anomalous situation resulting from it, a law was passed[47] which dispensed with the holding of a preliminary inquiry, provided that (a) the Attorney General certified in writing that the holding of such inquiry was not necessary and (b) copies of each prosecution witness's statement were served in advance on the accused or his counsel.[48]

---

[45] Criminal Procedure Law, s.90. See G. Pattiki and Another v. The Attorney General (2000) 1 C.L. R. 1669.

[46] See sections 92–106 of Criminal Procedure Law.

[47] Criminal Procedure (Temporary Provisions) Law 1974 (Law 42/1974 as amended by Law 44/1983).

[48] See a similar provision in the Canadian Criminal Code, s.577 ("Direct Indictments"), based on which the Attorney General has the power to directly indict the accused without the accused having the benefit of a preliminary inquiry.

This Law, 35 years later, is still in force. In fact, almost unexceptionally (the Deputy Attorney General, in the interview he gave me, stated that since 1974 only one preliminary inquiry has been held) all the defendants are committed for trial before the Assize Court without a preliminary inquiry.

3.2.4 Trial

The procedure at the criminal trial is mainly regulated by section 74 of the Criminal Procedure Law. Thoma (2000, pp. 479–480) remarks that "(b)uilding on its Common Law background, Cypriot law has adopted an adversarial system of trial. The judge acts as the referee between the two contending parties in their quest to win 'an evidence contest'.[49] Each party puts forward its own case and seeks to substantiate its case with the available evidence subject to the restrictions imposed by rules of law, evidence and procedure". The judge, who has the overall responsibility to see that all rules are properly followed, resolves any conflict arising out of the application of these rules. Section 74 of the Criminal Procedure Law in broad lines reproduces the same features of trial under the Common Law system and the principles followed in England and Wales. There are, however, two particular points that must be kept in mind:

The first relates to the criterion that the judge should apply to half-time submissions of no case to answer after the close of the prosecution case.[50] The Criminal Procedure Law provides that "if the court is satisfied that the prosecution has failed to establish sufficiently a *prima facie* case to require him to make his defence, it must order the acquittal and discharge of the accused". The meaning of the phrase "establish *sufficiently* a *prima facie* case" has troubled the courts on numerous occasions. In Azinas and Another v. The Police (1981) 2 C.L.R. 133, the Supreme Court declared that, in deciding whether a *prima facie* case exists, the court must use as a guide the Practice Directions that the Divisional Court of the Queen's Bench Division of the High Court of England issued in 1962, which provides that:

> 'a submission that there is no case to answer may properly be made and upheld: (a) when there has been no evidence to prove an essential element in the alleged offence; (b) when the evidence adduced by the prosecution has been so discredited as a result of cross-examination or it is manifestly so unreliable that no reasonable tribunal could safely convict on it'.[51]

---

[49] Loizou and Pikis (1975, p. 96).

[50] As will be shown in Chap. 6, it is this criterion that most of the Law Officers are referred to, when asked about the level of evidence that a case should satisfy in order to be sent to court.

[51] (1962) 1 All E R 448.

In the same case, however, there was a confusing reference to R. v. Galbraith,[52] which arguably[53] offers a lower criterion than the 1962 Practice Note according to which the evidence of the prosecution should be assessed. Although in later cases[54] the Supreme Court reconfirms the guidelines based on the 1962 Practice Note, in some cases there is still an additional reference to Galbraith.

It can be observed that the Supreme Court at least theoretically adopts the position that in order to require the accused to make his defence the prosecution evidence must be credited as at least provisionally reliable.[55] In the same way, as will be discussed in Chap. 6, when Law Officers argue that there should be at least a *prima facie* case in order for a case to be sent to court, most of them mean by this "enough provisionally reliable evidence".

The second point that must be kept in mind when referring to the criminal trial in Cyprus is that, as there is no jury system, the judge acts as arbitrator of both the law and the facts of the case. Considering that the jury is viewed by most as the ideal mode of conducting trials according to adversarial terms, the total absence of the jury in Cyprus may suggest some shifts in the character of the original adversarial trial.[56] It could be assumed that it may also affect the selection of the cases that are sent to court as well as the way prosecutors present them in court.[57] It should also be mentioned that the fact that the judges have the duty to provide a reasoned judgment in support of their decisions[58] (as opposed to jury decisions and somehow as a compensation for the absence of them) offers a valuable source of information on what type of cases "succeed or fail" in courts and the reasons why.

3.2.5 Evidence Law

Cyprus enacted in 1946 the Evidence Law (Cap. 9), which reproduced the legislation on evidence in force in England in 1914. The development of this Law, though, has not followed that of the English law of evidence. For example, the provisions of a series of Criminal Acts, which permit the introduction of hearsay evidence in a number of instances in England, have not been followed in Cyprus. Yet some flexibility has been permitted with section 5A of Evidence Law for

[52](1981) 2 All E R 1001.

[53]See Mansfield and Peay (1987).

[54]E.g. Attorney General v. Christodoulou (1990) 2 C.L.R. 133.

[55]See, *inter alia*, Attorney General v. Theodorou (2002) 2 C.L.R. 9.

[56]See Jackson and Doran (1995) for a discussion of the Diplock Trials in Northern Ireland.

[57]It has to be mentioned, though, that this book does not deal with the role of the Law Officers in presenting cases in court.

[58]Article 30.2 of the Constitution provides that the judgment of the Court shall be reasoned. Section 113.1 of the Criminal Procedure Law creates the same obligation, providing that reasons must be given for the judgment of the Court.

computer-generated materials which can be used as admissible evidence, provided that certain preconditions are satisfied. Apart from this statutory exception, until recently, the rules against hearsay have been subject to an inflexible interpretation by Cyprus courts.

A further characteristic of the Law of Evidence in Cyprus, which has been abolished in many of the common law jurisdictions, is the need for the prosecution to provide corroborative evidence in an extensive list of cases[59] (for instance, in the cases of procuration, perjury, claims on the estate of a deceased person, contradictory statements made during trial on information and until recently in the case of a child giving un-sworn evidence[60]). In some other cases (for example, in sexual offences, accomplices give evidence for the prosecution, identification evidence, etc.), the judge may convict an accused in the absence of corroborative evidence, provided that he has "warned himself"[61] of the dangers involved in reaching such a decision. Some argued that the need for corroborative evidence raises a number of obstacles for the prosecution in discharging their duty during trial and the application of this rule should be more limited in scope.[62]

The reform of the Law of Evidence has been a topic that has fuelled many arguments for years now in Cyprus. It is worth mentioning that absolutely all Law Officers I interviewed argued that the biggest problem they face presenting cases in court is the outdated Evidence Law. During the time of my fieldwork at the Attorney General's Office, there was a bill under consideration by the Parliament on hearsay evidence that caused much controversy. After fierce discussions, a law[63] was enacted in 2004 which introduced extensive exceptions in the law of hearsay evidence.

3.2.6 Concluding Remarks

From the foregoing it can be seen that the criminal justice process in Cyprus, although it evolved under the heavy influence of common law, developed its own particular characteristics under the influence of other legal systems and local needs but most importantly under the influence of a written Constitution which places great emphasis on the protection of human rights. It can be argued that the restrictions imposed by the Constitution on the gathering of evidence in criminal cases, as

[59] Similar provisions can be found in Scottish law.

[60] See, however, the changes introduced by Law 14(I)/2009. This recent Law, which modifies section 9 of Evidence Law, provides that there is no need for corroborative evidence in support of the sworn or un-sworn evidence given by a child.

[61] This is the exact – oddly sounding – phrase that the judiciary are using. Being both the arbiters of the law as well as the facts, they are obliged to warn themselves – instead of the jury – of the dangers that the acceptance of evidence without corroboration may involve.

[62] E.g. Thoma (2000) and Eliades (1994).

[63] Law 32(I)/2004 which amended the Law of Evidence (Cap. 9).

well as the complex law of evidence, imposes certain (arguably justifiable) difficulties upon the investigative duties of the police. These particular difficulties may partly explain the necessity of the prosecutors' involvement in the investigative stage, as will be shown in Chap. 5.

3.3 Prosecutions and the Attorney General's Office

3.3.1 Before Independence – 1960

3.3.1.1 Police Prosecutions

The history of criminal prosecutions in Cyprus charts a progression from a limited private activity to a unique system of prosecution in which broad and extensive powers are concentrated in the Office of the Attorney General. Unfortunately, there is very limited information available for the very early years of the British colonisation as far as prosecutions are concerned. The general conclusion that can be extracted from the study of historic sources is that the practice regarding prosecutions in Cyprus was similar to that in England at that time in that the initiation of criminal proceedings was the right of the private individual as well as one of the main duties of the newly re-organised police.

Since the importation of the common law to Cyprus, its fundamental philosophy that there is a responsibility as well as a right of each member of the community in the administration of the community's affairs began to be introduced in the criminal justice system. However, it could be argued that, initially, it was introduced more as a responsibility to assist in keeping the peace and apprehending the offenders rather than as a right to participate in the administration of justice.[64] Nevertheless, the right of every member of the public to initiate prosecutions was indisputable and very much encouraged. In fact, it is interesting to note that the 1882 Cyprus Courts of Justice Order introduced the "citizen's arrest", a power that authorised every person who had reason to believe that someone had committed an offence to arrest him (Kapardis 2001). Furthermore, it established a system of rewards and awards of costs to private prosecutions so they could cover witnesses' expenses and the other usually daunting costs of prosecutions.

Despite the encouragement of private prosecutions, it was very soon obvious that they were not effective. A system of criminal prosecutions which relied solely

[64] It should be noted that, as Kapardis (2001) remarks, this principle was introduced in Cyprus with the "necessary" adaptations suited for a colony: for example, although the High Commissioner had the power to appoint Justices of the Peace for the lower courts, Ordinance XXVI of 1879 provided for the appointment of police magistrates, rather than lay magistrates, while, as we saw earlier, jury trials were never introduced into Cyprus. "One could, therefore, surmise that the British simply did not think they could call upon 'good and lawful men' among the local population to administer justice ..." (Kapardis 2001, p. 60).

on the support, diligence and commitment of the general public would never have many hopes of success under a colonial regime, especially during the first years when there was a widespread suspicion and distrust of the administration of justice.[65] In fact, the colonial administration never relied exclusively on private prosecutions. One of their first tasks, as soon as they arrived on the island, was to reform and strengthen the police force in order for it to "serve as a constabulary force for the prevention and detection of crime, the apprehension of offenders, the maintenance of peace and good order ..." (Cyprus Police Augmentation Ordinance [No. XXX] of 1879, as cited by Kapardis 2001, p. 152).[66] Very early on, therefore, the police assumed the role of bringing offenders to justice. Although the Cyprus Police Ordinance (No. VIII) of 1880 established only one police force by placing under one command all the previous forces (e.g. municipal police, Ottoman *zaptiehs*), the prosecutions were initiated in the name of the Chief Constable of each district, obviously under the influence of the same practice followed in Britain.

3.3.1.2 The Attorney General's Office

The Office of the Attorney General existed throughout British rule.[67] The post was first created in 1878 under the title of the "Legal Adviser of the Government".[68] Loucaides (1974) remarks that, peculiarly, the first holder of the post occupied at the same time the office of the Chief Judicial Officer. The same author points out that "naturally, the execution of the duties resulting from these two posts by the same person was creating many problems and constituted a source of frustration for the (Colonial) Administration;[69] therefore, as a result, in 1881 a different person was appointed for each post and the post of the Legal Adviser of the Government was renamed to King's Advocate ..." (Loucaides 1974, p. 22). Gradually the duties and responsibilities of that office-holder were significantly expanded to almost equal the powers of the Attorney General in Britain and eventually in 1925 the same title ("Attorney General") was adopted in Cyprus.

The public records of those times show the holder of the office of the Attorney General as one of the three permanent officials (the others were the Colonial Secretary and the Colonial Treasurer) who, under the Governor, comprised the Executive Council. They also record that he participated in the Legislative Council as an *ex officio* member until 1935 when the Council was abolished and the power

[65] See in Chap. 2 the similarities with the situation in Ireland and Northern Ireland.

[66] See also Christodoulou (1994).

[67] See in Appendix 2 a list of all the post-holders during British rule.

[68] Cyprus Gazette, 5/11/1878.

[69] See the Governor's Annual Report for the year 1881 (Biddulft 1881).

to legislate was granted to the Governor. As is apparent, the Attorney General's post concentrated a wide range of powers and authorities and exercised a substantial influence on the general government policy. It has to be remembered, however, that he was always exercising his functions under the supervision of the English Ministry of Colonies and, therefore, his independence – which in England was regarded as a prerequisite for the proper execution of the duties of the Attorney General's Office – was seriously compromised. For example, Loucaides (1974) reports that regarding serious legal matters affecting the general policy of the Government, the Attorney General was obliged to ask for the directions of the Ministry of Colonies.

As Edwards (1964) shows, it has always been one of the functions of the Law Officers of the Crown and particularly of the Attorney General to enforce by prosecutions the criminal law. Casey (1996, p. 27) points out, though, that in England and Wales Law Officers had only a residual concern in this area, as "... their interest historically lay in prosecuting serious offences against the state, such as treason and sedition. At the local level, enforcement of the law was left to other persons – in particular, to the police when in the nineteenth century local constabularies began to be organised in modern lines". He contrasts the situation with that of Ireland where the Attorney General adopted a more active role in prosecutions and gradually became the apex in a system of public prosecutions. Even in the latter case, though, the Attorney General directed only relatively few prosecutions in the Assizes and even later, when the principle was extended and more cases were taken over by the Crown,[70] these were again a small minority compared to the cases that were prosecuted by the police.[71]

In Cyprus the situation initially followed the same lines of development as in England. Very limited information is available on the exact categories of cases that were prosecuted by the Attorney General during the first years of British rule but the general conclusion was that, apart from very serious crimes, the discretion to choose which cases were fit for the Crown to prosecute was vested entirely in the Attorney General.[72] Similar to the situation in England, different Attorney Generals had taken different approaches to the frequency with which the Crown would prosecute.[73] The Attorney General in Cyprus was additionally armed with the powers recognised for his English counterpart as far as the rest of the prosecutions were concerned, the most important being the power to intervene and enter a *nolle prosequi*, if he thought necessary to do so. It seems that, as time passed, the Attorney General and his Counsel dominated the Assize Courts. Later on, it was also stipulated in law that prosecutions on information

[70]See Bell (1989) and Casey (1996).

[71]See Chap. 2 for the history of public prosecutions in (including others) England and Wales and Ireland.

[72]Loizou and Pikis (1975).

[73]See Edwards (1964) and Casey (1996).

could be only instituted by the Attorney General.[74] Meanwhile, the police had assumed a virtual monopoly over prosecutions at the District Courts. One can speculate that the similar circumstances that prompted a more active role for the Attorney General in Ireland at the end of the nineteenth and in the early twentieth centuries encouraged the same development in Cyprus as well.[75] Furthermore, the size of the country and the relatively low level of very serious crimes made the handling of these cases by the Attorney General a not unmanageable task.[76]

3.3.2 After 1960

The prosecution system of Cyprus after Independence is not described or set out fully in any single document. It is grounded in the Constitution and on some sections of statute law, notably the Criminal Procedure Law and Police Law, but many aspects of it are just implied or speculated rather than clearly stated.

The history of prosecutions in Cyprus after 1960 is characterised from the affirmation on any given opportunity of the supremacy of the Attorney General over all the rest of the actors involved in prosecutions which, however, was never combined with a detailed and thorough appraisal of his exact role in the process. As time passed, and for a variety of reasons, new powers and responsibilities were added to the already broad duties of the Law Office, regrettably though without a concerted effort to examine the prosecution system as a whole and without a long-term perspective. As will be discussed later in detail, some of the powers that are recognised to the Attorney General resemble powers that prosecutors of more inquisitorial system possess and yet these are not acknowledged as such (for example the power of the Attorney General to intervene during police investigations).

3.3.2.1 General Status and Powers of the Attorney General

Before discussing the specific role of the Attorney General as the head of the prosecution system, it would be worth referring briefly to his status and general role in the legal system of the Republic. It is to be observed that although the direct historical lineage between the Attorney General of Cyprus and his

[74] See Krone (2003) analysing the reasons why the Australian Attorney General was also given the monopoly over prosecutions on indictment. See also the situation in Ireland and Northern Ireland in Chap. 2.

[75] See Bell (1989, p. 9): "In Ireland ... a deliberate policy was adopted to introduce a professional system of law enforcement, the main reason being that its impartial administration could not be otherwise guaranteed".

[76] See Machlouzarides (1970) and Kapardis (2001).

counterpart in England is expressly acknowledged in the rare official descriptions of the Office, in some aspects he departed quite significantly from the original model.

The post of the Attorney General was retained by the Constitution after Cyprus Independence (1960) and is recognised as one of the great offices of the State.[77] He (as well as the Deputy Attorney General, who serves on the same terms as the Attorney-General) is appointed by the President of the Republic from among persons who are qualified for appointment as Judges of the Supreme Court,[78] holds office until the attainment of the age of 68 and can be removed only in the manner and on grounds similar again to those for the removal of a Judge of the Supreme Court. He is an independent officer and not a political one, in as much as his office is not subject to any Ministry. Moreover, unlike the other statutory office-holders (e.g. the Auditor General of the Republic and the Governor of the Central Bank), the Attorney General is not obliged to submit an annual report to the President on the activities of his Office.

Apart from responsibilities concerning criminal prosecutions, the Constitution (supplemented by ordinary legislation) entrusts the Attorney General with a considerable and diverse body of other duties. The Attorney General is the Legal Adviser of the Republic and the head of its Legal Service. Therefore, he has to render legal advice to any organ or authority of the Republic, he has to draft or check all legislation proposed to be submitted to the House of Representatives by the Government[79] and he is called very often at the meetings of the Council of Ministers to advise them on the legality of proposed measures to be taken. All legal actions by or against the Republic are brought in the name of the Attorney General. Furthermore, he is the Chairman of the Legal Board, which supervises the organisation and operation of the legal profession, of the Advocates Disciplinary Board and of the Advocates Pension Fund and is Honorary President of the Cyprus Bar Council. He is a member of the Supreme Council of Judicature and he is also represented in various statutory bodies such as the Medical Disciplinary Board and the Dentists Disciplinary Board. In addition, it is on the recommendation of the Attorney General that the President acts in the exercise of his prerogative right of mercy as to the remission, suspension or commutation of any sentence passed by a court in the Republic.

There are a number of points resulting from the above account of the status of the Attorney General, worth highlighting. *First*, as is apparent, he is responsible for a

[77] Articles 112–114 of the Constitution.

[78] There is a similar provision in the Constitutions of other Commonwealth countries: see, for example, Article 76 of the Constitution of India, Section 88(I) of the Nigerian Constitution and Article 42 of the Constitution of Guyana (Casey 1996).

[79] The English and Irish Law Officers were relieved from their drafting responsibilities as early as 1869 and 1875 respectively, when the Parliamentary Counsel's Office was established. See Casey (1996).

wide and diverse variety of duties. Underlining his position in criminal procedure and prosecutions in particular, should not obscure the fact that his role in the Cyprus legal system is far broader. The various roles that he is called on to fulfil, apart from making him an exceptionally powerful and influential person in the Republic, are one of the main reasons for the particularly heavy workload with which the Law Office has to deal. As will be shown later in this book, successive Attorney Generals have admitted that this exercises some influence on the way the Attorney General's role regarding prosecutions is carried out.

Secondly, the drafters of the Constitution chose to make the Office of the Attorney General an independent instead of a political one, contrary to the original model of the English Law Officer.[80] It might reasonably be argued that the special circumstances of Cyprus, particularly the existence of two separate communities,[81] were the reason behind the choice of an independent Attorney General, free from political pressures.[82] While also in countries where the Attorney General is a political appointee it is regarded that he should execute his duties independently from the Government,[83] the *official* safeguard of the Office's independence in Cyprus, undoubtedly, fosters his position and gives legal ground for the right of the Attorney General to act independently.[84]

Thirdly, this independence, combined with the security of tenure that the Attorney General enjoys and the qualifications which he must possess in order to be appointed to the office, furnishes him with a quasi-judicial status which not only arguably generates the special respect of the public, but is also the basis on which courts have on many occasions stressed that his discretion is absolute and not reviewable. Therefore, the Attorney General enjoys a great independence regarding his relationship with both the Executive and the Judiciary.

---

[80] There are other Commonwealth countries that chose this path, for example, Kenya, Singapore, Pakistan, Seychelles, etc. (Edwards 1989).

[81] The two communities are the Greek-Cypriot community and the Turkish-Cypriot one. However, since the Turkish invasion in 1974 the two communities have been violently separated. The majority of Turkish-Cypriots are now living in the north part of Cyprus, which is under Turkish occupation.

[82] However, it should be noted that according to some officials at that time, the fact that the serving Attorney General (Mr Tornaritis) was part of the committee that drafted the Constitution, contributed towards the allocation of extremely broad powers and political independence to the Office of the Attorney General.

[83] For example, in England he is a Minister appointed by the Prime Minister but not a member of the Cabinet. It has been advocated that when executing his prosecutorial functions, he may seek the advice of the Cabinet but he is not required to do so. The most well known explanation of this relationship is the one found in a parliamentary speech of Lord Shawcross when Attorney General in 1951 (see H.C. Debates, Vol. 483, col. 683).

[84] On the contrary, in England and Wales the independence of the Attorney General is only a matter of convention. See, for example, Marshall (1984), cited in the Law Reform Commission of Canada (1990), commenting that it is difficult to find "any clear *legal* ground for asserting a right in the Attorney General to act independently".

3.3.2.2 The Attorney General and Prosecutions

Among the other roles that the Attorney General is entrusted with, the Constitution recognised him as the head of the prosecution system, entitled to intervene in and supervise any prosecution:

> 'The Attorney General of the Republic shall have power, exercisable at his discretion in the public interest, to institute, conduct, take over, and continue or discontinue any criminal proceedings for an offence against any person in the Republic'. (Article 113.2 of the Constitution)

While it is correct to say that with this provision the formal introduction of a system of public prosecutions was declared, it must be realised that this was grafted on to the previously existing system and therefore it coexists with the (infrequently invoked and circumscribed) power of private prosecution. The Constitution avoided a radical change of the existing prosecution system and chose instead to insert in it a highly powerful new Office of the Attorney General to supervise and control the whole system of prosecutions. Thus, although the Constitution gives primacy to the Attorney General empowering him to oversee all prosecutions in the jurisdiction, it does not give him the monopoly of instituting criminal proceedings. The Supreme Court took the opportunity to declare that:

> 'Article 113.2 (of the Constitution) is an empowering enactment conferring wide powers upon the Attorney-General with regard to prosecution, in addition and not in derogation of those vesting in other persons or authorities'. (Ttofinis v. Theocharides 1983 2 C.L.R. 369)

With section 107 of the Criminal Procedure Law, however, the Attorney General is given the monopoly as far as prosecutions at Assize Courts are concerned. This section provides that:

> 'No person shall be put upon his trial for any offence not triable summarily, although he may have been committed for trial, *except upon an information filed by the Attorney General* in the Assize Court in which such person is to be tried'. (emphasis added)

Furthermore, there are a number of other legislative provisions that require the consent of the Attorney General in order for prosecutions of some offences to be invoked.[85] "Consent provisions" have been used with increasing frequency since the British period as an additional means of exercising control over private prosecutions and their preservation itself confirms the preservation of the right to a private prosecution.

Thus, apart from prosecutions on information and "consent prosecutions", it depends on the Attorney General what other types of cases he wishes to prosecute. As will be shown later, different Attorney Generals have taken different approaches. Nonetheless, there are certain categories which have always been included in the

[85] E.g. Corruption and extortion by a public office s.105-6 of Cap. 154, Participation in an illegal union s.56, 67 of Cap. 154, etc.

Law Office's workload: complex cases, sensitive cases, cases that involve public officers, etc.

A further point that arises out of the consideration of Article 113.2 of the Constitution is that it is confirmed that Cyprus prosecution system is an expediency-based system (*in the public interest*). Apart from this broad statement in the Constitution, there is no published code stating the criteria which should be applied in prosecutorial decisions. On the contrary, it has repeatedly stated[86] that "it is the exclusive right of the Attorney General to represent the public interest" (The Police v. Athienitis 1983 2 C.L.R. 223)[87] and that the Attorney General in exercising his discretionary power is not to be subject to the direction or control of any other person or authority.[88]

3.3.2.3 Private Prosecutions

The courts have on many occasions been at pains to stress that "there is nothing in the Constitution neutralising the position at common law as regards private prosecutions" (Ttofinis v. Theocharides 1983 2 C.L.R. 363) and "neither the constitution nor the Criminal Procedure Law had abolished the valuable right of private prosecutions" (The Police v. Athienitis 1983 2 C.L.R. 194).[89] It was held that the right of a common informer to bring and conduct a prosecution for the trial of a summary offence derives from the common law and remains untouched, and indeed untrammelled, by any statutory provision. However, as the current President of the Supreme Court recognised extra-judicially, "a private prosecution is always subject to the control of the Attorney General through his power to control, take over, continue or discontinue criminal proceedings" (Artemis 1989, p. 4032). Furthermore, it only concerns summary prosecutions as prosecutions on information can only been carried out by the Attorney General. Therefore, if a common informer wants to prosecute an offence tried on information, he can only do so up to the point of the preliminary inquiry. There are no official statistics about the exact number of private prosecutions that are being invoked every year, but it is common knowledge that they are very few and mainly limited to those relating to the offence of dishonoured cheques or offences regarding breaches of local administrative law.[90]

---

[86] In Re Ttooulias (1984) 1 C.L.R. 885, Attorney General v. Ioannidi (1993) 2 C.L.R. 377, Attorney General v. Andrianou (1995) 1 C.L.R. 486.

[87] See Artemis (1989, p. 4033): "The power assigned to the Attorney General might be abused as there is a possibility of any power to be abused. As a general proposition that is true but it has nothing to do with this question. A law, either pre-existing the Constitution or enacted thereafter, cannot validly alter or abridge the powers of the Attorney General conferred on him by the Constitution".

[88] See Chap. 6.

[89] See also: In Re Koumougiouros (1995) 1 C.L.R. 805.

[90] Loucaides (1974), Loizou and Pikis (1975), Artemis (1989) and Pashalides (1991).

3.3.2.4 Agencies' Prosecutions

Various Government Departments, such as the District Administrations, the Social Insurance Department, the Inland Revenue and the Custom and Excise Office, as well as other non-governmental agencies (e.g. Local Authorities) have a power based on specific statutory provisions[91] to prosecute summary offences within their particular sphere of activity. Some of these statutory provisions clearly state that these prosecutions are instituted "subject to the directions of the Attorney General".[92] Nonetheless, even when this is not specifically stated, it is assumed, resulting from the power of the Attorney General to control all prosecutions (Louca & Another v. The Republic 1984 2 C.L.R. 141).[93]

3.3.2.5 Police Prosecutions

The police also have the right to institute criminal proceedings in the interests of law enforcement. Article 19 of the Police Law (Cap. 285) clearly states their right to institute prosecutions:

> '*Subject to any direction by the Attorney General*, it shall be lawful for *any police officer* to make a complaint or charge against any person before the Courts and to apply for a summons, warrant, search warrant or such other legal process as may by law be issued against any person, and to summon before the Courts any person charged with an offence and conduct *public prosecutions* and preliminary inquiries against such person'. (emphasis added)

There are a number of interesting points arising out of this provision of the Police Law. *First*, with this section the power of the police to institute prosecutions is grounded on a statutory provision, despite the fact that in some judicial decisions it is regarded as deriving from the common law right of private prosecutions. This latter attitude is reinforced by some writings of members of the judiciary[94] in the Cyprus Law Review in which they referred to police prosecutions as private prosecutions. This view could be further enhanced by the fact that the Chief Constable of each district institutes prosecutions in his own name, following the previous situation in England.[95] The difference in Cyprus, though, is that there is a single Police Force, which is hierarchically organised and although the Chief

---

[91] For example, Social Insurance Law 2/1964, Municipal Corporations Law 64/1964, Streets and Buildings Regulation Law Cap. 96, etc.

[92] For example, Law 82/1967 s.176.1: "Prosecutions against this Law ... are referred to as custom prosecutions and are made subject to any direction of the Attorney General of the Republic".

[93] See also Ttofinis v. Theocharides (1983) 2 C.L.R. 363.

[94] See, *inter alia*, Pashalides (1991) and Artemis (1989).

[95] As shown in Chap. 2, before the enactment of the Prosecution of Offences Act 1985, the vast majority of prosecutions were carried out by the police and normally by a constable in his own right as a private prosecutor. See, though, the principle of constabulary independence there.

Constable of each district enjoys considerable discretion, at least theoretically, he comes under the orders of the Chief of the Police and the common policy of the Force. Therefore, it can be argued that the practice according to which the Chief Constable of each district brings prosecutions in his own name is just a residue of the situation during British rule and does not reflect the current nature of police prosecutions.[96]

Secondly, it is clearly acknowledged that the police in the execution of their prosecutorial functions are subject to the instructions of the Attorney General. Based on this provision it is officially accepted that although the Police as an organisation come under the Ministry of the Justice, as far as their activities relate to criminal prosecutions, the Attorney General is their supervising authority. At least in theory, all police prosecutions remain throughout under the supervision of the Attorney General, who is the competent authority to give directions and review at any time all police decisions on prosecution. Article 19 of the Police Law is arguably a more empowering provision than the constitutional provision of Article 113.2, since it formally recognises the Attorney General as the *immediate* supervisor of the police and, therefore, as entitled to exert *direct* control over police decisions regarding both individual cases and also matters of general policy.[97]

Thirdly, the above general provision was interpreted as additionally giving power to the Attorney General to intervene during investigations and/or require further information, as well as to cause any matter he considers appropriate to be investigated by the police.[98] As was shown in Chap. 2, this is a power which used to be associated with prosecutors in inquisitorial prosecution systems.[99] This power of the Attorney General in Cyprus indicates the broader role that has been assigned to him in prosecutions compared to the role that his counterparts in common law jurisdictions until recently used to have.

3.3.2.6 Public Prosecutors Law 8/1989

Until 1989 criminal prosecutions on behalf of the police (summary prosecutions) were conducted by police officers serving in the Prosecution Department of each Police Division. As early as 1969, concerns had been voiced about the increasing difficulties in requiring non-legally qualified policemen to make legal judgments and exercise a quasi-judicial discretion as to who should be prosecuted and also

---

[96] See Chap. 4 for a further analysis of this point.

[97] It has to be remarked, though, that the exact meaning of this provision has not been properly analysed. See Chap. 4.

[98] See, for example, Circular GE 7/1969/2 issued by Mr Tornaritis, dated 12/06/1976. For detailed discussion on this topic see Chap. 5.

[99] See Chap. 2, however, for exceptions to this rule, either as matter of practice or new legislative trends.

present cases in court. With these concerns, formally expressed for the first time in Parliament by the Member of Parliament Mr Anastasiades,[100] it was indirectly submitted that the Attorney General did not or could not exercise control in every police prosecution. However, the brief reply of the Government to these fears was that the Attorney General, carrying the ultimate responsibility for prosecutions, is in a position to oversee police prosecutions as well and exert an effective control over them:

> 'Each case that there is a doubt or difficulty with is forwarded to the Attorney General's Office and directions are given to the police for its handling. Moreover, frequently, Law Officers are presenting summary cases at District Courts ... Only very simple cases are being handled by the police ... Under these circumstances, the change of the existing arrangements according to which police officers appearing in court for simple summary cases would cause additional costs without any valid reason'. (Reply of the Ministry of Justice in Parliament, dated 04/04/1969)[101]

It took more than two decades for the House of Representatives to deal with the same issue in some detail. In 1988, a Member of Parliament (Mr Efstathios Efstathiou[102]) pointed out that the merging of the investigative and the prosecutorial functions in the case of summary offences posed great dangers to the public perception of the impartial administration of criminal justice, and made a proposal for new legislation on the issue. The first draft of his proposal clearly demonstrated that he was influenced by the same concerns voiced in England prior to the 1986 reform of the prosecution system. It appeared that a golden opportunity was given to discuss in depth the entire prosecution system and adopt a strategy that would update the system in a structured and organised fashion.

Sadly, that opportunity was missed. It is remarkable that what could result in a major change of the prosecution process in Cyprus was dealt with briefly and with an apparent lack of consideration. In the Law that was finally passed (Law 8/1989) a half-hearted and confusing approach was taken which tried to avoid a disruption of the prosecution system. It only provided that (a) everyone who presents cases to court as a public prosecutor must be legally qualified, and (b) when a public prosecutor executes his duties he comes under the instruction of the Attorney General. A perusal of the Law reveals that considerably more attention and thought was given to the question of presenting cases in court, and the qualifications that one must possess in order to be so entitled, than was addressed to the question of the decision to prosecute. The power of the police to charge and institute criminal

---

[100] See Question in Parliament of MP Mr Anastasiades, dated 01/02/1969. See also Loucaides (1979).

[101] This reply of the Ministry of Justice appears to be based on the letter of the Attorney General Mr Tornaritis to the Ministry of Justice, dated 13/02/1969 (G.E. 18/30/3) and reflects his opinion on this matter.

[102] Mr Efstathios Efstathiou was Member of Parliament (1985–1996) and President of the Law Committee of the Parliament (1991–1996).

prosecutions *per se* was not discussed in the new Law and, therefore, it retained the same status as before.[103]

Indicative of this approach was the reaction of the police to this Law. The reason that it was not very welcoming was not so much the fact that they felt that with the new Law they were more "threatened" by the Attorney General's powers but the fact that police officers without legal qualifications were no longer permitted to appear in courts.[104] From this reaction one could see how a proposal that could change the whole structure of prosecutions resulted in focusing on the – still important but considerably minor – point of the legal qualifications of Public Prosecutors. On a more positive note, however, although the Law *per se* did not substantially modify the existing structure of prosecutions (or indeed the powers of the Attorney General), as an indirect result, the supervisory authority of the Attorney General's Office on police prosecutions became closer.[105]

3.4 Concluding Remarks

This chapter has given a brief historical background to the legal system in Cyprus, followed by an outline of the criminal justice process and a study of the evolution and legal framework of the prosecution system. It can be seen that ideas, practices and trends which have their roots in other jurisdictions have been borrowed, adapted and applied with distinctive results in the Cyprus legal system. The variety of influences from other legal systems which have been blended in a unique (but often also confusing) way, the total absence of the jury system and the primacy of a written Constitution over any statutory legislation are some of the noteworthy characteristics of Cyprus law.

In seeking an understanding of how successive office-holders have viewed their responsibilities as Attorney Generals (see next chapters), one element that arises frequently is their commitment to following British constitutional traditions. What, however, is becoming apparent, as the policies and practices followed within the Office of the Attorney General are examined in depth, is that declarations of adherence to British constitutional precedents have not always been followed through. As a matter of fact, they could not have been, since the Office in Cyprus has substantial differences from its counterpart in Britain.[106] This observation is

---

[103] As will be shown later, however, this power is not identical to the power of the police in England and Wales before the Criminal Justice Act 2003, as it is subject to the limitations and restrictions that the special relationship between the Attorney General and the police demands.

[104] In fact, in order to appease police reactions a special section of that Law provided that there would be an intermediate period during which police officers without legal qualifications would be able to appear in court provided that they would be qualified upon a certain date.

[105] See Chap. 4.

[106] And also from the DPP's Office which in 1879 acquired the role of the Public Prosecutor in England and Wales.

true for the whole of Cyprus law and it is one of the main issues that I wanted to illustrate in this chapter. Although sometimes there is a quasi-religious theoretical attachment to common law principles, the reality is that in many aspects there has been a considerable deviation from them.

As far as prosecutions are concerned, the Attorney General's role in the process appears far broader and more multifarious than his counterpart's in England and Wales has ever been. The system of prosecutions in Cyprus is based upon the primacy of the Attorney General who has a constitutional power to control all prosecutions in the jurisdiction and is entrusted with very broad powers in the execution of his role. However, the exact parameters of his powers and the principles according to which they are executed have never been clearly determined or appraised.

In the face of a paucity of detailed statutory provisions and in the absence of extensive guidelines, there is a sense that the prosecution system relies for its functioning on convention and informal regulation besides statute law and pronounced official policy. Most importantly, as will be demonstrated in the next chapters, much is dependent on the broad discretion of the Office of the Attorney General, as well as on the particular holders of the Office.

Chapter 4
The Workload of the Attorney General's Office

> 'Every decision relating to prosecution is ours. *We* decide whether a prosecution should be instituted or not or whether it should be interrupted . . . *Directly* or *indirectly*, this is the case for all prosecutions'. (Law Officer 13)

As was demonstrated in the previous chapter, the Attorney General in Cyprus is entrusted with the overall control of, and responsibility for, all prosecutions. However, the exact parameters of his role have not been specified in detail in terms of the categories of cases that he is closely dealing with, the specific powers that he is enabled to exercise regarding them, or the criteria that he applies. This chapter investigates the first of these issues,[1] namely the workload of the Attorney General's Office. Is the role of the Office confined to the prosecution of serious or exceptional cases? Or does the Law Office have a more systematic involvement in the bulk of prosecutions within the system? And what is its role in relation to the police who also occupy a significant place in prosecutions? This chapter attempts to make sense of which cases the Law Office is supposed to deal with; and which cases actually end up at the Law Office. It also throws light on the reasons behind this reality and examines how Law Officers themselves see and reflect on these issues.

The *first* and *second* sections will attempt to uncover the *rhetoric* and the *history* of the system regarding the Law Office's workload through the limited official accounts of the system, the standpoints of the various "actors" in the criminal justice system (judges, legislators, police), as well as the approaches that successive Attorney Generals have adopted over time. The latter will be achieved based on the results of an examination of the internal circulars, press releases and documents of the four out of five Attorney Generals who have served since the establishment

[1]The second issue (powers of the Attorney General especially during investigations) and the third one (formulation of prosecution policies and criteria) are discussed in Chaps 5 and 6, respectively.

D. Kyprianou, *The Role of the Cyprus Attorney General's Office in Prosecutions: Rhetoric, Ideology and Practice*,
DOI 10.1007/978-3-642-01921-0_4, © Springer-Verlag Berlin Heidelberg 2010

of the Cyprus Republic,[2] corroborated by the interviews I carried out with three of those four office-holders.[3]

The *third* and fourth sections will mostly deal with the situation existing during the time of my main fieldwork. I will firstly discuss the *ideology* that characterises the Law Officers' way of thinking regarding the cases that make up their workload. Given the vagueness in the rhetoric, is there a certainty among them in determining the limits of their responsibilities? Do they have a clear understanding of the type of cases they are dealing with and the reasons for dealing with them? And do they relate in the same way to all aspects of their workload? Valuable insight into the Law Officers' ideology is provided by the semi-structured interviews I carried out with them, as well as by the data I collected through my observation period at the Law Office and the less formal discussions I had with Law Officers during that period.

In the *fourth* and final section, I will describe the *practices* developed in the Law Office concerning the workload of the Attorney General's Office as I explored them through observation and the examination of a series of cases during my fieldwork period. In this part, I will classify the actual categories of cases that I observed reaching the Law Office and identify the common or distinctive characteristics of each category.

4.1 Rhetoric

It is widely accepted[4] that the "law in the books", or the official rhetoric about a certain area, does not correspond completely to the "law in action"; but since the former "constrains, enables, and channels" (Johnson 2002, p. 13) the actual reality – even if this is done through the context of many other factors – it still merits careful scrutiny. In Cyprus, the very broad legal provisions regarding prosecutions inevitably make the rhetoric that has been developed about them – and, thus, what has been interpreted as the law – more important. In the process of examining the rhetoric around the Law Office's responsibilities, it is important to seek to understand how different actors in the system appreciate the Law Office's role and, perhaps most importantly, how successive office-holders themselves have interpreted their role through time.

One of the crucial issues in this discussion will be the exact relationship between the Attorney General's Office and the police, since this heavily influences the workload of the Law Office. Depending on the way the relationship between these two services is perceived, either more or less cases are regarded as belonging to the Law Office's workload, or the justification for this varies considerably.

[2] Until the time of my main fieldwork. The sixth Attorney General of the Republic is Mr Petros Clerides. See also Footnote 39.

[3] See Appendix 1 for a detailed chapter on my research strategies and methodology.

[4] See McBarnet (1981a, b) and McConville et al. (1991).

4.1.1 Broad Legal Provisions

As shown in Chap. 3, although the Constitution gives primacy to the Attorney General, empowering him to control and oversee all prosecutions in the jurisdiction, it does not give him the monopoly of instituting criminal proceedings. Therefore, apart from the specific categories of cases for which the Law Office has acquired *exclusive* responsibility by statutory provisions – prosecutions before the Assize Courts and consent prosecutions – it is left to the Attorney General to choose what other type of cases he wishes to prosecute.[5] Consequently, while it is the unmistakable duty of the Law Office to prosecute serious crime, the same cannot be argued for "ordinary" or minor crime.

Additionally, Article 19 of the Police Law provides that the police carry out their prosecutorial functions under the directions of the Attorney General. The nature of these directions, however, is left open. Moreover, various other laws,[6] which give the right to several governmental departments to prosecute summary offences within their particular sphere of activity, also provide that these prosecutions are subject to any instructions by the Attorney General. Again, nothing specifies either the nature of these instructions or the categories of cases that might end up at the Law Office.

All these broad provisions do not spell out which cases the Attorney General chooses to deal with apart from the serious ones in front of the Assize Courts. Neither do they indicate in detail how he chooses to utilise his control over the police, which is, admittedly, the main service dealing with the bulk of summary prosecutions. Regarding the cases that the police are dealing with, does the Attorney General exercise oversight and control in exceptional circumstances or a day-to-day supervision? The approach that the Attorney General adopts regarding these issues is highly influential on the range and size of his Office's workload.

4.1.2 Vague Rhetoric/Interpretations

As is evident from the foregoing, the legal provisions about the Law Office's workload leave many questions unanswered, and clearly not the least important ones. Likewise, the rhetoric that has been developed around these issues is characterised by the same vagueness and the absence of a detailed examination.

[5]This is a similar position to the powers of the DPP in Northern Ireland before the reform of the Justice (Northern Ireland) Act 2002. Article 5(1)(c) of the 1972 Prosecution of Offenders Order provided that it shall be the function of the DPP "where he thinks proper to initiate, undertake, and carry on behalf of the Crown, proceedings for indictable offences and for such summary offences or classes of summary offences as he considers should be dealt with by him". For further analysis of the system of prosecutions in Ireland, see Chap. 2.

[6]See Chap. 3 for examples.

Over the years, the discussions around the Law Office's role in prosecutions left out a number of important elements crucial to the understanding of both its constitutional position and its workload.

The limited texts on the role of the Attorney General focus on the word "control", which signifies more oversight and accountability rather than minute direction.[7] It is repeatedly asserted that "the Attorney General is entrusted with the ultimate responsibility for, and control of, prosecutions" (Tornaritis 1969, p. 2), but it is also repeatedly deduced that his direct involvement is not expected in every prosecution:

> 'Most criminal cases are prosecuted by the police, who act under the legal direction of the Attorney General. Prosecutions in the name of the Attorney General are instituted only in serious cases before the Assize Courts and in some other cases where it is expected that serious or complex issues are going to arise'. (Papaioannou 1999, p. 4)

and

> 'The prosecution of crime is not the exclusive province of the Attorney General. It is also the right of other public authorities, as well as the police, upon whom a specific power has been conferred by the Police Law ... This right, however, is under the limitations which are determined by the powers of the Attorney General derived from the Constitution and the Laws'. (Loucaides 1974, pp. 43–44)

Great emphasis is placed upon the symbolism and potential of the power of the Attorney General rather than the everyday execution of his prosecutorial function:

> '(T)he constitutional powers of the Attorney General ... are due to the need for control, oversight and organisation of the prosecution system by an independent ... public prosecutor who will ensure the objective and fair functioning of the criminal justice system and will protect the public interest'. (Loucaides 1974, p. 44)

Similar wording is used in all of the rare official accounts of the system, as well as in articles authored by judges,[8] lawyers or other commentators.[9]

There is little detailed reference to the categories of cases that the Law Office is dealing with, besides its obvious workload (Assize Court cases). The Attorney General is regarded as having absolute discretion to decide which other cases he wishes to prosecute. However, there are certain categories which are always cited in portrayals of the Law Office's workload: complex cases, "sensitive" cases, cases that concern constitutional or novel legal issues, cases that involve public officers or "important public persons", etc.; and there is a general consensus among the different actors in the system regarding responsibility for these particular cases.

---

[7] Furthermore, the power to suspend prosecutions – to enter a *nolle prosequi* – is so central in the rhetoric of the Cyprus prosecution system that almost all the actors in the criminal justice system regard it as "the most important power of the Attorney General's Office". From this, someone could conclude that, again, the emphasis in the rhetoric of the system regarding the Attorney General's role in prosecutions is placed on the "control" function.

[8] See Loizou (1972) and Artemis (1989).

[9] See Neocleous (2000) and Thoma (2000).

The extent to which the Attorney General uses this power in practice is obviously dependent on the choices of each office-holder. However, the fact that his power to choose whichever categories of cases he wishes to be forwarded to his Office is widely acknowledged is of great importance. As will be shown later in this book, this theoretical common standpoint regarding the supremacy of the Attorney General, and the power he can exercise over the rest of the services involved in prosecutions, is an important narrative which informs the everyday actions of the officials in the prosecution system.

4.1.3 Law Office–Police Relationship

However, apart from the categorical and indisputable principle of the primacy of the Attorney General, if anyone attempts to scratch the surface of the arguments on which this principle is based, they will find a rhetoric riddled with some contradictions. This particularly relates to the relationship between the Law Office and the police.

It is clearly acknowledged that the police discharge their functions regarding prosecutions under the superintendence of the Attorney General. Based on Article 19 of the Police Law, it is officially accepted that although the police, as an organisation, come under the Ministry of Justice, as far as their activities relating to criminal prosecutions are concerned, the Attorney General is considered to be their supervising authority. Most commentators argue that the form of words in Article 19 – "subject to the directions of" – leaves no doubt as to the subordination of the police to the Attorney General: "Both in relation to setting general directives as to how discretionary powers are to be exercised and in the giving of specific directions with respect to the handling of an individual case, the ultimate authority lies with the Attorney General" (Pashalides 1991, p. 5588). This does not imply an obligation of the Attorney General constantly to assert this authority by intervening and giving directions for every individual case. It recognises that the police, in a great deal of their workload, enjoy broad discretion and are executing their functions without the constant control of the Attorney General. However, this in no way diminishes the recognition as to which office carries with it the ultimate authority in terms of making the final decision when it chooses to do so.

The confusion begins when some terms contradictory to the whole philosophy of the Attorney General's positions and powers are used, or when the judiciary insists on relying upon the readily available precedents of the British period in interpreting the powers of the police. More specifically:

4.1.3.1 Adherence to the Traditions of the British Attorney General's Role

The first cause of confusion is the reference and reliance upon the constitutional conventions and customs that prevailed before Independence. In some cases, when reading the terms in which the role of the Attorney General in relation to the police is described, it becomes apparent that we have a mere recapitulation of the traditional roles associated with the Attorney General's Office or the DPP Office in England of last century. This causes confusion and misinterpretation since the position of the Cyprus Attorney General differs in many aspects from his counterpart in England and Wales.

In England, neither the Attorney General, nor the DPP (even after the 1986 reform) have ever been regarded as the immediate supervisors of the police.[10] On the contrary, long ago, the principle of "constabulary independence"[11] was declared. The classic statement of the relationship between the Attorney General and the Police was made by Lord Denning in R. Commissioner of Police of the Metropolis, ex parte Blackburn ([1968] 2 Q. B. 118):

> 'I hold it to be the duty of the Commissioner of Police of the Metropolis, as it is of every chief constable, to enforce the law of the land ... He must decide whether or not suspected persons are to be prosecuted; and, if need be, bring the prosecution or see that it is brought. But in all these things he is not the servant of anyone, save of the law itself. No Minister of the Crown can tell him that he must, or must not, keep observation on this place or that; or that he must, or must not, prosecute this man or that one. Nor can any police authority tell him so. The responsibility for law enforcement lies on him. He is answerable to the law and to the law alone'.

Furthermore, according to the doctrine of "constabulary independence", each police officer has a legal right and duty to enforce the law as he sees fit, regardless even of the orders of his superior officers. Bennion (1986, p. 5) suggests that "the constitutionally correct position is that it is not the police force as a whole that is the prosecutor in 'police cases' but the police officer himself", and even that a police prosecution until the point at which it is taken over by the CPS (compulsory after 1986) is still regarded as a private prosecution. This fits the traditions and the origins of the English prosecution system.[12]

In Cyprus, however, the situation is not the same. The courts themselves clearly acknowledge that:

> 'Charges for offences triable summarily are filed by the Police (District Divisional Commander of the Police) ... but always under the supervision, instructions, and with the approval of the Attorney General'. (In Re Ttooulias 1984 1 C.L.R. 885, at p. 890)

[10] See Chap. 2 for further discussion on the English Prosecution System.

[11] See Jones (2003).

[12] "The present prosecution system in England and Wales, having grown up in an undirected fashion over the centuries, is notoriously ramshackle. At its heart lies the tenet that it is for the citizen to set in motion the criminal law. The state apparatus that of necessity grew up round this increasingly unrealistic idea lacked an accepted rational. Instead we have accustomed ourselves to the fiction that the police, who prosecute in the vast majority of cases, ... do so as private persons" (Bennion 1986, pp. 3–4). See however, in Chap. 2, the changes introduced by the Criminal Justice Act 2003.

However, at the same time, two former Presidents of the Supreme Court extra-judicially refer to police prosecutions as *private prosecutions*:[13]

> 'The District Divisional Commander of the Police has the right to institute criminal proceedings in the interests of law enforcement. This is implicit from a study of the wide powers vested in the police to ensure law enforcement. These prosecutions, *private in theory*, are of a public nature as the principal consideration for the institution is the safeguard of the public interest in law enforcement and not the satisfaction of the injured party. The process of police prosecution remains throughout under the supervision of the Attorney General'. (Loizou and Pikis 1975, p. 64) (emphasis added)

Furthermore, in the *In Re Koumougioros* case (1995 1 C.L.R. 805) the Supreme Court, using wording close to the philosophy of the "constabulary independence principle", justified the filing of an accusation by the District Divisional Commander of the Police instead of the Chief of the Police. In this case, and for the first time, the tradition according to which the District Divisional Commander of the Police appears on the charge sheet in summary trials – followed since the British years – was challenged. Instead of clarifying the situation, the Court stated that:

> 'Article 19 of the Police Law gives the right to each and every member of the Police Force to stay criminal proceedings . . . Executing his powers, each police officer does not act as a representative of the force or his superiors but as an organ of the law itself . . .'. (In Re Koumougioros 1995 1 C.L.R. 805, at pp. 808–809)

In the language of the foregoing judicial decisions one can observe the contradictory co-existence of two things: (a) the claim that police prosecutions are *private* prosecutions in form and that the police officers, when prosecuting, do not represent the whole force but only themselves, and (b) the declaration that they are under the *immediate* direction of the Attorney General. The question is therefore inescapable: How can they be under the direct control of the Attorney General, when it is argued indirectly that police officers are not even obliged to obey the orders of their immediate superiors?

If the first point is accepted (and thus, additionally, the fact that the police right to institute proceedings is similar to the traditions in England), it is also accepted that the principle of constabulary independence is applicable in Cyprus. Therefore, the Attorney General would not be able to order the police to prosecute or not[14] but could only intervene when a case reaches the court. However, everything else indicates the contrary: The police force in Cyprus is governed by a statute and comes under the Ministry of Justice. Legislation establishes the powers and duties of police officers who are placed within a bureaucratic structure, hierarchically organised. Furthermore, and most importantly, Article 19 of the Police Law clearly

[13] In their book on Criminal Procedure in Cyprus (until recently, the only book on this area in Cyprus) which has been widely used by courts as reference.

[14] See also Sanders (1985, p. 6) referring to ex parte *Blackburn*: ". . . the common law theory makes a police prosecution, in form, a private prosecution, at least at its inception. Thus, if the police do not wish to prosecute a case they cannot be forced to do so".

provides that police prosecutions are "subject to the directions of the Attorney General".[15] Also, as has already been said, the courts themselves have on many occasions declared that police prosecutions are under the *direct* supervision of the Attorney General. Therefore, it can be concluded that the police in Cyprus do not enjoy the independence that they traditionally have enjoyed in England and Wales regarding prosecutions, but rather that they are completely bound by the directions of the Attorney General throughout the whole process.

4.1.3.2 Constitutional Powers: Police Law Powers

Another cause of some confusion as to the nature of the Law Office's powers *vis-a-vis* the police is the reference to the Constitutional provision of Article 113.2 as the provision on which the governance of the relationship between the two services is based, without reference to the specific provision of the Police Law:

> 'The Attorney General of the Republic shall have power, exercisable at his discretion in the public interest, to institute, conduct, take over, and continue or discontinue any criminal proceedings for an offence against any person in the Republic'.

However, what the Constitution declares is the right of the Attorney General to exercise a retrospective control over all prosecutions by his intervention ("take over, continue, discontinue"), besides his right to institute his own proceedings ("institute"). It is the special provision (Article 19) of the Police Law that argues for a more direct relationship between the police and the Law Office and designates the Attorney General as the immediate supervisor of the police concerning prosecutions.

The difference is that without the special provision of the Police Law,[16] if the police failed or refused to prosecute in any case, the only thing that the Attorney General could do, would be to bring his own prosecution; he would not be able to countermand the police decision and force the police to initiate proceedings.

---

[15] See the Canadian case Bisaillon v. Keable and AG of Quebec (1980) 17 C.R. (3d) 193 (Q.C.A.). As the Law Reform Commission of Canada (1990, n.31) argued:

> 'In that case the Quebec Court of Appeal distinguished Blackburn on the facts from the situation in Quebec. Mr Justice Turgeon held that the police in England enjoy great autonomy; in Quebec, they were under the Ministry of Justice ... who has responsibility for all aspects of the administration of justice in the province. Turgeon also suggested that stricter prosecutorial control in Quebec meant that the decision whether to lay charges in that province lay with the prosecutor's office rather than with the police. As a result, he held that *Blackburn* was not applicable in Quebec'.

See also Stenning (1986) for a discussion on the legal relationship between the police and the public prosecutors in Canada. See also the Report of Patten Commission on policing reform in Northern Ireland where the constabulary independence doctrine was critically analysed (Independent Commission on Policing in Northern Ireland 1999).

[16] And similar provisions in the particular Laws that give to other Governmental Departments the right to prosecute.

Conversely, if the police decided to prosecute and the Attorney General thought that this was wrong, he would have the right to enter a *nolle prosequi* in court but could not prevent the decision of the police to send the case to the court in the first place. The first set of powers arises from the Attorney General's constitutional position as the official responsible for the oversight and control of all prosecutions, but it does not directly give him the right to define police prosecution policies or to give compulsory directions for everyday police functions regarding prosecutions. It can be logically argued that these latter powers are given to him by the special section of the Police Law.

It is interesting to note here that, as shown in Chap. 2, the hallmark that used to distinguish the Scottish prosecution system from the English, even after the 1986 change, was that it was the fiscal's ultimate responsibility to decide if and when the criminal process was set in motion by the laying of the charge. In England and Wales, even after 1986, the CPS could not prevent the police from charging someone; they could only discontinue (or take over) the proceedings.[17] In Cyprus, if it is claimed that the Attorney General is the immediate supervisor of the police, then it is also accepted that he can, if he wishes, order the police not to charge *anyone* without his prior notice. Even if it is acknowledged that because of practical and resource reasons he does not wish to do that in every case, nevertheless, he still has the right to order the police not to charge, as well as the right to order them to do so contrary to their will. Based solely on this interpretation, it can be argued that the Attorney General is justified in declaring that the Police are *obliged* to send to the Law Office cases which they do not wish to prosecute (see below).[18]

4.1.3.3 Legal Advisor

The Attorney General is the legal advisor of the Government according to Article 113.1 of the Constitution. It is his duty to advise all Government Departments on

[17]See, however, the changes with the enactment of the Criminal Justice Act 2003 and the introduction of the "statutory charging".

[18]There is another issue that must be addressed. The Greek text of the Cyprus Constitution provides that the Attorney General has the right to "institute, take over, continue or discontinue and *order* any prosecutions in the Republic". As Loucaides (1974) states, it could be argued that strictly interpreted, this provision enables the Attorney General to order any Service in the Republic to lay charges against someone, even if they wish not to do so. Therefore, it could be claimed that the relationship of immediate supervision between the Attorney General and the Police (or any other prosecuting service) is indeed based on the Constitution. However, the phrase "order the prosecution" is omitted in the Turkish and English texts of the Constitution as well as in the Draft of the Cyprus Constitution. The Cyprus Constitution was written in three languages: Greek, Turkish, and English. Article 149 of the Constitution provides that any contradiction between the different texts of the Constitution is resolved by the Supreme Court with reference to the Draft of the Constitution which was signed on the 6/4/1960. Therefore, as the same commentator argues, it can be concluded that this provision was introduced in the Greek text *per incuriam* and has no effect.

the legality of their actions and the correct interpretation of the Laws and the Constitution. Tornaritis (1981, p. 10) states that:

> 'The Attorney General of the Republic, as its legal adviser, has to render legal advice to any organ or authority of the Republic on any matter involving legal consideration. Our Constitution does not restrict such function either to specific matters or in a case where legal advice is being sought. In the absence of any such restriction, it follows that the Attorney General may on his own notion submit to the appropriate authority or organ ... his views as to the legality of any proposed course to be taken'.

As Loucaides (1974) argues, the seeking of his advice regarding the legality of their actions is compulsory for Government Departments and they are obliged to follow it.

As a result of this additional status of the Attorney General, at times, in the descriptions of some commentators, the impression is given that his relationship with the police (and other prosecuting authorities) is that of legal advisor–advisee:

> 'Most criminal cases are prosecuted by the police, who act *under the legal direction* of the Attorney General'. (Papaioannou 1999, p. 4) (emphasis added)

> 'The Law Office must direct and lead the police in the execution of their duties and should provide them with the necessary *legal assistance*. Because of the status of the Attorney General as the *legal advisor* of the state and his status as the Public Prosecutor, the police are obliged to consult with him, get his directions and his legal advice ... in order for their actions to be according to law ...'. (Loucaides 1974, p. 47) (emphasis added)

Nevertheless, as it should be obvious by now, the Attorney General's powers regarding police prosecutions are much wider than the concept of "legal advice" would ever permit. The contrary would mean that although guidance as to the legality of a police prosecution would be properly within the domain of the Attorney General, any attempt to direct on the exercise of police discretion could be resisted as exceeding the authority comprehended in the concept of legal advice.

4.1.4 The Police Approach

There are very few written accounts from the police describing their role or their relationship with the Attorney General's Office. Their official view, repeatedly declared in the media and consistent with the general rhetoric about prosecutions, is that they discharge their functions regarding prosecutions under the superintendence of the Attorney General. This is also stated in the Police Force *Standing Order 3/24*, s.1:

> 'Every police officer according to the Police Law has the power to charge any person before the Courts and to apply for a summons, warrant, search warrant or such other legal process as may by law be issued against any person ... *always under the directions of the Attorney General*'. (emphasis added)

The official police approach to the workload of the Attorney General's Office seems also to be consistent with the theory and the rhetoric of prosecutions described earlier. When asked about which cases they forward to the Law Office, they replied:

The following categories of cases are always forwarded to the Law Office:

(a) Cases that concern offences punishable with 5 years or more.
(b) Consent cases.
(c) Sensitive cases, for example when the accused is a senior public servant or "an important and well-known person".
(d) Complex cases where constitutional or other novel legal issues may arise.
(e) Cases where the accused is a police officer.
(f) Files during the investigation stage when the advice of the Law Office is required.
(g) Cases for which there is a suggestion to be classified as "otherwise disposed of".
(h) Cases for which the police are not sure whether there is enough evidence to send them to Court.
(i) All other cases that the Attorney General requires the police to forward to his office. (Interview with the Head of the Police Prosecutions Department)

Studying the *Police Force Standing Orders* (which are issued by the Chief of the Police and directed to the police officers) it can be observed that they are generally consistent with the above statement.[19]

It can be seen that very broad terms are used and, undoubtedly, without specific guidelines from the Attorney General, a wide discretion to interpret these terms is given to the police. It is important, though, that there is the recognition that the Attorney General is empowered to direct the police to send to his Office whichever categories of cases he wishes. However, it is also obvious that what the police regard as "the Attorney General's workload" is predominately whatever is serious, complex, sensitive or extraordinary.

There is one provision in *Standing Orders* not consistent with the above statement. *Standing Order* 3/5 s.10.3 provides: "Regarding minor cases the District Commander of the Police could dispose of a case as 'otherwise disposed of' or 'non-existent' and return it to the Police Department". However, when that was drawn to the attention of the head of the Police Prosecution Department, he replied that this Order applied only to very minor cases and the rule was that "when there is a suggestion not to prosecute a case, we have to ask the Attorney General".[20] The following conversation I had with one of the senior members of the Central Police Prosecution Department is illuminating:

Q: If there is a suggestion for a case to be "otherwise disposed of", even if this is a minor case, must the file be sent to the Attorney General?
A: Yes, because even for minor cases, there is always the possibility that the victim may complain to the Attorney General . . . Only very minor and very clear cases can be closed by the Chief Constable or by us without the consent of the Law Office.

This was in line with the attitude of the heads of the District Police Prosecution Departments as well, who argued that they were asking for Law Office directions even when the Attorney General himself allowed them discretion:

[19] See particularly *Standing Order* 3/5, s.7.2 and *Standing Order* 3/4, s.5 and s.6.3c.

[20] However, in discussions I had with other members of the Police Force, the previous view was not supported equally strongly and it was admitted that there was a certain degree of discretion that could be exercised.

> 'There is a circular by the Attorney General stating that we can discontinue minor traffic cases or minor assaults, etc. without the prior notice of the Law Office. To be on the safe side, though, I always inform the Law Office, even if this is only by calling them (I usually call the Deputy Attorney General). You have to be careful, because there is always the chance that the victim may change his mind and complain to the Attorney General about the discontinuance of a case. This occurred in the past, so I always inform the Law Office'. (Interview with the head of one of the District Police Prosecution Departments)[21]

This is indicative of how police practice might have been influenced by the power of the Attorney General to intervene in any police case. Without clear guidance from the Attorney General, it is obvious that it is only when the police wish to involve the Law Office that the latter become involved in cases that are not part of their monopoly. However, the theoretical potential that someone else – most probably the defendant or the victim – might draw the Attorney General's attention to a particular case and provoke his intervention (which would be justified) in a way forces the police to send problematic cases to the Law Office for their directions.

4.1.5 Concluding Remarks

Although there is some vagueness in the rhetoric as far as the workload of the Law Office is concerned and some inconsistency regarding the exact relationship between the Attorney General and the police, the conclusion that all appear to reach in the end is that the Attorney General, if he wished, could make his control of the police tighter and extend the workload of his Office as he sees fit. The primacy of the Attorney General is never doubted; it is just the logic behind it that varies in some issues and causes confusion. Therefore, what remains to be seen is how successive Attorney Generals themselves have chosen to utilise their apparently broad discretion and which cases have been regarded as fitting in with their Office's workload.

4.2 The Attorney Generals' Approach – History of the Law Office's Workload[22]

> 'However much care is taken in the formulation of the powers associated with the respective offices, there is little doubt that the experience, standing and personalities of the people occupying these positions . . . have to be carefully assessed if a realistic picture is to be gained of the day to day administration of justice'. (Edwards 1989, p. 101)

[21] The head of the second District Police Prosecution Department I interviewed argued that they used to adopt the same tactic.

[22] In this section, I will provide data relevant to the Attorney Generals' approach regarding only the workload of their Office. Information about their approach regarding their powers (e.g. investigatory powers) and their prosecution policies and criteria will be provided in Chaps. 5 and 6, respectively.

In Cyprus, due to the absence of specific regulation and the broad discretion that is afforded to the Attorney General, what constitutes the law is closely linked to what is interpreted as the law by the Attorney General himself. Through the study of the history of the Law Office, one can notice that successive Attorney Generals have been comfortable with the broad nature of their role and the fact that they have acquired complete freedom of action to define and pursue their tasks.[23] It is as though the mystique that surrounds the Law Office and the excessive latitude that characterises its powers have been regarded as essential in order to retain the respect and the symbolic role that it plays in the prosecution process.[24]

A general conclusion that can be also drawn is that, over time, the involvement of the Law Office in different categories of cases became greater, and its control over the police became more effective. As shown in the previous section, the theory had always been that the Attorney General would be entitled to intervene in any case. However, in the past there was less expectation of him to do so and there also grew a tendency by some Attorney Generals to reserve their involvement for only the most exceptional cases. It will be evident by what follows in this section that a number of reasons advocated for a gradual shift of this attitude and that not all of them were based on the conscious efforts of the officials involved to do so.

Even so, the personality and the choices of each Attorney General formed some of the most significant factors that shaped the Law Office's workload. There are two main issues that this section should focus on: Firstly, the way in which successive Attorney Generals chose to utilise their discretion to define other categories of cases – apart from those required by law – which they wanted to deal with systematically; secondly, the way in which they interpreted their relationship with the police, further to the obvious and common principle that the police carry out their prosecutorial functions under their supervision. The Attorney Generals' approach to the latter issue defines the way they discharge their supervisory and regulatory role over the so-called *police prosecutions*.

4.2.1 The Workload of the Law Office during Mr Tornaritis' Tenure

As Loucaides (1974) points out, before Cyprus gained independence (1960), the Attorney General's responsibilities were defined by statutory laws and

[23] As in any democratic country, in Cyprus, the Parliament has the formal authority to create and reform Laws. Officially the Attorney General has no right to propose legislation. However, the Law Office, as the legal service of the Government, is responsible for drafting all the important legislation and it contributes significantly to the passage of bills within the Parliament. As a matter of fact, on many occasions it is the Law Office that initiates the introduction of new Laws or the reform of the existing ones (see Tornaritis 1971). Therefore, it would be well within their powers if they wished, to at least try and clarify the uncertainties in the legislation or pass more detailed provisions which would specify their powers regarding prosecutions.

[24] However, see below Mr Markides' willingness to be more specific.

supplemented by the respective provisions of the Law Office in England. Mr Tornaritis was appointed to the office of the Attorney General in 1952 during British rule, and continued his service after 1960 as the first Attorney General of the independent Republic of Cyprus.[25] Unsurprisingly, even after independence, he was heavily influenced in the discharge of his duties by his counterparts in England.

Mr Tornaritis wrote a number of short reports on various legal issues, as well as on the general responsibilities of his Office.[26] Although he frequently referred to the singularities of the Cyprus System and to the additional powers that the Attorney General's Office in Cyprus acquired,[27] his adherence to the British constitutional conventions and the common law was evident in his writings:

> 'The Attorney General in Cyprus, in the execution of his duties deriving from Article 113.2 of the Constitution, follows the same principles and conventions as are followed in England'. (Tornaritis 1983a, p. 6)

> 'The Attorney General in Cyprus presently, as well as during the colonial period, has a similar status to the Attorney General in England ... He carries the responsibility for criminal prosecutions ...'. (Memorandum of the Attorney General regarding his relationship to the Ministry of the Interior[28] and the police, dated 22/01/1969, p. 1)

It is obvious in his accounts about the Law Office that he placed emphasis on the *control function* of the Attorney General over the prosecution system rather than on the everyday involvement of his Office in every case. He underlined the symbolic role of the Attorney General in the system deriving from his status as an independent official with quasi-judicial responsibilities:

> 'The Constitution entrusts the Attorney General, an independent official, with broad powers so he can exercise effective control over the system of criminal prosecutions. He can intervene when public interest requires it and interrupt any criminal proceedings which constitute an abuse of the right in private prosecution'. (Tornaritis 1983a, p. 44)

and

> 'The Attorney General is entrusted with the *ultimate responsibility* for, and *control* of, prosecutions'. (Tornaritis 1969, p. 2)

---

[25] With an interruption of his service during the years 1955–1959, during which an armed liberation struggle was deployed in Cyprus which aimed for the expulsion of British troops from the island, for self-determination and for union with Greece. The colonial administration judged that an Englishman should serve at the post of the Attorney General during that time and, therefore, James H. Henry was appointed, replacing Mr Tornaritis. See Appendix 2.

[26] See Tornaritis (1969, 1971, 1975, 1981, 1983a, b, c, 1984, 1985).

[27] See Tornaritis (1983c). As will be shown in a latter chapter, Mr Tornaritis defended repeatedly, in a series of articles in the Cyprus Law Review, the independent status of the Office and the quasi-judicial nature of many of its powers.

[28] Police was under the Ministry of Interior up until 1993 when the Ministry of Justice was renamed to *Ministry of Justice and Public Order* and acquired responsibility for the Police.

The power to suspend prosecutions – to enter a *nolle prosequi* – preoccupied all of the written accounts by Mr Tornaritis regarding prosecutions.[29] This may be due to the fact that, on several occasions, the exercise of his prerogative became the focus of controversy in discussions in Parliament.[30] However, this indicates again that his emphasis was placed on the "control" function and the potential to intervene in court at the trial stage rather than on an *a priori* policy and directions.

Although, during his time at the office, he issued a few circulars directed to the police about other issues (see, for example, in Chap. 5 his circulars about his power to direct police during investigations), I was not able to find any circulars defining certain categories of cases that the police should forward to the Law Office. Anecdotal evidence suggests that the institution of criminal prosecutions on behalf of the Law Office during that period – apart from those in front of the Assize Courts – was not very usual. Where there might, on occasion, be informal contact between the police and Law Officers regarding minor cases, such contacts were merely on an *ad hoc* basis. His supervisory role over the "police cases" was reduced to discussing individual cases and incidents. This was also confirmed by the discussions I had with some senior members of the Law Office who also served during the last years of Mr Tornaritis' tenure.

Loucaides (1974), who served as a senior Law Officer during Mr Tornaritis' tenure, authored a short book about the Attorney General's Office in Cyprus which was prefaced by Mr Tornaritis. In this publication, some information about the Law Office's workload as far as prosecutions are concerned can be found. The author (1974, p. 45) reports: "Criminal prosecutions on behalf of the Attorney General are limited to cases in front of the Assize Courts and some other cases where serious issues of public interest are raised". The only example of such a case that he refers to is a prosecution against a newspaper in 1963.[31]

A speech[32] by the same Officer at the annual meeting of the Cyprus Bar in 1978 is illuminating on the same issue:

> 'During the years 1975, 1976 and 1977 the total number of criminal cases that were tried by Cyprus courts reached 360,068. Of these, only 200 cases were presented in courts by members of the Law Office .... These numbers relate to the cases that reach the courts, but it is also well recognised that in the great majority of cases the decision to prosecute or not is being taken by non-members of the Law Office'. (Loucaides 1979, pp. 92–93)

It has to be mentioned, though, that apart from the ideological factors and the way the Attorney General interpreted his role, the reasons for the small *systematic* intervention of the Office in prosecutions may additionally lie in resource issues.

---

[29] Tornaritis (1983a, c, 1985).

[30] See Parliaments' Records (1983, p. 123) and the speech by Mr Kikis Talaridis published in the Cyprus Law Review Talaridis (1983).

[31] Attorney General v. KIRIX Publications LTD (CC 17393/63).

[32] The Loucaides' speech "Presentation of criminal cases in court by non-legally qualified advocates" was given on 01/10/1978 and it was published in the Cyprus Law Review (Loucaides 1979, p. 92).

It has to be recalled that the Law Office functions also as the Legal Service of the Republic. The newly established state of Cyprus appeared to generate a great deal of work for the Attorney General in its early days. He was called upon to give advice on a multitude of questions and he was responsible for drafting government bills and advising the parliament on the drafting of a large volume of new legislation.[33] In an era when controversy centered on constitutional issues and on the distribution of power between the two communities of the island,[34] one might presume that the Attorney General was too preoccupied with other affairs of government to prosecute frequently.

At this point, as a parenthesis, it has to be mentioned that the other post-holders also argued that the multiple roles that the Law Office is called upon to fulfil exert influence on the volume of criminal cases that the Law Office can deal with:

> 'We have to draft legislation proposed to be submitted to the House of Representatives, give legal advice to all public authorities, handle all civil and administrative cases in which the Republic is a party, apart from our duties regarding prosecutions. Inevitably, this affects the amount of criminal cases that we can deal with'. (Interview with Mr Triantafyllides, 01/02/2002)

> 'This year, especially during the coming months, as a result of the preparation of Laws, etc. regarding Cyprus accession to the European Union, the Law Office has to handle a particularly heavy workload.[35] Because of their urgency we have to prioritise them above the rest of our duties'. (Interview with Mr Markides, 15/05/2002)

In most of the common law countries[36] the responsibilities of the Attorney General's Office have been long ago transferred to a separate institution, the Office of Public Prosecutions. In Cyprus, successive Attorney Generals, while complaining about the resource problems caused by the diversity of their duties, have advocated against this choice.[37]

Concluding this section on Mr Tornaritis' tenure, it has to be remarked that Mr Tornaritis did not establish a proactive policy about which cases the police were obliged to forward to the Law Office (apart from the Assize Court cases). Nor did he set up procedures for systematic contacts with the police regarding the cases that they used to deal with. However, he did manage to impose his status as the ultimate prosecuting authority. It is interesting to note that since that period, the police had regarded themselves as being part of a chain of command headed by the Attorney General in relation to prosecutions (irrespective of the fact the Attorney General rarely intervened in "their cases"). A revealing example is a letter by the Chief of

[33] See Loucaides (1974) and Tornaritis (1981).

[34] See Papaioannou (1984) and Neocleous (2000).

[35] It is interesting that for the same reason in 1974 the Office of the Director of Public Prosecutors was created in Ireland as the Government of the day thought it absolutely necessary to alleviate much of the workload of the Attorney General's Office in consequence of the State's accession to the European Economic Community.

[36] For instance, in England and Wales, Ireland and Northern Ireland; see Chap. 2.

[37] Interviews with the Attorney Generals.

the Police (dated 21/01/1969) sent to the Attorney General in which he complained of the intervention by the Ministry of the Interior in a murder case and asked the Attorney General to clarify "that in a criminal case the *only* responsible person to give directions to the police is the Attorney General"![38]

4.2.2 *Mr Triantafyllides' Tenure*[39]

4.2.2.1 Public Prosecutors Law 8/1989

The passing of the Public Prosecutors Law 8/1989 marked the beginning of the tenure of Mr Triantafyllides as Attorney General. As was discussed in the previous chapter, with Law 8/1989 arose the opportunity to examine in depth the entire prosecution system and the relationship between the police and the Law Office. However, that particular Law did not clarify many of the problems enumerated in the discussion on the rhetoric of the system.[40] Once again, many issues were left unclear or unanswered:

Firstly, the Law provided only for those cases that reached the court and not for those that the police might decide to filter out of the system – and it was concerning those, as has been demonstrated, that the greatest confusion prevailed. Consequently, the situation as regards those cases remained untouched, and was interpreted as before. They were, however, always subject to the limitations and restrictions that the special relationship between the Attorney General and the police demanded.

Secondly, the Law appeared to confuse two issues, namely the question of the presentation of cases in court and the question of who was prosecuting. The Law did not clarify whether there should be a takeover of police prosecutions by the public prosecutors, or whether they were still considered as police prosecutions being carried out by "public prosecutors". The Law could have set the preconditions to establish a system, as far as summary prosecutions were concerned, similar to that

[38] As will be shown in the next chapter, this letter was also referring to the powers of the Attorney General to direct the police even during the investigations.

[39] Mrs Stella Soulioti was the second Attorney General of the Republic. She served for about 3.5 years between 1984 and 1988. Unfortunately, it was not possible to carry out an interview with her. Furthermore, my search inside the Law Office for internal circulars, press releases, memoranda, etc., issued during Mrs Soulioti's tenure did not produce sufficient documents for a proper analysis. This may be due to the relatively short period of her tenure but it may also indicate her position towards the publication and the specification of her policies. Since the information I collected regarding Mrs Soulioti's tenure was limited comparing to the information I had for the rest of the office-holders, I considered any attempt to draw rigid conclusions about her policies at the Law Office unsafe and unfair.

[40] As shown in the previous chapter, the Law only provided that (a) everyone that presents cases to court as a public prosecutor must be legally qualified, and (b) the "public prosecutors" – who appear for the police or any other governmental service – shall execute their duties under the instructions of the Attorney General and they are considered as members of the Law Office.

in England and Wales after 1986.[41] However, the Public Prosecutors Law 8/1989 left untouched three crucial issues which could have advocated for such a change: (a) prosecutions were still being instituted in the name of the District Divisional Commander of the Police, (b) "public prosecutors" continued to serve in the police prosecution services, and (c) their immediate supervisor was a senior police officer.

4.2.2.2 A New Era?

However, notwithstanding these uncertainties (and the fact that if the Law was correctly analysed, it would become clear that it did not give any extra powers to the Attorney General in addition to those he already possessed), that Law appeared to signal a new era in the tenor of the relationship between the police and the Attorney General's Office. It was not so much the wording of the Law which brought about that change, but the ideas and the issues of principle, that for the first time were discussed in a slightly more extensive way than before.[42] It was the beginning of a closer relationship between the police and the Attorney General and it provided the reaffirmation that the latter was the undoubted supervisory authority.

Mr Triantafyllides himself described the attitude he adopted once he took up his duties, comparing it to the previous situation:

> 'Under the previous state of affairs, control over the police had been very lax. They were left to do whatever they wanted with their cases . . . When I was appointed to office I made it clear to everyone that *I* was the supervisor. After a while, police officers understood that the Attorney General was their boss regarding prosecutions and that he was the only one responsible for giving them directions'. (Interview 01/02/2002)

Even his critics admit that things changed for the better during his tenure as far as the control of police cases were concerned.[43]

However, instead of defining specific directions and a systematic approach towards the categories of cases he wished to deal with, he consciously refrained from such actions. He believed that classifying categories of cases or defining guidelines would somehow compromise his broad powers to deal with whatever he chose. In a frank response he admitted:

> 'Why limit your powers voluntarily? Guidelines are not necessary'. (Interview 01/02/2002)

---

[41] According to the Prosecution of Offences Act 1985, in England and Wales public prosecutors were responsible and obligated to take over all criminal prosecutions instituted by the police; see Chap. 2.

[42] See Discussions in Parliament (Parliament Records dated 22/04/88, p. 123).

[43] See the article by a well-known journalist, Mr Drousiotis, in the magazine "Selides" 28/08/1993 where, although he criticised intensively Mr Triantafyllides on a series of issues, he admitted that the control that he exercised over the police was more effective than before.

Instead, he believed that interpersonal dynamics was a crucial factor that would enable him to exercise control over the police. He emphasised the great importance of trust and cooperation with the senior members of the Force:

> 'The Attorney General should have a good relationship with the Chief of the Police. If you achieve that, then it is easier to isolate the police officers who disobey the Attorney General's instructions'. (Interview 01/02/2002)

Inevitably, without, again, comprehensive requirements on the police to report specific cases, the role of the Attorney General was limited to the "control function" in relation to less serious cases. The only time that he dealt with these was when the police or someone else asked him to do so. Mr Triantafyllides believed that the jurisdiction was so small that he would always be informed of something that deserved his attention. Therefore, he argued that:

> 'The important thing is to consolidate the position not only among the police but among the rest of the actors in the criminal justice system that you have the authority to intervene and to act that way . . . '. (Interview 01/02/2002)

It is true that during his tenure, police sought his directions more frequently than before and he intervened on many occasions in cases that did not belong to his regular "Assize Court" workload; always, however, on an *ad hoc* basis.[44] The documentary survey carried out at the Law Office came across several records which prove his intervention in libel cases, cases against journalists, cases against public officials, cases concerning economic scandals and fraud as well as cases concerning accusations against police officers of violence against suspects.

Nevertheless, towards the end of his tenure, the previously sporadic complaints about police actions and the way police were dealing with criminal cases multiplied. This did not necessarily mean that police actions had worsened but rather that people felt more secure to reveal things and journalists more free to expose police abuses.[45] Most of the criticism was levelled towards the police practice of filtering cases out of the system[46] ("let off well-known suspects or powerful persons").[47] The Law Office was also criticised for either tolerating police

[44] Source of data: Interviews with Law Officers who served during his tenure and with defence advocates.

[45] This must also be related to the fact that during that period, privately owned media were introduced to Cyprus for the first time.

[46] It is very interesting to note that in Cyprus, the main focus of controversy has always been on the cases that are filtered out of the system. In the past, there was criticism that too many of them are filtered out of the system in contrary to the situation in England, for example, where there was criticism that the police were sending too many cases to courts. Undoubtedly, this is one of the main reasons why successive Attorney Generals have placed particular emphasis on this category of cases.

[47] See, *inter alia*, a series of articles in the newspapers "Alithia", "Simerini", "Phileleftheros" between November 1993 and June 1994.

practices, or even contributing towards them.[48] Indeed, the criticism was so pronounced that the Attorney General felt compelled to issue one of his rare statements to the media stating that police did not have the power to filter out cases without his approval. [49]

4.2.3 Mr Markides' Tenure

During Mr Markides' tenure at the office, the way he interpreted his role together with a combination of other factors advocated the extension of the Law Office's workload in terms of both the variety and the number of cases that they were dealing with.

As soon as he assumed office, he made it clear that he was willing to follow a more structured approach to the workload of his Office, to systematise his communication with the police, and to consider improvements to the presentation of summary cases in the District Courts. Indicative of this approach were the following measures he introduced:

(a) He created specialised divisions in the Law Office which corresponded to their various responsibilities (e.g. Legislation Drafts division, and Civil Law, Administrative Law and Criminal Law divisions) and appointed one senior Law Officer as the head of each. Although Law Officers did not strictly come under one of these divisions, for the first time, some Law Officers were dealing exclusively with criminal cases. A very important development was that one Law Officer for each Police District was appointed with responsibility for communicating with the police on every-day matters and directions.[50]

(b) For the first time, he defined in writing some specific categories of cases that the police should forward to the Law Office, apart from the Assize Court cases: (1) domestic violence,[51] (2) corruption by public officers, (3) fraud/Stock Exchange, (4) fatal traffic accidents,[52] and (5) all sensitive or complex cases or cases where constitutional issues arise. It was also the first time that separate records for certain categories of cases were kept in the Law Office, under his directions.[53]

---

[48] Anxieties were also voiced about the increasing number of *nolle prosequis* that the Attorney General was entering.

[49] Statement A.F 7/69/3, dated 02/12/1993.

[50] For each of the busiest districts (Districts of Nicosia and Limassol), there were two Law Officers appointed as heads. See Circular G.E. 74/72/6, dated 15/04/96.

[51] See Circular G.E. 50(C)/1992/N.42, dated 11/06/1998.

[52] Another category, for a brief period, was cases of unlawful hunting.

[53] Previously, there was only *one* record for *all the cases* that were forwarded to the Law Office.

(c) During the first months of his tenure, he held a number of meetings with all the public prosecutors[54] serving in Police Prosecution Departments, as well as with senior police officers and the Chief of the Police,[55] during which they discussed prosecution policies and communication procedures between the two services. It is interesting to note that as a result of the meetings with the public prosecutors, he issued a circular defining certain steps that had to be followed when prosecutors faced problems presenting a case or when they judged that the case should be discontinued.[56] At the end of that circular the Attorney General made the point that: "It is emphasised that the public prosecutors discharge their duties under the directions of the Attorney General and the head of the Prosecution Department ONLY" (original emphasis).[57]

He soon realised, however, that it would not be easy to exercise effective control over the public prosecutors simply because Law 8/1989 and his circular declared that they had to obey his directions. Since they were still police officers, and they were serving in a police prosecution department under the immediate supervision of a senior police officer, there was always the danger that they would be influenced by police directions. The Attorney General himself admitted:

> 'We didn't think that the situation with the public prosecutors was the right one. Although the Law says that when dealing with prosecutions they should obey *my* directions as though they were members of my service, the reality is that they are still members of the police force and, at any time, the Chief of the Police could remove them or transfer them to another department'. (Interview 15/05/2002)

Therefore, he decided that the best solution was to appoint lawyers directly under his service, charging them with the duty of prosecuting the "police cases" in front of the District Courts, and placing them within the District Police Prosecution Departments:

> 'We have already appointed eight public prosecutors and eight more are to be appointed next year. It will take a few years before all the current public prosecutors/police officers

---

[54] See also a later announcement by the Attorney General (G.E. 9/52/309), dated 30/10/2001: "In a meeting at the office of the President of the District Court of Nicosia, the problems that courts are facing have been discussed and analysed and it was concluded (*inter alia*) that there is a need for the court to be relieved of cases concerning offences that had been committed a long time ago. As a result of this meeting, myself and the head of the Prosecution Department of Nicosia have examined a series of cases – which are referred to in the attached catalogue – and I have given the required directions for their further handling in court".

[55] See Memorandum G.E. 124/73/2, dated 03/05/1996.

[56] See Circulars G.E. 50(B)/87/N.35.3, dated 07/05/1996 and G.E. 50(B)/87/N.35, dated 23/12/1996.

[57] He also issued a number of other circulars directed to public prosecutors, dealing with issues related to the cases they were handling: e.g. Circular G.E. 19(M)/1964, dated 16/02/1999 concerning the priority of cases that were based on testimonies by foreigners, Circular G.E. 9/52/309, dated 30/10/01 concerning the discontinuance of a series of cases pending in courts for extended period of time and Circular G.E. 74/72/7, dated 15/10/01, concerning general procedural issues regarding the handling of cases in court.

are replaced with prosecutors who are coming, also formally, under our service. We will do this gradually because of the cost that is generated'. (Interview 15/05/2002)

Mr Markides seemed to realise the absurd situation that was created with Law 8/1989, and the inconsistencies that it produced and attempted to take some steps towards a more rational approach. However, once more, that attempt was done in a piecemeal fashion and without adequate reflection. Again, more thought was given to the presentation of cases in court rather than the actual decision to prosecute, and the status of the public prosecutors – although stronger than before – was still compromised by the fact that they were serving in *Police* Prosecution Departments.[58] On the first issue, the Attorney General admitted:

'I know this is not the ideal situation. However, in order to change that (the fact that the police takes the decision for prosecution in most of the summary cases), huge resources are required. For the moment, we don't plan to change that . . . Instead, I define certain categories of cases that I judge to need my attention and I give directions to the police to forward cases when they need my advice. In addition to the Assize Court cases, the police do send many cases here asking for our directions . . . And in any event they should send the cases that they want to filter out of the system for public interest reasons'. (Interview 15/05/2002)

And:

'There is no way that we can supervise and give directions on the thousands of cases that police are dealing with . . . However, we already have a much more extensive workload than the Law Office has ever had before'. (Interview 15/05/2002)

When asked how they could ensure that the police do send to the Law Office the cases that they should, Mr Markides was very honest:

'We can't be absolutely sure. There is no perfect way to check, unless someone draws our attention to that. There are instances when the victim or the defendant complains about the police decision and we ask the police to send the file so we can review their decision . . . We may not have pre-emptive control of all cases but we can certainly exercise control afterwards, when someone informs the Law Office'. (Interview 15/05/2002)

4.2.3.1 Contextual Factors

It is evident from the above that Mr Markides' approach certainly pointed towards a more extensive workload for the Law Office. In addition to that, it is interesting to refer here briefly to three other factors that appeared to contribute to the growth in the Law Office's workload:

1. Complexity has always been a criterion that advocated for the Law Office's involvement but, as time passed, complex crimes seemed to increase as new

[58] An absurd situation was created with public prosecutors having to answer both to the head of the PPD and to the Law Office. Even during Mr Markides' tenure, and despite the improvement observed compared to the previous situation, some circulars (e.g. G.E. 65/1993/3) directed to the public prosecutors were sent to the Chief of the Police to circulate to the PPD, instead of directly to them. Later, however, such circulars were sent directly to the PPD, albeit with a notification to the Chief of the Police.

forms of criminality appeared (e.g. organised crime, especially money laundering and drug trafficking). Especially during the period of the opening of the Cyprus Stock Exchange (1999) and immediately afterwards, a huge rise in economic crime was observed.[59] The low level of police experience[60] regarding those cases made the Law Office's intervention more frequent.[61]

2. The second catalyst appeared to be the increasing challenge to and criticism of police decisions by the media which on a number of occasions forced the Attorney General to intervene in police cases and, in a way, constituted an additional source of information for him.[62]
3. Defendants or victims themselves played a significant role in the tendency of the Law Office to intervene more frequently in summary cases. As will be seen in section four of this chapter, a great deal of the Law Office's involvement in cases that usually did not belong to their ordinary workload was provoked by the defendants' or victims' requests to review police decisions on prosecution. As was shown above, that appeared to have influenced police practice as well. The police themselves admitted that they were more inclined to send problematic cases to the Law Office.[63]

4.2.4 Mr Nikitas' Tenure

After Mr Nikitas' appointment, a different philosophy for the running of the Office was adopted which influenced more dramatically the way in which cases were handled and decided (as will be discussed in Chap. 6). But it also appeared to have some effects on both the variety and the volume of cases that reached the Law Office.

His approach was characterised by an emphasis on the independence of the Attorney General and on the quasi-judicial status of his role and responsibilities.[64] However, Mr Nikitas appeared more preoccupied with the establishment of solid

---

[59] See Kapardis et al. (2001).

[60] Rossidou-Papakyriakou (2001).

[61] See the next chapter for the cooperation of the police and the Law Office as far as the investigation for these crimes are concerned.

[62] This was a phenomenon which began to emerge from the last years of Mr Triantafyllides' tenure.

[63] Interviews with the heads of the PPD of Limassol and Nicosia and the Central PPD.

[64] The language he used in describing the role of the Attorney General is reminiscent of the wording of the Supreme Court decisions on the issue:

> 'The powers of the Attorney General are defined by Article 113 of the Constitution. He has the right to initiate prosecutions and to discontinue them with what is defined as '*nolle prosequi*'. The police have the right to carry out prosecutions but they are under the guidance of the Attorney General ... I have to underline this: every citizen has the right to institute criminal prosecutions – courts have been very clear on this. Of course, the Attorney General's right to intervene – by entering a *nolle prosequi* – is undoubted'. (Interview 11/01/2004)

Mr Nikitas was a Supreme Court Judge before appointed to the Office of the Attorney General. His critics accused him of being unable to escape from the judicial mentality.

principles on which cases should be decided rather than with which cases reached his Office. It is interesting to observe that the great majority of circulars that he issued concerned the way cases should be judged and the criteria by which the forum of trial should be chosen.[65] Although he appeared very strict and detailed regarding these guidelines, he did not seem to pay the same attention to which cases his Office was, and should be, dealing with:

> A: In studying the total number of cases, we can say that a relatively small number are reaching the Law Office. The police have *their own department* so they can institute proceedings. Only the serious or extraordinary cases are forwarded here ...
> Q: Have you given directions as to which other cases should be forwarded here?
> A: ... Some ... There is a huge number of criminal cases ... You cannot control all of them ... How could you? (Interview 11/01/2004)

Of the public prosecutors serving in the Police Prosecution Departments, he remarked:

> 'Theoretically, they are under the Law Office. For practical reasons, their immediate supervisor is the head of the Police Prosecution Department ... It is not an ideal system. They should have been integrated into the Law Office ...'. (Interview 11/01/2004)

During the first months of his tenure, he changed the structure of the Office, abolishing the positions of the Law Officers responsible for each of the District Police Prosecution Department – who until then served as the link between the District PPD and the Law Office – and ensured a more direct supervision of the PPD.[66] However, he later[67] went back to the previous situation, taking also the further step of placing two Law Officers in two of the remotest PPDs so that they could exert more effective control over the presentation of "police cases" in court.

Mr Nikitas argued that the Law Office's workload did not change significantly from the situation under his predecessor, but he did not find it necessary to give explicit directions to the police or the public prosecutors on this issue.

There are indications that his more general views on the criteria that should be applied to prosecution decisions influenced the workload of the Law Office. More specifically, as will be further discussed in Chap. 6, Mr Nikitas strongly believed that neither the Attorney General nor the police had the right to filter cases out of the system due to mitigating factors concerning the defendant. He argued that these cases should be decided in an open forum and all the relevant factors could be taken into consideration by the judge.[68] Thus, during the first months of his tenure, every request by defendants asking him either to enter a *nolle prosequi* or review a police

[65] See Circulars G.E. 41(K)/1947, dated 11/06/2003 and G.E. 41(K)/1947, dated 15/07/2003.

[66] Circular G.E. 74/72/8, dated 19/06/03.

[67] Circular G.E. 50(B)1987/N.35/7, dated 17/05/04.

[68] See his Circulars in Footnote 65, Circular G.E. 124/73/2 dated 11/03/04 and the quotations from his Interview (11/01/2004) in Chap. 6.

decision to prosecute was either refused or returned unanswered.[69] Inevitably, such requests reduced dramatically (see, e.g. Table 1).[70] Therefore, as a result of that policy, a significant part of the Office's workload – involving mostly "police cases" – almost disappeared.

4.2.5 Concluding Remarks

Whilst the statutory duties and powers of the Attorney General have changed little over the last 45 years, the way in which subsequent office-holders have interpreted them has varied to some extent and inevitably affected the workload of the Law Office. Undoubtedly, though, as the time passed, other factors – not directly relevant to the approach of each Attorney General – have influenced the kinds of cases that the Office is dealing with. The tendency up until Mr Nikitas' appointment was towards the expansion of the Law Office's workload. However, some specific approaches by the last Attorney General raise some concerns that they might hold back a further extension, and confirm once again that the personality and specific choices of the office-holder still hold considerable influence over the Law Office's workload.[71]

[69] Information from the Criminal Records Department of the Law Office.

[70] See also in Table 1 that domestic violence cases also significantly reduced, most probably as a result of the absence of a clear direction by the Attorney General that they be sent to the Law Office, as was the case during Mr Markides' tenure.

[71] However, towards the end of 2005, Mr Nikitas resigned and Mr Clerides (the Deputy Attorney General since Mr Markides' tenure) was appointed as the new Attorney General. Although this research does not include the tenure of Mr Clerides, it can be said that since his appointment there have been a return to the philosophy of Mr Markides' running of the Law Office, especially regarding prosecutions. This is based on four points: (a) During Mr Markides' tenure, Mr Clerides was in charge of Prosecutions in the Law Office and, as admitted by Mr Markides himself (interview data), was responsible for a great number of prosecution decisions, often replacing the Attorney General (especially during the period that the latter was preoccupied with his duties as the advisor to the President of the Republic during negotiation discussions on the solution of the Cyprus political problem); (b) During Mr Nikitas' tenure, Mr Clerides on several occasions disagreed with Mr Nikitas' choices and policies regarding prosecutions (see, e.g. statements by Mr Clerides reported in the newspaper "Politis" on 20/12/2003, in the newspaper "Simerini" on 20/12/2004 and in the newspaper "Fileleftheros" on 12/02/05 and 13/03/05); (c) His speech the day of his appointment in the Presidential Palace was revealing of his intention for a more "flexible and humane" prosecution policy (see, *inter alia*, comments in the newspapers "Phileleftheros", "Simerini" and "Politis" on 12/05/2005 and 13/05/2005); (d) Some limited research I carried out concerning circulars and memoranda that Mr Clerides has issued since his appointment, as well as several discussions I had with Law Officers dealing with criminal cases and Mr Clerides himself, confirmed – at least *prima facie* – the above assumption.

4.3 Ideology in the Attorney General's Office: The Law Officers' Approach to Their Workload

In the previous sections, it has been shown that the workload of the Attorney General's Office has never been unproblematic, given either the rhetoric developed regarding the prosecution system or the history of the Office. In this section, how Law Officers themselves approach the Law Office's workload will be examined. Given the vagueness of the rhetoric, is there a certainty among them in determining the boundary limits of their responsibilities? Do they have a clear understanding of which cases they are dealing with and the reasons for that? And do they connect equally with all aspects of their workload? For any legal theory or any policy of an Attorney General to be properly implemented, significance dependence (among other factors) has to be placed on the extent to which they are understood and internalised by the agents involved, and on the commitment of these agents to support them. Furthermore, arguably, Law Officers' adherence to the role they associate with each aspect of the Law Office's workload both defines and limits their sense of what they can and should properly do in each category of cases. This, however, is a matter that will be discussed extensively in Chap. 6 and it will be touched on here only indirectly.

4.3.1 Ultimate Responsibility for Prosecutions

The observation period in the Law Office, and particularly the interviews with the Law Officers, indicated their broad and strong awareness that the Attorney General held ultimate responsibility for all prosecutions. It was something that they stressed emphatically in all of their accounts of the Office's role in prosecutions:

> 'The Attorney General's responsibilities regarding prosecutions are defined by Article 113 of the Constitution. He has the ultimate authority for all prosecutions ... the general direction of the prosecution processes'. (Law Officer 02).
>
> 'Every decision relating to prosecution is ours. *We* decide if a prosecution should be instituted or not or if it should be interrupted ... *Directly* or *indirectly* this is the case for all prosecutions'. (Law Officer 09)
>
> 'We may not have the monopoly on prosecutions ... but what we certainly do have is the right to control *all* prosecutions. Therefore, anytime we wish, we can stop a prosecution instituted by another organ, as well as take over a prosecution ... '. (Law Officer 01)
>
> 'The Attorney General is dominant ... And that's how it should be ... He is an independent, unbiased authority ... '. (Law Officer 10)

4.3.2 Assize Court Cases: Their Main Workload

The more serious cases are considered as the core of the Attorney General's workload. Law Officers appeared to have a strong understanding that these cases were the exclusive responsibility of their Office and therefore deserved priority. As will be argued in Chap. 6,[72] Assize Court cases were given fuller consideration and more time and resources than the rest:

> 'Assize Court cases are our main job and take up most of our time . . . '. (Law Officer 12)
>
> 'We have so many responsibilities as far as prosecutions are concerned and all have to be arranged to fit into our schedule regarding the Assize Court cases'. (Law Officer 01)

4.3.3 *Exceptional Cases v. Run-of-the-Mill Cases*

As far as the rest of the cases were concerned, it was obvious from Law Officers' accounts that "exceptional, complex or sensitive" cases were regarded as "Law Office's material" in contrast to "ordinary or run-of-the-mill" cases:

> 'The cases that we are dealing with in District Court are not simple routine cases . . . These are not what we are here for'. (Law Officer 13)

They were unanimous in what they described as cases that deserved the Law Office's attention:

(a) Cases with complex /difficult legal issues
(b) Cases in which constitutional issues may arise
(c) Cases in which issues of greater public interest can arise
(d) When the accused is a public servant or an "important and well-known person"
(e) When the accused is a police officer
(f) Exceptional/sensitive cases that can potentially create problems
(g) Cases with "strong political overtones"

Their attitudes towards a more systematic involvement of the Law Office in more categories of cases varied. Most of them argued that it would have been good theoretically but due to resource issues, it could not be applied:

> 'It's a situation forced by circumstances. Theoretically, there should be the involvement of the Office in all criminal cases because the opinion of our service as to what should happen to each case is by nature – arising from our independence – a more objective opinion. Additionally, we have the legal knowledge and that's very important. However, the number of criminal cases is such that a decision stating that all of them should be sent here would create bigger problems than the ones it would solve. Cases would be stuck here forever and things wouldn't move with the speed that they should . . . '. (Law Officer 10)
>
> 'If all cases are forwarded here, then with the organisation and the resources we have now, chaos would be created'. (Law Officer 17)

For some Law Officers, however, that disengagement from minor or routine cases was not purely a resource issue. It seemed to be a part of the culture of the Law

[72] In Chap. 6, how the role that Law Officers associate with each category of these cases influences their decision-making will be discussed in detail.

Office that for years dictated their engagement with cases that were exceptional or serious or had some particular sensitivity:

> 'You cannot deal with trivial cases here. If that were the case, you would not have time to deal with the *real ones*'. (Law Officer 03)

> 'Run-of-the-mill cases are not really *our* job ... There has to be something extraordinary about them, or something that calls for attention. Sometimes they send very trivial things here and the increased workload prevents us from dealing with the more serious cases as thoroughly as we should'. (Law Officer 11)

4.3.4 Police Prosecutions

The rhetorical position that the Attorney General was responsible for the cases which the police were dealing with was theoretically adopted by the Law Officers. But the way they reflected on it was characterised by the same contradictions as the rhetoric itself, and probably as a result of this.

As a rule, all Law Officers declared categorically their ultimate responsibility for those cases:

> 'Police execute their prosecutorial functions under the directions of the Attorney General. He has every right to give them directions ... '. (Law Officer 02)

> 'We are responsible for all criminal cases, even the ones that the police are dealing with ... Most of them come here at some stage ... Very few don't ... For example, ordinary traffic cases do not come here, but fatal traffic accident cases do'. (Law Officer 09)

However, it was striking that the justifications for that were not equally clear to all of them. More senior Law Officers appeared to have a more sophisticated approach as to why they were dealing with summary cases and what their exact powers regarding them were, while the rest were less clear and, at times, self-contradictory.

For example, in reflecting on their exact *relationship with the police*, the terms they used mirrored some of the same misinterpretations or confusion that were observed in the rhetoric surrounding the Attorney General's role in prosecutions:

> 'If the Attorney General decides that all criminal cases should come to the Law Office, he is empowered to ask for that ... It is his right *according to the Constitution...* '. (Law Officer 15)

> 'Theoretically we have *parallel roles* ... in practice it is the relationship of a supervisor and a supervisee'. (Law Officer 17)

> 'We are the *legal advisors* to the police'. (Law Officer 12)[73] (emphases added)

---

[73]It is interesting to note here that Law Officers who did not deal with criminal prosecutions exclusively but had additional duties in the Law Office (e.g. legal advice to Government Departments) were more inclined to use the term "legal advice" when referring to their relationship with the police, obviously because they equated it to the relationship they had with the other services they were working with.

Perhaps as a result of this confusion over the justifications on which they based the exercise of their control over "police cases", a couple of Law Officers admitted that they were not in a position to define exactly which categories of cases the police were obliged to send to the Law Office apart from the "obvious ones":

> 'I'll be frank with you. I am not sure which specific cases the police have to forward to the Law Office apart from the serious ones and exactly why our intervention is obligatory for them . . . When I have these minor cases in front of me, I am just answering what the police are asking . . .'. (Law Officer 01)

Some Law Officers appeared to regard this issue as the exclusive responsibility of the Attorney General himself, who was in power to define the terms and limits of the dealings of the Office with the police:

> 'I've never considered this matter from such a theoretical point of view but deal with whatever comes along, knowing that we have the last word even in police cases. Anyway, this is an Attorney General's matter or policy . . . *He* has the authority to order the police to send here specific categories of cases'. (Law Officer 17)

It was striking that while all of them were quick to declare their certainty that if a case was forwarded to the Law Office, they had the final word on it, not all of them seemed equally enthusiastic to consider thoroughly the question of which cases police *did* send them.

Even the Law Officers who had a clearer view of their relationship with the police seemed to prefer to let the police decide which other cases deserved the Law Office's attention:

> 'Minor cases are practically *their* cases. Therefore, when they think that they need our advice, they contact us and ask for our directions. You cannot predefine everything anyway . . . '. (Law Officer 12)

The same applies to the stage where "police cases" reach the public prosecutors at the Police Prosecution Departments:

> 'Public prosecutors who are dealing with cases in the District Courts contact us when they need advice or directions. Or we could ask them to send here the file of a case they are dealing with when we need to investigate something. There should be a special reason, or something that calls for our attention. . .There is not a structured method of control . . . there couldn't be any . . . '. (Law Officer 09)

> 'Very often, public prosecutors ask me to authorise them to discontinue some cases or withdraw some charges when they are facing difficulties in presenting the case in court'. (Law Officer 12)

All of the Law Officers argued that since the appointment of public prosecutors by the Attorney General, their cooperation with the Police Prosecution Departments had been closer and more effective. Again, though, they admitted that usually it was when public prosecutors needed their advice that they contacted them:

> LO: In everyday dealings with criminal cases, public prosecutors are in touch with us and they are taking instructions from us.
> R: Do you think that you can exercise everyday control over them?

LO: No. After we give instructions about a case, we are not informed of the outcome of it. It's when *they* need advice and guidance that they contact us; we don't contact them. (Law Officer 12)

4.3.5 Police Discretion and "Control Potential"

Law Officers accepted that there was a considerable degree of flexibility regarding police reporting procedures, although they pointed out that the serving Attorney General (Mr Markides) was far more specific in his directions than his predecessors.

Even regarding categories of cases where most of the Law Officers were clear on the obligation of the police to forward them to their Office, they seemed to acknowledge that the police had considerable discretion:

R: If the police decide not to prosecute a case, do they have to send the case here?
LO: Yes.
R: Even minor cases?
LO: For minor cases, not always ...
R: But theoretically they should, shouldn't they?
LO: They should...but sometimes, for very trivial cases, the police may deviate .... (Law Officer 02)

R: If the police decide not to prosecute, do they send the case here so you can approve this decision?
LO: This is the tactic ... but I am not in the position to check if they follow it. How could I? Having said that, I can say that we receive *many* cases where the police ask for directions from the Law Office, arguing, that for some reason, they should not prosecute .... (Law Officer 01)

Nevertheless, most of them appeared to believe that human dynamics and trust were more important than predefined rules:

'You should trust them to send you whatever needs attention. In a small society like Cyprus, it is more important to know the person you are dealing with and whether you can trust him. It is more important than saying to the police, 'you must send these cases here, or you must ask for our advice on that'. That's why, for example, the heads of the (Police) Prosecution Departments should be trustworthy ... and the Attorney General ensures that they are'. (Law Officer 09)

They acknowledged, though, that not all of the police officers involved in prosecutions deserved their trust, and some of the Law Officers were particularly cynical about that. For example, discussing a certain head of a Police Prosecution Department, a Law Officer was emphatic:

'... He does whatever he wants ... he is corrupt ... Once, he asked me about a case involving a relative of his ... to give a direction for discontinuance ... in so many other cases, he doesn't ask ... I don't know why he asked that time'. (Law Officer 14)

'There were various problems with the police regarding cases of domestic violence. There were a couple of times when public prosecutors discontinued a case without our direction...We decided that some of them would not be prosecuting such cases ... we excluded 2–3 public prosecutors ... '. (Law Officer 16)

'It is strongly emphasised that the police cannot close a case ... On some occasions we ordered investigations against police officers who were closing cases of domestic violence.

. . . In the future, they will be more sensitive with these issues, when they see that we are serious about this and we order investigations against officers who don't obey our directions'. (Law Officer 08)

Generally, although they acknowledged that the police sometimes stretched the standards, and did not exclude the fact that, sometimes, the police exploit their powers, most of the Law Officers appeared confident that worrisome abuses were rare, for three reasons:

(a) They believed that, because of the size of the jurisdiction, it was easy for the Law Office to become aware of special cases that required their attention, even if the police chose not to inform them:

'Cyprus is a small place. We find out about the extraordinary cases very easily. Even Judges sometimes inform us that a case which the police are dealing with is not being properly handled and we should intervene'. (Law Officer 09)

(b) They argued that since it was widely appreciated that the Attorney General was the primary authority in prosecutions, victims or defendants made sure that he was informed whenever they felt that their cases were not dealt with properly by the police:

'You can see that it is standard procedure to receive requests from the defendants to review their cases'. (Law Officer 04)

(c) With public prosecutors – appointed by the Attorney General – serving in the Police Prosecution Departments, they claimed that there was more security and that they were notified about what required their intervention.

4.3.6 Concluding Remarks

In summary, it can be stated that the Law Officers' attitude and ideology regarding their workload focus on the ultimate responsibility of the Office to control and oversee all prosecutions, even if the justifications they offer for their powers are fairly unclear. Although they theoretically accept that the Law Office can also deal with the most minor of cases, they connect more with the most serious ones since they regard these as the core of their workload. They realise that they cannot exercise everyday control in all cases mainly because of resource issues and therefore, they focus on their control function and their ability to intervene. Law Officers acknowledge that this allows the police a wide discretion, but they believe that if something really important needs their attention, there are sufficient mechanisms to find out.

4.4 Practice

In this section, I will provide an account of the categories of cases that actually reach the Law Office on an everyday basis and make up its workload. These data are based on my observation and the examination of cases I carried out during my fieldwork period in the Attorney General's Office and they are supplemented by available records of cases which the Law Office dealt with over an extended period of time.

4.4.1 Preliminary Remark

It is essential to make a note here about the records system in the Law Office. In the Records Department, separate records are kept only for the following categories of files:[74]

(a) Files concerning the cases that are committed for trial before the Assize Courts.
(b) Cases presented at the District Courts.
(c) Applications by defendants (or victims) asking the Attorney General to review a police decision (usually applications on the entering of a *nolle prosequi*).
(d) Domestic violence cases.
(e) Fraud/stock exchange cases.
(f) Corruption by public officers cases.
(g) There is a large record in which the rest of the files are included without being separated:
    (ga) Cases where the police are seeking the consent of the Attorney General for the summary trial of indictable offences.
    (gb) Cases where the police are not sure whether there is enough evidence for a prosecution, or believe that there is not enough evidence, and cases where they believe there are other ("public interest") reasons for not prosecuting.
    (gc) Cases at the investigation stage for which the advice of the Law Office is sought.
    (gd) Fatal motoring offences.
    (ge) Offences committed by juveniles.
    (gf) Cases which have been investigated after a complaint-report to the Attorney General.

Table 1 shows the number of files forwarded to the Law Office for each category of its workload during the years 2000–2005.

[74] Therefore, although the total number of cases that the Law Office is dealing with can be calculated for the cases for which there are separate records, the same cannot be achieved for the cases coming under category (f). For example, we cannot say how many of the 2,681 cases that were forwarded to the Law Office in 2002 by the police and recorded under this category were indictable cases for which consent for a summary trial was requested, or how many were summary cases with a suggestion to refrain from prosecution for public interest reasons. For these cases, the numbers included in my sample provide an indication of the real distribution of each category of cases in the Law Office's workload. However, I cannot argue that this is a very strong indication since, as I will show later, a significant part of Law Officers' workloads is not file-based. Nevertheless, from the beginning (see Chap. 1 and Appendix 1) I have stressed that my study does not aim to provide a strict statistical analysis – but rather a qualitative description – of the Law Office's workload.

Table 1 Files forwarded to the Law Office for each category of its workload (2000–2005)

Categories of cases	2000	2001	2002	2003	2004	2005
Files of cases committed for trial before an Assize Court	135	104	71	97	137	96
Cases presented at the District Court by Law Officers	36	72	48	45	49	51
Requests for a *nolle prosequi* – review of police decision	1,276	1,412	1,316	686	349	744
Domestic violence cases	192	136	192	147	72	86
Fraud/stock exchange cases	13	205	400	394	247	442
Corruption by public officers cases	3	14	42	14	14	3
Files concerning cases for review, consent, advice, etc.	2,774	2,877	2,681	2,616	2,769	2,776

4.4.2 Prosecution of All Cases Before the Assize Courts

This category formed what was characterised by all the agents in the prosecution system as the principal workload of the Law Office. As was observed in practice, a significant part of the time and resources of the Office were invested in cases coming under this category. By virtue of Article 117 of the Criminal Procedure Law, the Attorney General has a monopoly over prosecutions on information.[75] Therefore, cases concerning indictable offences (offences punishable with imprisonment of 5 years and above) with a suggestion to prosecute were always sent to his Office. After a positive decision for prosecution was taken, the Law Officers themselves (who were all qualified as advocates[76]) were responsible not only for the preparation of the case and the pre-trial stages, but also for the conduct of the trial in court.[77] During my fieldwork period, I observed 18 such cases at various stages and I examined 60 attachments to the Attorney General after the completion of the cases in court (these concerned cases finalised during 2001). The most common offences prosecuted in Assize Court were: Robberies, rape or other serious sexual offences, manslaughter/murder/causing grievous bodily harm, conspiracies, serious forgeries, serious drug offences, arson, unlawful possession of firearms and explosives, burglary, destroying property by explosives, serious frauds, and stealing by a servant.

[75] "Prosecutions on information" is the term used for prosecutions on indictment in Cyprus.

[76] In Cyprus the division between barristers and solicitors does not exist within the legal profession.

[77] In Cyprus the Attorney General's Office does not instruct counsel to handle cases in court on its behalf. Law Officers themselves have rights of audience not only in District Courts but also in Assize Courts.

4.4.3 *Prosecution Before the District Courts*

4.4.3.1 "Sensitive" and Complex Cases

Despite the rule that most of the cases before a District Court were handled by Public Prosecutors serving in the Police Prosecution Departments, there were a number of cases which were presented by Law Officers. These were usually cases that were sent to the Law Office for consideration and the Attorney General, after a positive decision for prosecution, decided to keep them in the Office so they could be handled by members of his staff. These were the cases that had been characterised as complex or "sensitive" in my interviews with the Law Officers and the Attorney General. During my fieldwork (2002), these were:

(a) A case of stealing by a public servant and abuse of his power
(b) A case concerning the offence of forgery by a public servant
(c) A case concerning stealing electricity regarding which publicity was generated by the media
(d) A case concerning the offence of causing death by want of precaution or by carelessness (s.210 of Criminal Law) (the accused was the driver of a private minibus who caused an accident resulting in the death of all eight passengers)
(e) A case concerning serious offences of domestic violence
(f) A case of indecent assault against a journalist
(g) Nineteen complex economic or Stock Exchange cases

In order to extend the picture of what usually constitutes complex or sensitive cases, the records for the years 2000, 2001 and 2003 were additionally collected and studied. In 2000 the following cases were presented to District Courts by Law Officers: a case concerning the offence of corruption and extortion by two senior public officers; a case of a lawyer obtaining money by false pretences; a case of illegal trespassing in a Shelter for the protection of juveniles by the parents of one of the children kept in the Shelter; and 14 complex economic or Stock Exchange cases. In 2001: a case of extortion by a public servant; a case of assault by a police officer; two cases concerning fatal motoring accidents (one of them causing the death of six persons), three cases of conspiracy; two cases concerning the offence of corruption and extortion by public officers (a senior doctor at a Public Hospital), a case against a Metropolitan Bishop of conspiracy to ruin one's reputation; a case concerning the offence of Contempt of Court against a well-known journalist; a case concerning offences under the Adoption Law against a gynaecologist; and 19 complex economic or Stock Exchange cases. In 2003: two cases of assault by police officers; a case of conspiracy to defraud; a case concerning the offence of forgery by a public servant; a case of forgery; a conspiracy to defraud case; a case concerning serious offences of domestic violence; five interrelated cases concerning offences of conspiracy to defraud and illegal importations (this was a widely publicised scandal); a case of extortion by a public servant; a case of medical negligence; and four complex economic or Stock Exchange cases.

As can be observed, this category is not made up of ordinary, run-of-the-mill cases, but rather by cases that are either difficult to prove, involve a well-known person/a public official/a police officer, or attract extensive media attention.

4.4.3.2 Government Department Prosecutions

As was stated earlier, various Government Departments have the power to prosecute summary offences within their particular sphere of activity. During the time of my fieldwork (but also before and after that for an extended period of time), at the Ministry of Labour and the Department of Environment there was a shortage of qualified (according to Law 8/1989) prosecutors who could present cases in court and, as a result, many cases were sent to the Law Office in order to be presented by Law Officers. In 2002, Law Officers handled 23 cases on behalf of Government Departments (which equates to 50% of the total number of cases before a District Court which were handled by a Law Officer).[78] These were relatively simple cases (mainly concerning regulatory offences) compared to the cases that Law Officers used to handle before Assize Courts, or the rest of the District Court cases. It is curious that the limited resources of the Law Office were spent in that way because of the shortage of staff in other Government Departments.

4.4.4 Requests to Enter a Nolle Prosequi or to Review Police Decisions

It was observed that a special aspect of the Law Office's workload concerned the consideration of requests submitted to the Attorney General by defendants asking him to exercise his power to terminate criminal proceedings or to review a decision for prosecution before a charge is preferred in court. These requests concerned mainly summary offences which were handled by the Police Prosecution Departments and a small number of them, prosecutions by other Government Departments. With these requests, defendants would ask the Attorney General to overrule a decision to prosecute made by the police (or by other authorities), stating various reasons. Most of them were based on *public interest factors* (health reasons, remorse, disproportionate consequences of a possible conviction, abuse of process/oppressiveness in prosecution, reconciliation between offender and victim), but a number of them were based on *evidential reasons* (total absence of evidence, unreliable evidence, abuse of process by the police). In my sample, *53 applications* were included which related to cases concerning the offences listed in Table 2.

These were cases that would not normally be part of the Law Office's workload and they were only forwarded there because defendants took the initiative to ask for

[78] In 2000, 24 such cases (61%) were presented and in 2001, 40 cases (58%).

Table 2 Requests to Enter a Nolle Prosequi (type of offences)

Type of offences	No of cases	Type of offences	No of cases
Assaults causing actual bodily harm	6	Reckless and negligent acts	1
Reckless or careless driving	5	Offences against exchange control law	1
Affray	3	Offences against Cyprus Athletic Organisation Law	1
Issue of a cheque without	3	Offence against Streets and Buildings Regulation Law	1
Theft	3	Disturbance	1
Motoring offences	3	Offence under Dogs Law	1
Drug offences	2	Burglary	1
Domestic violence	2	Offences against Antiquities Law	1
Offences against law and regulations relating to driving licence	2	Poaching	1
Employing unlawful immigrants	2	Various regulatory offences	4
Common assault	2	Forgery and extortion	1
Public insult and threatening violence	2	S.105 of Criminal Law	1
Indecent assault and criminal trespass	1	Causing grievous bodily harm	1
Carrying arms to terrorise	1		

the Attorney General's intervention. They represented the best example of the Law Office's "controlling potential" (constantly referred to by the Attorney General and the Law Officers) which was activated by the actions of other agents in the prosecution system. The large number of those cases also indicated that there was a widespread appreciation among the public of the Law Office's role and powers in the process; especially its power to intervene and overrule a police decision. Furthermore, defence lawyers I interviewed confirmed that the Law Office, in comparison to the police, was regarded as a far more objective and independent service, which they referred to so that a biased or unfair police decision could be corrected.

4.4.5 *Domestic Violence Cases, Fraud/Stock Exchange Cases, Corruption by Public Officers Cases/"Consent" Cases and Fatal Motoring Offences, Offences Committed by Juveniles*

All these cases formed categories that the Attorney General had clearly and specifically directed should be forwarded to the Law Office. They included offences where he was of the opinion that particular attention was required or were "cases that might reveal important considerations of public policy". For the three first categories, a separated record was being kept at the Law Office and thus, the total number of cases for each category could be easily calculated (see Table 1). On the contrary, the cases coming under the last two categories were recorded under the general record (g).

4.4.5.1 Domestic Violence Cases (Seven Cases in my Sample)

Since 1998, according to a circular from the Attorney General,[79] all Government Department officers (police officers, social workers, doctors, etc.), to whose attention came a case of domestic violence, had an obligation to submit a report to the Attorney General within 7 days. A team of Law Officers would examine the reports and give directions. Until 2000, all criminal files were forwarded to the Law Office after the police investigations and Law Officers decided whether to prosecute or not. Due to the large amount of files arriving at the Office, the police were directed to send only those cases in which *they had decided not to prosecute or they were not sure whether they should prosecute*.

4.4.5.2 Fraud/Stock Exchange Cases

As a result of the opening of the Cyprus Stock Exchange (1999) and immediately afterwards, a huge rise in economic crime was observed. A special unit operated within the Law Office responsible for economic crime and money laundering offences which closely cooperated with the police department for economic crime. After a positive decision for prosecution was taken, these cases were usually presented in court by Law Officers (see category b).

4.4.5.3 Corruption by Public Officers Cases/"Consent" Cases (Five Cases in my Sample)

There are certain provisions in the Criminal Code, as well as in a few other statutes, which require that the Attorney General's consent be obtained for the prosecution of particular offences. The almost exclusive category of "consent cases" which was observed reaching the Law Office were offences relating to corruption and extortion by a public officer. There was a clear direction by the Attorney General that the police should forward such cases to the Law Office, even if it was thought that there was not enough evidence for prosecution. These cases were always presented in court by Law Officers.

4.4.5.4 Fatal Motoring Offences (Two Cases in my Sample)

For motoring accidents which involve loss of life, two charges could be preferred; either "causing death in a traffic accident", which is a minor offence, or "causing death by want of precaution or by carelessness", which is a serious one. As the border between these two offences had not been clear, the Attorney General directed the Police to forward all such cases to the Office.

[79] Circular G.E. 50(C)/1992/N.42, dated 11/06/1998.

4.4.5.5 Offences Committed by Juveniles (12 Cases in my Sample)

There was a special procedure followed for this category of cases. There were Committees comprised of the Police Constable and representatives of Social Services for each District, responsible for reviewing all juvenile cases. Their suggestion as to the proper disposal of the case and a review of the Social Services' report were forwarded to the Attorney General's Office with the relevant criminal file. Law Officers could endorse or overrule the decision of those Committees.

4.4.6 Summary Trial of Indictable Offences

A large number of files referred to the Law Office by the Police concerned the suggestion for the summary disposal of indictable offences, a procedure for which the Attorney General's consent is obligatory. In the Cyprus Legal System, there are no "triable either way" offences. The District Court has jurisdiction to try summarily all offences punishable with a term of imprisonment not exceeding 5 years and/or a fine not exceeding £5,000. For the most serious offences, the accused must be committed to the Assize Court for a trial "on information". By Law, the Attorney General may consent to the summary trial of every offence.[80]

These files related mainly to offences of forgery of cheques, drug offences and Firearms Law offences. For these offences, the maximum sentence in Law is very high and there are no predefined subcategories, i.e. the maximum sentence in Law for the forgery of a cheque of £15 is the same as for the forgery of a cheque of

Table 3 Type/number of indictable offences proposed for summary trial

Type of offences	No of cases	Type of offences	No of cases
Forgery of a cheque or uttering false documents	11	Stealing by trustees and persons in a position of trust	4
Unlawful possession, supplying or cultivation of drugs (Narcotic drugs Law 29/77)	18	Stealing by clerks and servants, s.268 of Criminal Law	1
Unlawful possession of firearms (Law 38/74) or unlawful possession of explosive substances (Law Cap. 54)	16	Stealing by persons in public service, s. 267 of Criminal Law	1
Breaking into a building and committing a felony (burglary)	10	Causing grievous bodily harm, s. 231 of Criminal Law	1
Violence within family Law 47(1)/94	2	Trespass in restricted areas, s. 50B of Criminal Law	1

[80] Section 24 of the Courts of Justice Law (Law 14/1960).

£150,000! *65 files* of this category were examined and they involved the offences listed in Table 3.

4.4.7 Cases Which the Police Want to Filter Out of the System

Many files were forwarded to the Law Office regarding cases where (i) the Police suggested that a prosecution was not required due to public interest factors or (ii) they were not sure that there was enough evidence for a prosecution. This category formed an absolutely critical aspect of the Law Office workload. It validated the argument by the Attorney General, the Law Officers and the police[81] that the police do not generally filter cases – apart from very minor ones – out of the system without the directions of the Law Office. Included in this category were not only cases concerning indictable offences (which is less debatable due to their being the exclusive responsibility of the Law Office), but also cases concerning less serious crimes:

4.4.7.1 Indictable Offences Cases: Mainly Evidential Issues[82]

(a) A rape case
(b) A rape case of a mentally defective girl
(c) A case of forgery and fraud
(d) A case of arson (not sure whether it was intentional or accidental)
(e) Two cases of stealing by a servant
(f) Three cases of forgery
(g) A case of stealing by a trustee

4.4.7.2 Indictable Offences Cases: Mainly Public Interest Factors[83] (21 Cases)

(a) Two cases of unlawful possession of a weapon
(b) A case of forgery of a public document
(c) Two cases of forgery of a cheque
(d) A case of unlawful possession of explosive substances
(e) A case of unlawful importation of explosive substances

---

[81] See the interviews earlier in this chapter.

[82] As will be shown in Chap. 6, public interest factors and evidential issues were quite often mixed.

[83] Most of those cases were cases which only technically concerned indictable offences. The circumstances of the offences would normally argue for a suggestion of a summary trial.

(f) A case of burglary
(g) Thirteen cases of drugs offences

4.4.7.3 Summary Offences Cases: Mainly Evidential Issues (11 Cases)

(a) Two cases against two companies for unlawful possession of explosive substances relating to the type of games they were selling
(b) A case of breach of banking regulations
(c) A case of unlawful possession of drugs
(d) A case of fraud
(e) A case concerning offences against Foreign Currency Law
(f) A case concerning offences against Bankruptcy Law
(g) A case of stealing
(h) A case of receiving stolen goods
(i) A case of criminal impersonation
(j) A case of extortion by a police officer

4.4.7.4 Summary Offences Cases: Mainly Public Interest Factors (34 Cases)

(a) Nine cases of drug offences
(b) Seven cases of regulatory offences
(c) Five cases of assault causing bodily harm – the victim withdrew the complaint
(d) Two case of common assault
(e) A case of affray
(f) A case of obtaining a formal document by false pretences
(g) A case of obtaining goods by false pretences
(h) A case of a motor accident
(i) A case of selling counterfeit CDs
(j) A case of illegal cutting of trees (Forest Law)
(k) Two cases of assault causing bodily harm
(l) A case of employing an unlawful immigrant (Immigration Law)
(m) A case between a father and a son of threatening violence/carrying arms to terrorise
(n) A case of a psychological disturbed individual carrying arms to terrorise

Law Officers' decisions in these cases could be either a direction for prosecution or non-prosecution based on public interest or evidential reasons, or a direction for further investigations.[84]

[84] See Chap. 6.

4.4.8 Files Referred to the Law Office for Advice During the Investigation Stage[85]

This part of the Law Office's workload concerned files referred by the police during the investigation stage and it will be discussed in detail in the next chapter. The police quite often sought Law Officers' advice on the kind of information needed to sustain certain charges, on legal provisions or even on investigation techniques and strategies. This part of the Law Office's workload was not solely file-based. During my fieldwork, I noticed that, for serious cases, police investigators used to come to the Office in person and consult with the Law Officers. Typical cases that were included in this category were: cases of forgery, cases of obtaining goods by false pretences, fraud/Stock Exchange cases, murder/manslaughter cases or cases where a well-known person was involved.

4.4.9 Cases Which Have Been Investigated After a Complaint-Report to the Attorney General

The Law Office from time to time received correspondence from various sources, e.g. Members of the Parliament, other elected representatives or simply members of the public, who felt that a certain incident required a prosecution. The type of reports received this way amounted to very serious allegations of criminal conduct (e.g. exercise of violence by police officers against arrested persons in custody), but it also concerned information regarding trivial offences. When the Attorney General considered it appropriate, he would request the police to carry out investigations and, depending on their outcomes, he would decide whether to prosecute or not:

(a) A case of unlawful possession of antiquities – after a report by the Ministry of Transportation
(b) A case of unlawful disclosure of bank accounts – after a complaint by a member of the public
(c) Two cases of Contempt of Court – after a letter from the Ministry of Finance
(d) A case of malicious prosecution by the Police – after a complaint by a member of the public
(e) Accusations of police violence against suspects in custody – by a Member of Parliament

[85]This is not representative because I observed many other cases where police officers came in person asking for advice or called the Law Officers for the same purpose (see next chapter).

4.4.10 Concluding Remarks

It is evident that the Law Office's workload is incredibly diverse and multifarious. The following are some general conclusions that can be derived by studying the actual cases that reach the Law Office:

Firstly, the workload of the Attorney General's Office includes an interesting mixture of high-profile cases, complex crimes, "sensitive cases", as well as the more ordinary/run-of-the-mill cases.[86]

Secondly, there is a *variety of reasons* which explain which categories of cases are forwarded to the Office. Some of them are sent because it is mandatory by law (a, ga, f); some because of clear and specific directions by the Attorney General, (b, d, e, f, gd, ge); some because of police initiative – influenced by the policy of each Attorney General (gb, gc) – and others because agents involved in the process (usually the defendants) ask for the Law Office's intervention (c, gf).

Thirdly, there are cases in which the Law Office are *systematically* involved (e.g. Assize Court cases) and others in which they are only involved (*control potential*) if someone else draws their attention (e.g. when the police ask, the defendants request, or the public inform).

Fourthly, there are cases that are under the immediate control of the Attorney General's Office from the beginning to the end (e.g. Assize Court cases) and others that are forwarded to the Law Office only for a limited period of time (e.g. advice during investigation, requests for *nolle prosequi*).

4.5 Summary

Based on this chapter, it can be concluded that the workload of the Attorney General's Office has never been straightforward, not even in the rhetoric developed around the system, let alone in its everyday practice. However, it can also be understood that it has been as varied and multifarious as the broader role of the Law Office in prosecutions appears to be.

In the *rhetoric*, great emphasis has been placed upon the symbolism and potential of the power of the Attorney General rather than the everyday execution of his prosecutorial function. The very broad powers that the Office is given by the Constitution, as well as the absence of any detailed statutory legislation, allowed sometimes varied interpretations not only by the rest of the actors in the criminal justice system, but also by the different office-holders themselves. A reluctance to be detached from terms and customs associated with the common law tradition of prosecutions in the last century was observed, when even in the

[86] Which, in a way, become extra-ordinary because either it is suggested that they should be filtered out of the system, or because the defendant takes the initiative to involve the Attorney General in them.

country of their origin things have changed. This contrasts with the indisputable recognition – by the same actors – of characteristics and powers of the Attorney General's Office, which are not compatible with the "strict" common law tradition.

However, although there is some vagueness in the rhetoric as far as the Law Office's workload is concerned, and some inconsistency regarding the exact relationship between the Attorney General and the police, the conclusion that is unanimously reached is that the Attorney General, if he wished, could make his control over the police tighter and extend the workload of his Office as he sees fit. The primacy of the Attorney General is never doubted; it is just the logic or the justifications behind it that vary on some occasions and create confusion.

It is obvious that successive Attorney Generals have been comfortable with their broad discretion, as it permitted them to be flexible with the categories of cases they were dealing with. At the beginning, there was less expectation from the Attorney General to be involved in cases other than the most serious ones, even if the law, right from the start, enabled him to do so. Gradually, as time passed, and due to a number of reasons – practical ones as well as the specific choices of some office-holders (mainly Mr Markides') – this approach started to change and, as a result, the Law Office's workload has been significantly extended.

Given the vagueness in the rhetoric and the varied interpretations of successive office-holders, it is not remarkable that the Law Officers' approach towards their workload (*ideology*) is relatively unclear as well – especially regarding the justifications of their powers. Although theoretically they accept that the Attorney General oversees the whole prosecution system and can also deal with the most minor of the cases, they connect more with the most serious ones since they regard *them* as the core of their workload. They realise that they cannot exercise everyday control in all cases, mainly because of resource issues, and, therefore, they emphatically focus on their "control function" and their ability to intervene. Law Officers acknowledge that this gives the police a wide discretion (which might result in abuses), but they appear confident that if something really important needs their attention, there is always a way to find out.[87]

In *practice*, it has been observed that the workload of the Attorney General's Office is very mixed, consisting not only of the most high-profile cases, but also of minor ones that reach the Law Office sometimes as a matter of purely accidental practical arrangements (see prosecution on behalf of Government Departments). Apart from the cases that it is obliged by law to deal with, the Law Office also deals with those categories of cases that the Attorney General has clearly specified *a priori* or chosen *ad hoc*, cases for which the police request advice or directions,

[87]The way and the criteria upon which cases are decided in the Law Office are issues that will be discussed in the next two chapters (especially in Chap. 6). At this point, it is sufficient to say that the Law Officers' adherence to the role they associated with each aspect of their workload and how strong they feel that a category of cases is "Law Office material" are some of the most influential factors that affect their decision-making.

as well as cases for which other agents in the process (usually the defendants) ask the Law Office's intervention – usually to overrule a police decision.

Although the serving Attorney General (at the time of my fieldwork) has been more specific than his predecessors in defining categories of cases that should be forwarded to the Law Office, he has not fully utilised his powers. Admittedly, as a result, the police have enjoyed a broad discretion; apart from specific categories of cases, they are left to judge semi-autonomously what is important and problematic enough to be sent to the Law Office. However, the fact that there is a strong consensus on the matter of principle – namely that the Attorney General is the ultimate authority in prosecutions and has the authority to give directions regarding all prosecutions – appears to inform the practices of all the actors in the system. Victims and defendants quite often request the Law Office's intervention in cases that do not regularly belong to its workload and the police practices appear to be influenced by this theoretical potential.

Therefore, as a first general conclusion, it can be stated that the Law Office's role in the system is not confined to the prosecution of serious crime. The theory, as well as the practice, proves that the Attorney General is expected to, and does, play a much broader role in all criminal prosecutions, even if he is not closely dealing with all of them. One of the most crucial aspects of this role is the "controlling mechanism" he offers to supervise and intervene dynamically in the bulk of criminal prosecutions.

Chapter 5
The Role of the Attorney General's Office Regarding Investigations

> 'The true independence of the prosecutor from the police is not to be found in the total separation of the investigative and prosecutorial functions, but rather in the prosecutor's authority over the police in relation to the evidential side of the criminal investigation . . .'.
> (L. Robb 1988, p. 28)

In the previous chapter the categories of cases that the Cyprus Law Office is dealing with have been examined, placing particular emphasis on the sharing of its workload with the police regarding prosecutions. In this chapter, another aspect of the Law Office's relationship with the police will be studied. This relates to the role and the powers of the Law Office as far as the investigation and the collection of information for a case are concerned. Therefore, it explores the Law Office's participation in the stage that cases are still being formed as potential "prosecutable edifices".[1] It is widely accepted that whatever takes place during this phase exerts considerable influence on the later decision of prosecution, but also on the progress of the case overall.

In common law jurisdictions investigations have been traditionally regarded as the preserve of the police, contrary to the pure continental tradition which has placed prosecutors in charge of the investigatory as well as the post-investigatory stage. However, as was shown in Chap. 2, both models have been compromised over time by a variety of factors. In the *first section* of this chapter the standpoint of the Cyprus prosecution system regarding the involvement of the Attorney General's Office in investigations will be reviewed. Once again, since there are no detailed statutory provisions relating to this issue, a study of their interpretation and the rhetoric that has been developed over time, as well as of the Attorney Generals' approach regarding prosecutors' involvement in investigations, is essential.

In the *second section* the Law Officers' viewpoint will be examined. Given the broad nature of the legal provisions and the great discretion they enjoy regarding their involvement in criminal investigations, it is crucial to explore how Law Officers themselves approach, interpret and reflect on their role.

---

[1] Sanders (1988a, p. 35).

D. Kyprianou, *The Role of the Cyprus Attorney General's Office in Prosecutions: Rhetoric, Ideology and Practice*,
DOI 10.1007/978-3-642-01921-0_5,

Finally, in the *third section* the role that is carried out by the Law Office in investigations in practice will be described, drawing on observation of the everyday life of the Office, as well as on the examination of cases during the fieldwork period in the Law Office.

5.1 Rhetoric – History

The involvement of prosecutors in investigations is directly related to the constitutional position of the police in relation to the prosecution service. As was discussed in detail in Chap. 2, pure *inquisitorial systems* traditionally place the police, when investigating a crime, under the authority of the prosecutors. Usually, in those systems, there is a line of command between the two services. According to the traditional *common law*, by contrast, the responsibility for the investigation lies exclusively in the hands of the police. In most common law countries there is no direct line of authority between the police and the prosecution service and the former enjoy a considerable independence in the execution of their duties.

However, this clear-cut division of work between the constitutionally separate institutions of the police and prosecutors has recently begun to change, because of a number of factors. For example, the appearance of new forms of criminality and the ever increasing complexities of substantive and procedural law made the police dependent on the prosecutors for legal advice, a fact which in many jurisdictions has evolved into forms of cooperation that have provided the prosecutor with some influence in the investigation process itself. Nevertheless, in most jurisdictions the appropriate boundary between the police and the prosecutor's involvement in investigations has not yet been set in theory, let alone achieved in practice, and certainly remains a controversial issue in the discussions about the relationships of these two institutions.

5.1.1 Legal Theory in the Cyprus Prosecution System

In Cyprus the Attorney General, right from the beginning, in contrast to his common law background, was entrusted with a role in investigations as well as in prosecutions.[2] This is in accordance with the wide powers that were delegated to him generally as far as prosecutions are concerned and which rendered him so important in the Cyprus prosecution system. However, also in line with the broad nature of the rest of his powers, his role in investigations was not prescribed in detail in the statutory provisions.

[2]This is an additional role that has been acquired by the Attorney General in Cyprus that did not appear to exist during the pre-independence period.

The Criminal Procedure Law (Cap. 155 s.4.1) gives police the primary responsibility for investigations but it also confers on the Council of Ministers a complementary authority to appoint independent investigators in any case (s.4.2). Sections 4–34 regulate the conduct of investigations, placing particular emphasis on the powers of the police to arrest and search a suspect.[3] As was shown in Chap. 3, there are strict exclusionary rules regarding the collection of evidence and its admissibility in court (imposed by the constitutional provisions) but the framework of procedural rules determining how interrogation is to be conducted is rather limited. There is a section in the Criminal Procedure Law providing that the Judges' Rules, which are in force in England, apply in Cyprus as well (Section 8). A new Law (163(I)/2005) has been recently enacted, however, to safeguard the rights of people detained for interrogation,[4] in part reiterating – and also specifying – the relevant provisions of the Constitution, which have been already strictly applied by the courts.

Statutory legislation does not give the Attorney General, and thus the Law Officers, *direct* investigatory powers. Therefore, Law Officers themselves are not empowered to undertake any specific investigative actions, such as interrogating witnesses and suspects or collecting any other evidence. However, a special provision of the Police Law (Cap. 285, Art. 19), as well as the general constitutional relationship between the Police and the Law Office, places the investigation of crimes by the former, formally, subject to the instructions of the latter.

In particular, Article 19 of the Police Law specifically provides that police officers applying for summons, arrest warrants, search warrants or any other legal process, which can be issued against any person during an investigation, are "subject to the directions of the Attorney General". Therefore, regarding these specific investigatory actions, there is a clear provision in law, which empowers the Law Office to give directions or authorisation to the police. The rest of the same section widens even further the powers of the Law Office regarding investigations. As examined in the previous chapter, Article 19 (combined with the constitutional provision of Article 113.2) is the cornerstone on which the relationship between the two services is based. By this provision, it is clearly acknowledged that the police in the execution of their prosecutorial functions are subject to the instructions of the Attorney General. Based on this section, it is officially accepted that, although the Police as an organisation come under the Ministry of Justice, regarding *all* their activities that relate to criminal prosecutions (and not only the ones that concern the presentation of the cases in court), the Attorney General is their supervising authority.[5] This general provision, therefore, has been interpreted as *additionally* giving power to the Attorney General to intervene during investigations and/or require further information, as well as to cause any matter he considers appropriate to be investigated by the police.[6]

---

[3]See Chap. 3 for a further analysis of these powers.

[4]E.g. the right for legal advice in the police station.

[5]See Papaioannou (1999).

[6]See similar wording in s.17 of the Scottish Police Act 1967: "... in relation to the investigation of offences the chief constable should comply with such lawful instructions as he may receive from the appropriate prosecutor".

The logic of this interpretation is consistent with the situation in other jurisdictions: wherever there is a line of authority between the public prosecution service and the police, the former are empowered to issue directions to the latter regarding investigations.[7] Loucaides (1974, p. 48) argues that "since the investigation of an incident constitutes the first step of a procedure leading to the institution of a prosecution, the control and the responsibility for which bears with the Attorney General, Police even during the investigative stage are obliged to follow the instructions of the Law Office".

The question arises as to whether there are any direct mechanisms for enforcing these directives in the event that the Law Office are not satisfied with the response of the police, given the fact that they themselves have no immediate investigation powers enabling them to carry out the actions that the police do not. Apart from having available the very simple expedient of refusing to prosecute if the quality of the police investigations fails to satisfy their directions,[8] Loucaides (1974) claims that the Law Office could initiate a criminal or a disciplinary procedure against investigators who refuse to obey their orders.

Loucaides (1974) based most of his arguments on a memorandum[9] published by the first Attorney General of the Republic, Mr Tornaritis, in the early years of his tenure. In this memorandum for the first time[10] the relationship between the police and the Law Office was formally analysed. It was made clear that the Attorney General was the supervising authority of the police regarding investigations (as well as prosecutions) and the only one authorised to give directions. It is remarkable that a police initiative caused the issue of this document. In a letter that the Chief of the Police sent to Mr Tornaritis[11] he complained about the intervention of the Ministry of the Interior during the investigation of a murder case and he asked the Attorney General to direct that no one else except him can give instructions regarding investigations and prosecutions. It is interesting to observe that, from the beginning, the police themselves regarded the Attorney General as their supervisor for the investigations they carried out.

In 1976, after a discussion in Parliament regarding the way police and prosecution authorities handled the case of an attempted murder committed against a well known politician, Mr Tornaritis issued another memorandum directed to the police,[12] in which he repeated and further analysed his position stated in his previous memorandum. He emphasised that the investigative stage constitutes the first and

---

[7] See, for example, Germany, France and the Netherlands.

[8] Law Officers have the power to prevent the police from prosecuting and not only the power to discontinue prosecutions with which they do not agree (see previous chapter). Therefore, once the Law Office have this power, it is reasonable that they can require the police to investigate further before agreeing to the commencement of criminal proceedings.

[9] G.E. 7/1969, dated 22/01/1969 (attached to a letter sent to the police on the same date).

[10] This was the first and the only time that an Attorney General issued a formal document stating in a relatively explicit manner the relationship of his Office with the police.

[11] A.F. E/274/34, dated 21/01/1969.

[12] Memorandum G.E. 7/1969/2, dated 12/06/1976.

essential step of a procedure leading to the prosecution. Therefore, even during that stage the police is obliged to follow the instructions of the Attorney General. He argued that this position was based not only on the constitutional powers of the Attorney General but also on the explicit provision of Article 19 of the Police Law.

Although different views about the exact legal relationship between the police and the Attorney General regarding investigations can be found,[13] these days it is generally and formally accepted that the Law Office can exert control over the police even during investigations. See, for instance, a relatively recent declaration of the powers of the Attorney General in a formal document by the Government:

> 'In exercise of his constitutional powers, the Attorney-General of the Republic of Cyprus, can *ex-proprio motu* ask the Police to initiate, and carry out an investigation into the commission of any criminal offence . . . for the purpose of determining whether to institute criminal proceedings against any person, and can give instructions to the Police regarding the conduct of the investigation (collection of evidence and interrogations), both in the case of an investigation initiated in pursuance to his own instructions, and also in the case of an investigation carried out in performance of the Police's duty to detect and bring offenders to justice'.[14]

Apart from the general position that places the police under the control of the Law Office during investigations, there are a number of cases where a *direct* investigative power has been clearly conferred with legislative provisions on the Attorney General:

1. According to the Military Criminal Procedure (Law 40/1964), which resembles the continental Greek Military Code, the Attorney General supervises and directs the investigations of crimes under the Military Criminal Code.[15] In this case, the legality of the investigation is directly connected to the oversight and final control of the Law Office and a specific procedure is provided for the execution of this control. Therefore, the involvement of the Law Office is obligatory and not just discretionary.[16]
2. As was stated above, the Criminal Procedure Law (Cap. 155, s.4.2) allocates to the Council of Ministers a complementary – to the general police power – authority to appoint independent investigators in any case they consider

[13] See, for example, Malachtou-Pamballi (2005, p. 482): "The Police are under no legal obligation to consult the Office of the Attorney General in relation to investigations that they are carrying out". However, the same writer later comments that "in practice . . . such a consultation takes place on a daily basis . . . In any event, the Attorney General may ask the police to inform him of progress made and issue specific instructions at any stage during the investigation process" Malachtou-Pamballi (2005, pp. 482–483).

[14] National Report of the Republic of Cyprus on the Implementation of the Conclusions of the European and World Conferences against Racism (Ministry of Justice and Public Order, Republic of Cyprus 2003, p. 27).

[15] See Daskalakis (1966) for an analysis of the Cyprus Military Criminal Law.

[16] In practice, the Attorney General has appointed a Law Officer who serves at the Military Prosecution Department and executes all the responsibilities and duties of the Law Office deriving from the Military Criminal Procedure Law. It has not been possible, due to limited resources and time, to examine how this part of the responsibility of the Law Office is carried out in practice.

appropriate. In 1996, for the first time, the Council of Ministers delegated to the Attorney General the power to appoint criminal investigators to investigate instances of alleged commission of criminal offences by members of the police and also economic offences punishable with more than one year imprisonment.[17] The prerequisite that a written complaint must be submitted to him has been eradicated through a decision of the Council of Ministers taken on 22 March 2001.[18] The new decision adopted a recommendation by the Attorney General "to extend the ambit of the delegation so as to afford the power of appointment of criminal investigators in all instances concerning the relevant offences coming to his knowledge in any manner whatsoever (e.g. through newspapers reports, television broadcast and reports by any organisation, committee, body or tribunal domestic or otherwise)".[19] The proposal of the Attorney General was submitted as a result of the report of the European Committee for the Prevention of Torture and Inhumane and Degrading Treatment or Punishment (CPT) of 2000. In that report[20] the CPT recommended that "steps (should) be taken to ensure that investigations into cases involving complaints of ill-treatment by police officers are, and are seen to be, totally independent and impartial" and "the Attorney General (should) be accorded the power *proprio motu* to appoint independent investigators, in cases where he deems this necessary".

Since 1996, the Attorney General has exercised his right to appoint independent investigators several times, on an *ad hoc* basis.[21] However, legislation has recently been enacted (Law 9(I)/2006) which provides for the establishment and operation of an Independent Police Complaints Commission, invested with the responsibility to investigate certain criminal and disciplinary offences allegedly committed by members of the police. Even in this Law, though, it is provided that the members of the Commission and the independent investigators appointed by them, when carrying out a criminal (as opposed to a disciplinary) investigation, are obliged to follow the Attorney General's directions

3. Under Law 31(I)/1995 for the Prevention of Crime (Controlled Delivery and Other Special Provisions), as far as certain serious offences are concerned (e.g. drug and weapon trafficking), the police are empowered to make use of a special investigation method known as "controlled delivery". This Law ensures that the

---

[17] See Decisions of the Council of Ministers 44.874, dated 03/10/1996 and 44.448, dated 07/10/1998.

[18] Decision of the Council of Ministers 53.406, dated 22/03/2001.

[19] Letter of the Attorney General, Mr Markides, to the Council of Ministers, dated 14/03/2001.

[20] Report to the Government of Cyprus on the visit carried out by the European Committee for the prevention of Torture and Inhumane and Degrading Treatment or Punishment (CPT) (European Committee for the Prevention of Torture and Inhumane or Degrading Treatment or Punishment 2000, p. 41).

[21] E.g. there are records within the Office which suggest that the Attorney General exercised this right in more than 30 cases within the period April 2001 to July 2002.

use of this technique is under the supervision of the Attorney General. More specifically, although s.6 of the Law provides that the decision for the use of this special investigation procedure is taken by the Chief of the Police or the Director of Customs and Excise, s.6.3 clearly provides that: "the Attorney General is notified in advance for any decision for controlled delivery and upon notification he may give any directions he considers proper or necessary". As Malachtou-Pamballi (2005, p. 483) points out "this is a concrete example of the legislator's anxiety to ensure that, when using drastic investigation methods, the police operate under the vigilant eye of the Attorney General".

4. Under Law 183(I)/2007 (Retention of Telecommunication Data Law),[22] the police, during the investigation of serious crime, can apply to Court for the issue of a warrant which authorizes access to certain telecommunication data. Section 4.2 of this Law provides that the Attorney General's consent is a prerequisite for this application.
5. Law 95(I)/2001 for the Protection of Witnesses and Informants, s.16, provides that the Attorney General will control, oversee and be responsible for the execution and utilisation of the Plan for the protection of witnesses and informants of justice.
6. Law 61(I)/1996 provides for the establishment of a special interagency investigation team to deal with cases of money laundering and economic crime. This Unit consists of police officers, Custom officers, accountants and Law Officers, operates within the Law Office and is granted all the powers recognised to the police investigators by a specific legislative provision (sections 53 and 54).

What is concluded from these examples is that legislative provisions have gradually been introduced to ensure the obligatory (and not just discretionary) involvement of the Law Office in certain investigations, especially in areas where either coercive measures could be used or sensitive/complex issues may arise.

In contrast to the effect of these specific legislative provisions, however, in all other cases, the position that generally places the police under the directions of the Attorney General during investigations is less imposing than it sounds. The legal text is framed very broadly and does not make the Attorney General's intervention in investigations obligatory. It does not set out specific duties and responsibilities for the Law Office during the investigatory period, neither does it associate the legality of the investigation with the authorisation or the final control of the Attorney General.[23] What it does ensure, however, is that there is a theoretical potential and power of the Attorney General to act in such a way if he wishes to do so. Once again, the extent to which, and the way that, this power is used is left open to the Attorney General to define.

[22] This Law was enacted after Directive 2006/24/EC of the European Parliament and of the Council, adopted on15 March 2006.

[23] As is the case, for example, in France and in Germany.

5.1.2 The Attorney Generals' Policy

The law does not stipulate which specific powers the Attorney General could use within the context of his general role in investigations. It is very difficult to find out how exactly this power has been utilised or indeed interpreted by the different Attorney Generals in the past since, apart from Mr Tornaritis' memoranda mentioned above, no other Attorney General has issued any similar documents explaining his policy *vis-à-vis* the police regarding investigations.

The examination of relevant circulars in the Law Office and letters of correspondence between them and the police, as well as the interviews with the former and the current Attorney Generals I carried out,[24] revealed that the Law Office for many years hardly developed any *active* or at least publicly pronounced policy on investigations in practice. Once again, the succeeding Attorney Generals preferred to deal with cases on an *ad hoc* basis instead of formulating a deliberate and comprehensive policy regarding all investigations.

Having said that, it is noticeable that it appeared not to be unusual for the Law Office to direct the police to initiate investigations regarding particular incidents. Several letters of all the successive Attorney Generals directed to the Chief of the Police requesting the investigation of allegations of crimes were found in the Law Office's records.[25] In a number of other cases, the Attorney General took the initiative in requesting information regarding the investigation of particular cases and sometimes required to be constantly informed about the investigation of a particular case.[26] These mainly concerned cases that created media attention and publicity, something that had not been unusual in a small society like Cyprus, or cases of particular sensitivity or complexity that came to the attention of the Law Office. The following are selective examples of such actions:

> A press announcement stating that the Attorney General (Mr Tornaritis) gave directions to the Police to investigate certain allegations for serious violation of Banking Law.
>
> A direction for investigation of the offence of Publication of false news/information against a newspaper (Mr Tornaritis).
>
> A letter of the Attorney General (Mr Triantafyllides) to the police requesting the investigation of the offence of libel against a well-known journalist after the publication of extensive articles in the newspapers.
>
> A document confirming the investigation of allegations of violence committed by police officers against civilians which was ordered and supervised by the Attorney General (Mr Markides).

---

[24] Complemented by interviews with police officials and defence attorneys.

[25] Documentary survey in the Attorney General's Office.

[26] See, for example, a press release by Mr Tornaritis (Press Release G.E. 61/1984 dated 17/03/1983) stating that the Attorney General called at his office the police investigator of a very serious drug case, asked him to inform him about the progress of investigations and gave directions for further steps to be taken. A further meeting with the investigator regarding the same case was also announced to the press (see Press Release G.E. 61/1984 dated 26/03/1983).

A direction for investigation of allegations against a senior doctor of the Government Hospital for negligence (Mr Markides).

Directions for investigation of the offence of contempt of court against a Minister of the Government (Mr Nikitas).

Directions for investigation of an economic offence allegedly committed by employees of the Ministry of Communications and Works after the publication of articles in the newspapers (Mr Nikitas).

There were also a number of circulars expressing criticism of the police conduct of investigations. For example, in a circular by Mr Nikitas[27] addressed to the Chief of the Police, a concern was expressed about the delay of the investigation of offences committed by juveniles. The Attorney General underlined the negative effects on the prosecution of a case that the unduly delayed investigations might have and he gave relevant directions to the police on that issue.

There were not, however, any circulars by any of the Attorney Generals detailing specific policies about the investigation of crimes. The only exception was a circular by Mr Markides indicating the procedure of requesting the revelation of bank documents.[28] He directed the police that whenever they wanted to proceed in such an action they should get the authorisation of one of the Law Officers. This was a procedure that was agreed after consultation with all the major banks and regarded as an effort to avoid the abuse of that power by the police investigators.[29]

The impression that was given from the wording used, and generally from the content of the correspondence between the police and the Attorney General, was that the police had always regarded themselves – at least theoretically – as absolutely bound by an instruction from the Law Office, at least concerning these serious or high profile cases. The wording used in that correspondence included phrases like: "Please give us directions as to what we should do in this case" or "Shall we investigate further in this case?". However, it was equally noticeable that until recently, apart from rare exceptions, serious issues that created friction between the two services regarding the investigation of crimes appeared not to exist.[30] This may be interpreted as indicating a good cooperative relationship

[27] Circular G.E. 41(A)/1947/17), dated 17/10/03.

[28] Circular G.E. 41(A)/1947/15, dated 14/02/2002. See also the recent confirmation of this procedure by the current Attorney General with Circular G.E. 41(A)/1947/18, dated 05/06/2005.

[29] This power derives from s.6 of the Criminal Procedure Law but in the past banks threatened to dispute such actions in court. Eventually, they agreed to accept requests to reveal bank documents provided that the police investigator had the authorisation of the Law Office. This is another indication of the integrity that the Attorney General's involvement in the process ensures.

[30] However, during Mr Nikitas' tenure, there was some friction in the relationship of the Law Office and the police concerning investigations against a Minister of the Government. It was apparent that the Attorney General disagreed with the way the police were investigating the matter and gave repeated and strict directions as to how the investigations should proceed. Although, as a result of this, there had been some police frustration, it was obvious that the police acknowledged that the Attorney General had every right to give directions: "We are obliged to obey the directions of the Attorney General, even if we disagree" (Statement of the Deputy Chief of the Police on 29/09/04).

between them. It may be also attributed to the fact that generally, apart from those special cases, the Law Office did not interfere regularly and systematically in the day-to-day work of the police unless their advice was sought.

On the contrary, there were some incidents in the past when they preferred to keep a distance from police investigations and expressed contradictory positions as to their appropriate role regarding them. For instance, Mr Triantafyllides on one occasion, when asked if he was willing to order the police to initiate investigations against a Chief Constable, stated that investigations were mainly the responsibility of the police and the responsibility of the Law Office started when the police forwarded the completed file to the Office.[31]

It has to be observed, that this curious statement contradicted previous actions and positions of the same Attorney General. Nevertheless, it is indicative of an ideology – more or less adopted by all the Attorney Generals – that afforded a flexibility regarding their role in investigations and preferred at times not to promote – or to declare – a very interventionist policy in the investigative role of the police.[32]

The following (deliberately extensive) quotations from the interviews I carried out with the Attorney Generals illustrate the approach they adopted regarding their role in investigations:

> Q: Is there a Law Office's role and intervention during the investigative stage?
> 'A: Absolutely; investigations are subject to our directions. The fact that we do not intervene that often is a matter of discretion ... The investigator is obliged to follow the directions of the Law Office. The Attorney General *is empowered* to give directions for the issue of a search warrant or an arrest warrant or to prevent the police from doing so. In practice, we have *never prevented* the police from issuing warrants but we have often directed them to carry out *further* investigatory acts, issue search warrants, or investigate other lines of inquiry. There are some *complex or sensitive cases* that *should* be forwarded here from the very beginning so we can study them and give directions for further inquiries'. (Interview with Mr Markides) (emphasis added)

> Q: Are you involved in investigations?
> 'A: *Not regularly*, unless our opinion or advice is sought. Of course, police during investigations could ask for our *legal advice* at any time. The Attorney General also has the right to direct the police to undertake further investigations. We could send a file back with directions for *additional or other evidence*. For example, if we see that an argument of the accused has not been investigated, we can send the case back and ask the police to make further inquiries in relation to that'. (Interview with Mr Nikitas) (emphasis added)
> 'A: In a number of cases I have directed the police to investigate allegations of an incident ... I was *empowered* to do that ... During the investigations of all crimes *they could* also

[31] See Statement G.E. 61/85/IV, dated 13/07/1994.

[32] See also an interview of the Deputy Attorney General in the newspaper "Fileleftheros", dated 26/08/2001:

> 'Police should acknowledge and respect the fact that the Law Office has the crucial role (in prosecutions). And from our side, we respect the responsibilities and powers that the law entrusts the police with, for example their role in the investigations where we don't usually intervene'.

> come here to ask our advice . . . After they send the file here we *must* check the evidence and possibly ask for further inquiries'. (Interview with Mr Triantafyllides) (emphasis added)

There are some interesting points arising out of these comments, which reflect the Attorney Generals' philosophy regarding investigations. First, they all declare their theoretical potential to intervene in every stage of an investigation but they are careful not to claim that this is a regular job for their Office to execute inescapably and on a systematic basis. Secondly, they talk more about legal advice, rather than supervision of investigations, apart from specific categories of cases ("sensitive cases", cases involving public figures, allegations against police officers) when they choose to use a more authoritative terminology. Finally, during the stage that a case is forwarded to the Law Office for a decision for a prosecution to be taken, it is then clearly considered as their duty to thoroughly examine the evidence and order further inquiries if this is required.

5.2 Ideology: The Law Officers' Approach

In this section, the ideology that has been developed within the Law Office concerning their powers over investigations will be explored. It is crucial to study here how Law Officers themselves approach, interpret and reflect on their role in investigations. In the next section, it will be shown how these attitudes, combined with a number of other contextual and structural factors, are translated into practice and form the actual role that the Law Office plays in investigations.

5.2.1 A Right, Not a Duty, to Intervene

Law Officers appeared uncertain about determining exactly the boundary lines of the Law Office's role during investigations. Although most of them acknowledged that, at least in theory, the Attorney General could direct the police even during the investigative stage:[33]

> 'The rule is that the police are under the direction of the Attorney General during the investigative stages as well'. (Law Officer 04)

they stressed that this was more of a right to intervene whenever he deemed proper rather than a duty to do so in each and every case:

---

[33]However, a couple of Law Officers appeared to deny even that:

> 'The Attorney General is responsible for the decision of prosecution, not for the investigations. He is in charge of all the services that are related to the presentation of a case in court. There is no involvement in the investigative stage unless the police ask for our advice'. (Law Officer 05)

> 'In principle, the Attorney General could direct the police during the investigative stages as well. However, the Law Office does not have to intervene in all the thousands of cases which the police investigate at the same time'. (Law Officer 12)

> 'Of course, we have the right to intervene in investigations. We are not, though, obliged to do so'. (Law Officer 01)

Further questioning revealed that this attitude was based on a reluctance to accept a role which would dramatically increase their workload without an analogous increase of their resources. They argued that under the given circumstances it was inevitable that they limited their role to those cases that were complex, difficult or regarding which the police chose to ask for their advice:

> 'Inevitably, given the current arrangements, our role can only be reactive ...' . (Law Officer 02)

> 'Our resources could not possibly allow us to get involved in each and every case. This happens when there is a special reason for it to happen, e.g. when a case is particularly complex or sensitive ... or when the police ask for our advice'. (Law Officer 10)

5.2.2 Positive Attitude

Nevertheless, in general, Law Officers were very much in favour of their participation in the investigative phase and emphasised the advantages of their early involvement in a case:

> 'It would be ideal to have control of the case from the beginning. In other countries prosecutors are systematically involved in the investigations. These are different systems, though; there are different arrangements there ... But, still, it would be very effective to be able to do this in every case'. (Law Officer 12)

> 'The Law Office should be involved in the process of investigation of a case from the early stages more substantially ... I believe that these stages are the most important and the most crucial stages of a criminal case'. (Law Officer 05)

5.2.3 "Police Have the Primary Investigative Role"

Law Officers appeared to acknowledge that, regardless of whether it was a matter of practice or theory, the police bear the burden of the investigative stage in a case. Therefore, investigations were regarded as primarily a police job and responsibility, at least up until the point that they would send a file to the Law Office.

Therefore, some Law Officers argued, it was the responsibility of the police to seek directions from the Law Office when they needed advice or assistance for their job, and, most of the time, it was after police initiative that this occurred:

> 'The police role is to investigate. Our role usually begins after the completion of the investigation. However, in complicated cases it is not unusual to be involved during the investigative stage. They usually ask for our advice and direction. It is their responsibility to do that when needed ... We have a cooperative relationship'. (Law Officer 12)

> 'In serious cases we assist the police from the early stages. It's better to control things from the beginning. However, it is usually at the *investigator's initiative* that a case comes here during the investigative stage. They usually come to the Deputy Attorney General and ask his advice. Unfortunately, this is not a practice followed in all cases'. (Law Officer 06)

Some Law Officers admitted that police investigators did not always come to the Law Office for advice and, as a result, crucial mistakes were sometimes made during investigations. However, they did not seem to think that there was anything at the moment that the Law Office could do in order to correct this situation, other than (a) refusing to prosecute improperly investigated cases:

> 'When a case fails to be prosecuted due to mistakes they committed during the investigation, it makes investigators realise how important it is to contact the Law Office for advice early enough'. (Law Officer 04)

and (b) encouraging more cooperation with the police.

5.2.4 Cooperation Rather than Supervision

This is obviously an additional reason why the Law Officers tended to talk more about assistance and cooperation with the police during the investigative stage rather than supervision or authority to give orders:

> 'It is in the best interests of both services to have a *cooperative* relationship. We encourage the police when they are investigating a serious allegation to contact us at an early stage so that we can discuss the case and provide our *assistance* with any evidential or other problem that they may deal with in an investigation'. (Law Officer 01)

Moreover, they referred constantly to the importance of police officers' practical experience:

> 'The role of the police during investigations is crucial. Without their assistance we cannot do many things. They have the experience. We realise their value in cases where we are appointed as independent investigators, e.g. cases against police officers. Without their help our job is very difficult, so, it is not useful to declare and boast that we are the leaders in an investigation'. (Law Officer 13)

> 'You have to show respect for the work that the police investigator is doing and take into serious consideration his experience. He is the one who 'lives' the case, right from the beginning, and in addition knows how to handle certain circumstances'. (Law Officer 07)

5.2.5 Legal Assistance: Their Main Role

However, almost everyone pointed out that police investigators' input, although crucial and vital was not, these days, enough for the proper execution of investigations. They believed that while legal knowledge and advice had always been helpful in collecting the right evidence, the complexity of new forms of criminality besides the strict exclusionary rules of the Cyprus Constitution had currently rendered them essential:[34]

> 'It is necessary that experienced lawyers are involved in the process of investigation from the beginning in order to ensure that the provisions of the Laws and the Constitution regarding the collection of evidence are not violated ... Police ... are not qualified to do that ... They do not have lawyers or people with legal knowledge to lead them during investigations ... for example, how to collect exhibits ... In Cyprus we have strict exclusionary rules ... The Constitution does not allow the courts to take into account illegally-obtained evidence'. (Law Officer 05)

> 'Nowadays, some criminals adopt sophisticated methods for their crimes. You have to be very careful from the beginning in order to collect the right evidence'. (Law Officer 04)

Law Officers pointed out that police officers were not legally trained:

> 'Sometimes there are gaps in the evidence. We have to keep in mind that investigators are not legally qualified. There have been occasions when it was obvious that certain evidence should have been obtained and the investigators did not act that way. Sometimes they don't have the ability to predict things or to evaluate some evidence in the right way'. (Law Officer 12)

> 'Sometimes police officers make mistakes when they investigate. Under the circumstances though, it could be worse ... They don't get special training for that, it is all what they learn in practice ...'. (Law Officer 09)

They, therefore, viewed their main role in investigations as providing legal advice to the police investigators and offering the legal knowledge that police were lacking:

> 'Our role is to provide them with legal advice during the investigations. Some issues regarding the collection of evidence require legal knowledge'. (Law Officer 09)

> 'Evidence should be collected at the right time ... In order to achieve that, you need legal knowledge and experience ... Police may have experience but they don't have legal knowledge and a combination of the two is essential. *We* have the legal knowledge'. (Law Officer 05)

Furthermore, although there were several favourable comments about the expertise of police officers working in the field, Law Officers talked about variable competence. Some Law Officers described a few police investigators as incompetent and therefore saw their own assistance as more essential.[35] Due to the relatively small

---

[34] Another reason why they believed that their help was becoming more vital to the police, and therefore their role in investigations more crucial, was that:

> 'Now that we don't have admissions as often as before, everyone is skeptical about investigations and the collection of the evidence'. (Law Officer 12)

[35] See for example the comments of one Law Officer:

> 'Some investigators are totally incompetent. There have been occasions when it was obvious that certain evidence should have been obtained and the investigators did not act that way'.

number of police investigators (especially those serving at the CID dealing with serious crime), Law Officers had personal knowledge of almost all of them.

As far as intentional breaches of the law by police investigators and police malpractice were concerned, most Law Officers appeared to correlate them again with individual investigators, adopting the theory of "bad apples" in the police force. They considered it as their indisputable duty to exclude evidence which had been obtained improperly, but they admitted that their role could not extend to preventing such incidents from occurring.

5.2.6 A More Proactive Role?

The last observation is directly related to the above-mentioned issue. Apart from the legal direction that they were more than happy to provide the police with, Law Officers appeared divided in their views about a more proactive role in investigations that would extend to choosing the methods or techniques for investigations, defining policies or even watching over the legality of investigators' actions.

Some Law Officers argued that this was not feasible anyway because there were simply insufficient resources for them to engage in a more proactive way with the police investigation:

> 'In order to be able to control every movement of the investigator you need a Law Officer for each investigator'. (Law Officer 04)

Some of them claimed that such a systematic involvement was not even desirable because it would compromise their objectivity. They believed that a valuable consequence of the fact that they did not appear too involved in the investigations was the maintenance of a more independent and objective status. Their independence was seen as arising from their separation from the day-to-day concerns of the police and the investigation process combined with their ultimate control over investigations:

> 'When you don't have to deal with the everyday concerns of an investigation you can keep a certain distance, be more objective and have a clearer picture of the situation sometimes ... And at the end of the day you can always give directions for certain things to be done while still keeping a distance ...'. (Law Officer 09)

5.2.7 Duty to Order Further Investigations

Law Officers appeared to separate the stages during which they could intervene in (a) the main investigative stage before a complete file was formed and (b) the stage when a case was forwarded to the Law Office.

For Law Officers, in accordance with the views of their superiors (see earlier), once a file was forwarded to the Law Office for a prosecution decision to be taken, the *right* to intervening and ask for further information or order other lines of inquiries also became a *duty*:

> 'In almost all cases I ask for further evidence ... There are always some gaps in the evidence. Our *duty* is to check for gaps and see if the case has been investigated properly or whether more needs to be done'. (Law Officer 03)

> '*At this stage*, we have the duty to make a decision about prosecution and, if there are gaps in the evidence or if the evidence is obviously illegally obtained, we cannot proceed ... Therefore we should either ask them to proceed to further inquiries or decline to prosecute'. (Law Officer 09)

Most of the Law Officers argued that at that stage alternative lines usually suggested by defence lawyers could also be explored, if they appeared reasonable. They further claimed that generally, defence comments or information about the evidence collected by the police, when offered, were taken into consideration when evaluating the evidence:

> 'Information from the defence attorneys could prove very useful in making us review the police file with a more vigilant eye. Sometimes, when you have in mind certain factors you can read between the lines and discover other things'. (Law Officer 04)

5.2.8 Concluding Remarks

In conclusion, it could be argued that the Law Officers' approach to their role in investigations reflects the policies that succeeding Attorney Generals have promoted over time. They regard their involvement in investigations more as a power rather than a duty and although they consider it as extremely beneficial, they acknowledge that due to their heavy workload this cannot be particularly extensive. They emphasise the good cooperation and trust that should characterise their relations with the police so that police investigators seek their assistance when needed. However, when a file is forwarded to the Law Office for a prosecution decision to be taken, Law Officers consider it as their duty to ask for further information or order other lines of inquiries (often suggested by the defence) when necessary so that a justified decision can be taken.

5.3 Practice

In this section, an insight into the role that is actually carried out by the Law Office in investigations will be attempted, drawing on observations of the everyday life of the Office, as well as the examination of cases during the fieldwork period. It will be explored how the approach of the Law Officers and the Attorney General himself to their powers is combined with a number of other factors, including the attitudes of other actors in the system, to construct the role that the Law Office plays in investigations in practice.

There are three stages[36] during which the Attorney General's Office could potentially exert its power to intervene in the building up of a case, or in what can be described as the investigation and collection of information based on which a decision would be made as to whether a case would be sent to court or not:

(a) *Stage 1*: The Attorney General is empowered to order the *initiation* of investigations.
(b) *Stage 2*: He is able to intervene *during* the conduct of investigations.
(c) *Stage 3*: He can order *further investigations* after the file of a case is forwarded to the Office for a decision to prosecute or not.

5.3.1 *Direction for the Initiation* of Investigations

> 'We don't have the ability to watch everything in order to be able to know when and where a certain crime is being committed. When we have a complaint and we find out that there is something that *prima facie* is worth being investigated it is then a matter of a routine action: we give directions to the police to investigate it'. (Mr Markides' Interview in the newspaper "Neos Typos" on 18/03/01)

As mentioned before, there is evidence (resulting from the previous circulars and letters of correspondence between the Law Office and the police) that Attorney Generals have been using the power to instruct the instigation of investigations in cases of particularly serious crimes or crimes that created publicity.

In the field, it was observed that the power of the Attorney General to order the initiation of investigations was a power exercised either by him personally or by the Deputy Attorney General. It did not form a part of the ordinary, everyday workload of the Law Officers.

What usually caused the exercise of the Attorney General's power was the receipt of information that a certain incident had occurred and investigation was required, or the media coverage of an event that contained allegations of a crime. This kind of correspondence would usually come from a Government Department, a Member of Parliament or simply a member of the public who claimed that he had been the victim of a crime. It was observed that the type of reports received in this way amounted to very serious allegations of criminal conduct but, surprisingly, they also concerned information regarding relatively trivial offences. That indicated awareness on the part of the public that the Attorney General had the authority to order the initiation of investigations, even contrary to the police will, as well as trust and

[36]Regarding the cases that Law Officers present to the court, there is another opportunity to elicit further information, at a later stage though. After the committal, there is a practice followed by the Law Officers of seeing the main witnesses before testifying in Court and, thus, checking on the quality of the evidence personally.

belief that they would secure a fairer decision; people usually turned to the Attorney General when they felt that there had not been a proper police reaction to the allegations of a crime.

In all the cases that I observed, the Attorney General considered it appropriate to request that the police (or independent investigators) carry out investigations, after which he was informed of the results and decided whether to prosecute or not:Case IN1: a case of unlawful possession of antiquities – after a report of the Ministry of Transportation.

> Case IN2: a case of unlawful disclosure of bank accounts – after a complaint by a member of the public.
> Cases IN3 and IN4: two cases of contempt of court – after a letter from the Ministry of Finance.
> Case IN5: a case of malicious prosecution by the police – after a complaint by a member of the public.
> Case IN6: accusations for police violence against a suspect in custody – letter by a Member of Parliament and extensive media coverage.

For the last case, the Attorney General activated the power conferred on him by the Council of Ministers (see earlier) to appoint independent investigators. Two senior Law Officers and a former judge were selected and granted the authority to conduct investigations.

It was also observed that the Attorney General could sometimes set priorities as to the initiation or the process of investigation of particular cases. That concerned serious cases – when there was an exceptional public outcry – regarding which speedy investigation was a necessity. For example:

> Case IN7: A direction of the Deputy Attorney General to a Chief Constable asking him to speed up the investigations of a particular case, widely covered by the media, concerning forgery by a public servant. He specifically ordered the police to give priority to the investigation of that case over the other cases that the same investigators were dealing with during the same time.

5.3.2 Intervention During the Conduct of Investigations

There was no formal or static structure to facilitate the Law Office's involvement in police operations from the beginning. Most of the time, but not always, the decision to request advice from the Law Office during investigations depended upon the judgment of the investigator or his seniors. However, it was observed that there was a well-developed culture of cooperation that was encouraging police officers to seek the Attorney General's advice regularly. During my fieldwork, I noticed that the police investigators would come to the Law Office in person quite often to consult with the Law Officers, would call Law Officers on a daily basis asking questions about different aspects of their investigation, or would send files in the middle of an investigation asking for directions.

As far as complicated cases were concerned, they would seek Law Officers' directions from the very beginning of the investigation. For example:

> Case LP: A case involving a series of complex offences of stealing electricity power and frauds. A particular newspaper had caused the initiation of investigations with the publication of some information they discovered and, accordingly, great publicity was created. Because of the complexity and the novelty of the case, police investigators sought the Law Office's help from the very first day of the investigation.

There were a number of particularly complex cases where the police required almost continuous advice throughout the investigation:

> Case MM: A case of a series of frauds relating to the importation of a large number of luxury cars from abroad violating *inter alia* the tax laws. An innovative way of committing those offences was involved as new cars were imported in parts and after being assembled in Cyprus were sold as used cars.

Furthermore, in a number of cases, the Attorney General himself took the initiative in requesting information regarding the investigation of particular cases and sometimes required to be constantly informed about the investigation of a particular case. This mainly concerned cases that created media attention and publicity or involved public figures.

> Case PK: A case of forgery by a public servant widely covered by the media. The Deputy Attorney General, after giving advice on that case, asked the police to keep him informed about further investigations. The file was forwarded to the Law Office three times during the investigation period and at the end a Law Officer handled the case in the District Court.

In those cases, supervision and directions were far more comprehensive than in the rest of the cases. Law Officers would give orders, check on progress, coordinate tactics and hold regular briefings. There was a sense that, regarding those cases Law Officers and the Attorney General himself[37] were actually leading the investigation.

In many other – not necessarily very serious – cases, police officers would send the file to the Law Office in the middle of the investigation, asking advice about how to proceed and Law Officers had the chance to give directions and order the collection of more information. Police investigators usually asked for directions about the kind of information that was needed to sustain certain charges or regarding the applicability of certain legal provisions. Furthermore, they sometimes took Law Officers' advice concerning disputed points of law, especially regarding the collection of evidence with special investigative techniques. Typical cases that were included in this category were cases of forgery, cases of obtaining goods by false pretences, fraud, Stock Exchange cases, etc. They also used to send files concerning "sensitive" (as they called them) cases:

> Case GP: This concerned the rape of a mentally handicapped girl. The investigator described the evidence collected up to that time and asked for directions on how to proceed, expressing some doubts about the strength of the evidence, the ability of the girl to testify in court and the harm that may be caused to her by a possible appearance in court. The Law

[37] In fact, most of the time, it was the Deputy Attorney General.

Officer asked the police to take the opinion of a second expert, to take further statements from the mother and the doctor of the girl and to examine the possibility of finding other independent evidence so that the girl would not have to testify in court.

As was explained in Chap. 3, according to the constitutional provisions, flagrant crimes excluded, the police are not empowered to arrest or search someone without a judicial warrant. Therefore, the police were often seen to seek Law Officers' assistance when wishing to obtain judicial authorisation for their activities. As a police investigator remarked:

These days, judges make it more difficult to grant warrants than in the past. Thus, legal assistance from the Law Office is often essential.

Responding to this "police need", and also in an attempt to encourage even more the police-Law Office liaison at the level of the investigation of a case, a catalogue with names and telephone numbers of Law Officers (an on-call list) who were available any time that advice was needed (especially regarding the issue of warrants of arrest or search) had been sent to the Police Departments by the Attorney General.

Finally, it is important to note that for serious economic crime cases the Law Office's involvement in the investigation process was much more systematic and regular. A Fraud Investigation Team had been established, in which Law Officers, accountants and police investigators participated and, under the immediate control of the Attorney General, they were dealing with the investigation and prosecution of all serious and complex economic crimes.[38]

5.3.3 *Directions for Further* Investigations

During the stage that a file was forwarded to the Law Office so that a decision for a prosecution could be taken, Law Officers appeared, as was seen in the last section, more willing to play their "investigative role". This is a good point at which to explore how this role was translated in practice and whether there were appropriate circumstances which facilitated such an action.

5.3.3.1 The Investigation File

'If all materials collected by the police in the course of the investigation were handed to crown prosecutors, then they would be in a much stronger position than at present to provide some real direction to enquiries'. (Baldwin and Moloney 1992, p. 78)[39]

---

[38]Such investigation teams consisting of experts, investigators and prosecutors have been established in most countries because of the need for special knowledge and expertise on financial matters when investigating complex economic crimes.

[39]Research studies suggest that review bodies cannot effectively review earlier decisions or processes of other agencies without access to the raw material that those agencies have considered, or at least submissions from other agencies other than those which they are reviewing (Leng et al. 1996).

It was logical that in order for the Law Officers to be able to exercise any meaningful role during that stage, they should have had a real sense of what had happened up until that point. In cases where they had not been personally involved in the investigations from the beginning (see previous section), the investigation files were their main source of information. Therefore, it is worth examining here the type of information included in those files.

It was observed that when the police forwarded cases to the Attorney General's Office they would almost always send the *original* investigation files. Those were firmly settled. Each file was divided into three parts. The *first* consisted of the "activity calendar", a detailed chronological record of the progress of a case under investigation from the time the police were notified of a crime and investigations began until the day the file was forwarded to the Law Office. That was accompanied by a summary report by the investigating officer which recorded the relevant personal details of the suspect, described the evidence collected and summarised the main witnesses' statements. It also recorded whether the suspect had been charged or not and/or whether any other evidence was still to be obtained and any additional observations that might have been relevant. It concluded with the recommendations of the investigating officer regarding the decision to prosecute and/or his suggestions as to what charges, if any, should be laid. In the "activity calendar" the recommendations of at least three more senior officers were included (which were not necessarily the same as those expressed by the investigating officer), as the file had to reach the Law Office through the hierarchical structure of the police force (investigating officer to officer in charge of the police station, to Chief Constable, to officer in charge of the Prosecution Department of the Police Headquarters).[40] The *second part* of the file consisted of statements by the various witnesses. It might run from a few pages to hundreds of pages, depending on the complexity of the particular case. This part also contained copies of documentary evidence, for example, copies of invoices or bank statements in fraud cases or copies of maps and sketch plans in road traffic cases. The *third part* of the file might contain any other miscellaneous papers, such as the detention schedule showing the number and length of interviews of an accused person by the police, and the criminal record of the accused.[41]

---

[40] This structure within which a file proceeds is similar to the situation existing in England before the Criminal Evidence Act 1984, which gave custody officers a critical role in the decision to charge. Before 1984, a police officer was supervised by his Sergeant during the investigation of a crime. The file of a case was then sent to the Inspector and after that to the Detective Inspector who would make the decision whether to prosecute. See in Baldwin and Hunt's (1998, pp. 530–531) interviews with police officers their comments that the earlier situation was enabling quicker and more efficient identification of evidential weaknesses in a case, since there was the input of three senior people in the hierarchy of the police before the case reached the court system.

[41] See, in comparison, Sanders (1986c, p. 27) commenting about the great use of *abbreviated files* as the only available base for prosecutors' decisions in England: "They are little more than police précis and the defendant's statements, rendering much prosecution screening perfunctory ... Some cases in my research underwent six or more hearings before a full file was produced".

As is obvious, the investigation files were usually very long and appeared to constitute a detailed account of "what happened" until that stage. However, as McConville et al. (1991, p. 12) state: "... at each point of the criminal justice process 'what happened' is the subject of interpretation, addition, subtraction, selection and reformulation". Prosecution files were the product of the police investigation and they reflected the quality of their work and the resources and effort they invested in the investigation of the case, as well as their interpretation of certain facts and their inferences from others. As will be shown later, however, Law Officers appeared to acknowledge the implications of this reality. Furthermore, the fact that in the investigation file Law Officers were able to find the views on the evidence not only of the investigator of the case but also of all his superiors proved on occasions very useful in locating inconsistencies in the police accounts of events.

5.3.3.2 Police Prompting

There were occasions when, even at that stage, the police themselves appeared to alert Law Officers to possible problems or weaknesses in the cases and ask them to consider whether, in view of those difficulties, a prosecution was desirable. Law Officers' decisions in these cases could be either a direction for prosecution or non-prosecution, or a direction for further investigations (for example, they would direct that a witness should make an additional statement giving fuller details of an event, they would ask the police to arrange an identification parade to be held or they would request further documentary evidence):[42]

> Case SE: A case of arson – The police investigator wrote in the file that, based on the evidence collected, it was unclear whether the action was intentional or accidental. The Law Officer found further gaps in the evidence and decided not to prosecute.
> Case FF: A case of forgery and fraud – The police suggested that the evidence was weak. The Law Officer asked for further documentary evidence and additional witnesses' statements.
> Cases HG and HE: Two cases against two companies for unlawful possession of explosive substances relating to a type of games they were selling – The police were not sure whether a regulation allowing the possession of certain explosive substances in certain circumstances was applicable in those cases. The Law Officer argued that it was applicable: Decision to refrain from prosecution.
> Case FT: A case of criminal impersonation – The Law Officer did not agree with the police suggestion of weak evidence: Direction to prosecute.

[42]There were 21 cases of this category in my sample which included: two rape cases, a case of forgery and fraud, a case of arson, two cases of stealing by a servant, three cases of forgery, a case of stealing by a trustee, two cases against companies for unlawful possession of explosive substances, a case of breach of banking regulations, a case of unlawful possession of drugs, a case of fraud, a case concerning offences against Foreign Currency Law, a case concerning offences against Bankruptcy Law, a case of stealing, a case of receiving stolen goods, a case of criminal impersonation and a case of extortion by a police officer. See the complete catalogue in Chap. 4, under Sect. 4.4.1 (gb).

5.3.3.3 Law Officers' Practices

Law Officers appeared to use their power to order further investigations and information on a case quite often, especially regarding the serious cases that they were going to present to court themselves.

Regarding those cases the investigation file was not approached as an unproblematic given but was sufficiently scrutinised so that any weaknesses or gaps in the evidence could be uncovered.[43] It must be observed, however, that this approach was not adopted for all cases with the same vigilance. For the so-called "ordinary cases" the degree of scrutiny that the investigation file was subjected to was directly correlated to the amount of time they had available (or to the information that another source – usually the defence – provided). Organisational pressures and practical constraints required the Law Officers to prioritise the cases which they considered to be more important.

It was also true that even for the serious cases, often their directions for further investigations concerned only clarification of details, correction of internal inconsistencies or the taking of statements which had for some reasons been overlooked by the police. However, it was not unusual for Law Officers in various cases to order new lines of inquiry or to challenge the "police construction of a case".[44] When the latter occurred it was largely the result of one of the following two factors:

1. Law Officers Alert to Police "Biased Information"

Some Law Officers seemed to be more alert than others to the possibility that the police may present "biased information", omit crucial evidence or conceal facts either intentionally or unintentionally:

> Case AK: possession of drugs with intent to supply – The case was committed for a trial before the Assize Court. The Law Officer confirmed 'the instinct he had that something was wrong with this case' when he had the chance to meet the police undercover agent before the opening of the trial. 'After a couple of questions I realised that he was lying about certain things. I confronted him and he told me the truth. I realised that the evidence was very weak and probably illegally obtained. We entered a nolle prosequi'. (Law Officer 04)

[43] See in comparison Baldwin and Moloney (1992, p. 64) describing the totally different approach of the English prosecutors: "Despite the relative gravity of the offences in question, the investigations were for the most part viewed as straightforward, unproblematic and satisfactorily conducted by the officers concerned. There was not a single case in which the Crown Prosecutors had requested that further information be collected or had criticism of the way an enquiry had been conducted".

[44] This was contrary to research findings in England and Wales regarding the prosecutors' requests for further information. See, for example, Baldwin (1997, pp.547–548) commenting on the results of his own research: "In few of the files were there examples of imaginative questioning of the evidence. Instead, requests to the police, in so far as they were made at all, were overwhelmingly for clarification of the detail . . . There were only isolated instances in the files where suggestions had been made by reviewing lawyers about the need to pursue fresh lines of inquiry".

> Case AB: a case of unlawful possession of firearms and explosives – On this occasion the case appeared strong on paper, as witnesses' statements were given great value. However, the real 'confidence' the police had about this case – arising from 'informal information' that they had about the certain suspect – was not explained at the beginning, and gaps and weaknesses in the evidence were left aside. The case was withdrawn.

Law Officers correlated the standard of information received from the police with the personal competence or integrity of the investigator. They seemed to be more alert and suspicious whenever particular police officers were in charge of the investigations:

> 'There are certain investigating officers that I can absolutely trust. When I receive their cases I know that at least I will have a carefully prepared file'. (Law Officer 01)

> 'Some investigators do not perform their duties adequately. They make serious mistakes, which occasionally prove damaging for the case. As time passes, you know who they are and you are more careful when reviewing their cases'. (Law Officer 06)

2. The Defence's Input

> 'Whatever system may be adopted it is the defence solicitor who will have to stimulate the critical intellect of any judicial or prosecutorial intermediary, in the investigative process and at the pre-trial stage in general. We cannot rely on the examining magistrate or prosecutor to do so without the assistance of one whose adversariness in interest stimulates critical reflection'. (Leigh and Zedner 1992, p. 73)

The drawing of ambiguity or impropriety to the attention of the Law Officers by defence attorneys was a key factor that used to prompt them to challenge the police's construction of a case. During my research period, I observed that the Attorney General and the Law Officers were frequently informed about gaps and inconsistencies in the evidence by the defence lawyers. Defence lawyers could also provide further information, not included in the police file, or prompt the Law Officer to ask the police to investigate new directions in their inquiries:[45]

> Case AG: A drug case – The suspect's explanation was left out of the summary. After a meeting with the defence lawyer and the information he gave him, the Law Officer realised that there were various gaps in the evidence and, therefore, he decided not to proceed with the case.

[45]Research studies in Britain (McConville and Mirsky 1992; Baldwin 1985; Baldwin and McConville 1977) have been particularly critical of the defence attorneys' attitude and role in the prosecution process. They commented on their failure to act in an adversarial way and their often uncritical acceptance of the prosecution case. McConville et al. (1991) suggest that defence lawyers quite often judge their clients' cases in the light of the police case, while Sanders (1992) argues that although quite often police constructions are weak, the police are saved from exposure because of the legal defence community's inability or unwillingness to challenge those constructions. For a more focused empirical study, which confirms the lack of active pre-trial investigation by defence lawyers in England and Wales, see McConville et al. (1994).

> Case AV: A case of an alleged rape of a 14-year-old girl – The case was forwarded to the Law Office with the suggestion not to prosecute based mainly on the victim's lack of credibility and some inconsistencies in her testimony (this case is further analysed elsewhere). A direction of no prosecution was issued initially. The victim's attorney sent a number of letters to the Law Office asking for explanations for their decision and offering evidence and reasons why the case deserved to go to court. He repeatedly asked for a meeting with the Attorney General and the Law Officer who reviewed the case. As a result of this meeting and a second review of the case by another Law Officer, the Attorney General directed for the case to be prosecuted. The accused was convicted but after an appeal he was acquitted.

There are two interesting points related to Case AV: Firstly, this case shows that not only do the defence attorneys provide the Law Office with information that advocates *against* prosecution, but the converse situation occurs as well: the victims' attorneys provide the Law Office with information which advocates *towards* prosecution. Secondly, it highlights a phenomenon observed on a number of occasions during my fieldwork period: the fact that the Attorney General and (more often) the Deputy Attorney General are personally and actively involved in very serious cases.

In most cases, even when a defence attorney did not offer specific information or tangible evidence on a case, his comments on a possible misuse of police powers or on suspicious police practices urged the Law Officers to question the police construction of a case. The following was an example of a situation where the persistence of the defence attorney led the Law Officer to go behind the police account and discover information that the police, in order to strengthen their case, had not disclosed:

> Case CF: An armed robbery – There were two perpetrators, of whom one was arrested in the act and the other escaped. The defence attorney contacted the Law Officer and strongly argued that the case was a police 'set up' and giving a number of indications as to why this might be. The Law Officer confronted the police and they admitted that the Central Intelligence Service knew about the planning of the robbery beforehand. They were informed by the perpetrator who was left to escape! The charge was reduced to attempted robbery. The accused pleaded guilty and the whole story was revealed to the court.

It was obvious that Law Officers were regarded by the defence attorneys as much more trustworthy and objective than the police and, therefore, the defence felt comfortable contacting them and suggesting alternative accounts for a case. Those accounts were sometimes effective in challenging the police story and opened up new lines of investigation. The Law Officers' response to such claims, namely the fact that they used to appear willing to take them into consideration and act upon them, strengthened even more the independent and the "ministry of justice" status that the Law Officers were promoting.

5.3.4 Concluding Remarks

The role that the Law Office plays in practice regarding investigations corresponds to the way Law Officers themselves approach their powers, but it is also responsive to the needs and actions of other actors in the system (as well as constrained by practical limitations). Therefore, the Law Officers: (a) order investigations where allegations of crimes are not properly investigated by the police; (b) provide extensive legal advice to the police during investigations, usually when the police sought such advice but sometimes because they judged that because of the sensitivity of the case they should intervene; and (c) order further inquiries and additional evidence after the case is forwarded to the Law Office, and ensure that defence information is taken into account.

The Law Office's early involvement in a case, apart from providing a valuable assistance to police investigative actions, ensures a better understanding of the case[46] and provides an obstacle to the absolute control of the investigative stage by the police:

> 'Much research evidence from England and Wales concludes that prosecutors cannot effectively monitor police investigations via police-constructed files. But this need not necessarily be the case in jurisdictions where there is a greater diversity of influences on the file; the difficult trick is to ensure that diversity'. (Field 1994, p. 126)

5.4 Summary

The Attorney General in Cyprus, in contrast to his common law background, is entrusted with an important role in investigations. This is in accordance with the wide powers that are delegated to him generally as far as prosecutions are concerned and which have rendered him so important in the Cyprus prosecution system.

Apart from some specific legislative provisions, the legal text that governs the Law Office's general role in investigations is framed very broadly and does not make the Attorney General's intervention in investigations obligatory. Nevertheless, it ensures that there is the theoretical potential and power of the Attorney General to act in such a way, if he wishes to do so. Once again, the extent and the way that this power is used are left open to the Attorney General to define. However, a gradual introduction of legislative provisions which confer on the Attorney General a direct investigative power or which make his intervention in investigations obligatory can be observed.

The Law Office for many years hardly developed any *active*, or at least publicly pronounced, policy on investigations in practice. Successive Attorney Generals preferred to deal with cases on an *ad hoc* basis instead of formulating a deliberate and comprehensive policy regarding all investigations. However, an examination of past circulars and letters in the Law Office revealed that the Attorney Generals used to exercise their power quite often and that the police had always regarded

[46] As Sanders (1988a, p. 35) points out, "involvement in the early stages could assist ... in understanding cases prior to their construction by the police as prosecutable edifices".

themselves as absolutely bound by an instruction from the Law Office, at least concerning serious or high profile cases.

Law Officers, generally, were very much in favour of their participation in the investigating phase and emphasised the advantages of their early involvement in a case. However, their limited resources made them reluctant to adopt a more proactive role in all investigations. They, therefore, appeared to consider investigations as predominantly a police job and their role usually as complementary, providing legal knowledge in the investigative process. They talked more about legal advice rather than supervision of investigations, apart from specific categories of case ("sensitive cases", cases involving public figures, allegations against police officers, etc.) when they chose to use a more authoritative terminology. Furthermore, at the stage that a case was forwarded to the Law Office for a decision for a prosecution to be taken, it was then clearly considered as their duty to thoroughly examine the evidence and order further inquiries if this was required.

In practice, Law Officers:

(a) Would order investigations where allegations of crimes were not properly investigated by the police after the receipt of information that a certain incident had occurred or after media coverage of an event.
(b) Would provide extensive legal advice to the police during investigations. There was no formal or static structure to facilitate the Law Office's involvement in police operations from the beginning. There was, however, a well-developed culture that encouraged the police officers to seek the Attorney General's advice.
(c) Would quite regularly order further inquiries and additional evidence after a case was forwarded to the Law Office. It was true that, very often, this only concerned clarification of details and correction of internal inconsistencies, but sometimes Law Officers, especially when they were prompted – usually by the defence attorneys – ordered new lines of inquiry or challenged the police construction of a case. Moreover, their actions generally served to enhance confidence in the integrity of investigations:

> 'While prosecutors may not play an investigative role in all or even most criminal cases, the majority of which are probably reactive as well as routine, the importance of the investigative role lies not in the number of cases it affects, but in the significance of the role in the matters where it arises'. (Little 1999, p. 728)

Chapter 6
Prosecution Policies and Decision-Making Within the Attorney General's Office

> 'The highest authority within the prosecution service is the Attorney General. He alone prescribes prosecution policy and supervises its implementation ... The Constitution expressly provides that the Attorney General exercises his powers 'in the public interest' and he himself is the sole judge of that'. (Malachtou-Pamballi 2005, p. 486)

The extent to which a prosecuting agency is regarded as responsible for the investigatory stage is a matter of great variation across different prosecution systems. The special status of the Attorney General's Office in Cyprus in that area has been discussed in the previous chapter. This chapter deals with what is regarded as the central function – the *sine qua non* – of *every* prosecuting authority: the power to decide whether a particular case should be forwarded to court or filtered out of the system, and inevitably the power to define the answer to a number of other issues that result from this initial decision (e.g. choice of charges, selection of the mode of trial, discontinuance of prosecution, acceptance of a plea).

In the *first section* of this chapter, the legal standpoint of the Cyprus prosecution system on the issue of prosecutorial discretion will be examined. The great latitude that is afforded to the Attorney General to formulate prosecution policies and exercise his prosecutorial discretion will be highlighted.

In the *second section*, an analysis of the way the Law Office has approached this broad discretion through time will be attempted. Based on the results of the examination of the Attorney Generals' internal circulars, their press releases and the documents they authored, as well as the interviews I carried out with them, I will attempt to provide answers to a number of questions: Have the succeeding Attorney Generals developed any specific criteria/policies by which prosecution decisions should be made? Have they publicly announced these policies? Have these criteria been consistent over time and through the succession of different Attorney Generals?

In the *third section*, the approach of the Law Officers themselves towards prosecutorial discretion will be examined. An analysis will be attempted into the way Law Officers approach prosecution decisions and into the values and principles they aspire to promote with their decision-making. Furthermore, and more

D. Kyprianou, *The Role of the Cyprus Attorney General's Office in Prosecutions: Rhetoric, Ideology and Practice*,
DOI 10.1007/978-3-642-01921-0_6, © Springer-Verlag Berlin Heidelberg 2010

specifically, an examination of the factors that they consider to be important in their decision making will be performed.

Finally, in the *fourth section*, a more empirical approach into both the way prosecutorial decisions are taken within the Law Office and the factors that are considered will be provided. This section will mainly draw on the results of the examination of cases that was carried out in the Law Office, as well as on the conclusions extracted from the observation period that was spent there.

6.1 Rhetoric

As shown in Chap. 2, prosecution systems have traditionally been characterised as adhering to either the legality or the opportunity principle, depending on the extent of the discretion that prosecutors are allowed in the decision to prosecute, and the permission to take into account factors other than evidence in making this decision. Once it is admitted that a certain amount of discretion should be allowed to prosecuting agencies, a number of issues arise regarding the formulation of prosecutorial policies, which different jurisdictions have dealt with in different ways. In some countries, prosecutors are obliged to issue a code stating their policy and criteria by which prosecution decisions should be made. Other jurisdictions, however, have adopted a different approach, which allows a broader discretion, while at the same time significantly limiting the number of decision makers. Furthermore, the formulation of prosecutorial policies in some countries is the responsibility of the prosecution service itself, while in others it comes under the control of the Executive who also defines the Government's criminal policy.

6.1.1 Legal Theory in the Cyprus Prosecution System

The Cyprus prosecution system, given its common law origins, adheres to the opportunity principle. There has never been an unavoidable obligation placed by law on the prosecuting authorities to institute proceedings for all crimes that come to their notice.[1] Therefore, it is accepted that the prosecuting authorities enjoy a certain amount of discretion in deciding whether or not to institute criminal proceedings and, thus, to develop their policies and/or criteria by which this discretion is exercised.

As shown in previous chapters, apart from the Attorney General's Office, there are various other authorities empowered to institute prosecutions within the sphere of their activity, the most important being the police. Nevertheless, as it has also been established by now in this book, the system of prosecutions in Cyprus is based

[1] See Loucaides (1974) and Tornaritis (1985).

upon the primacy of the Attorney General who has a constitutional power to control all prosecutions in the jurisdiction.

There are, therefore, two issues that merit discussion regarding the formulation of the prosecution policy in Cyprus. The first issue concerns the extent of the discretion that is allowed to the Law Office to formulate a certain policy regarding prosecutions, and the second concerns the question whether the Law Office is empowered to define the prosecution policy of the rest of the prosecuting authorities (especially the police) and thus, the question of the role that the Law Office has to play in the formulation of the *overall* prosecution policy of the jurisdiction.[2]

The Constitution specifically declares that the Attorney General exercises his prosecutorial powers "at his discretion, in the public interest" (Article 113.2) and, therefore, entrusts him with a broad discretion in the area without imposing any terms or conditions for the execution of this power. Neither the Constitution nor statutory legislation oblige the Attorney General to declare publicly the principles upon which he acts in exercising his discretion in prosecuting;[3] neither do they oblige him to give reasons for his decisions in particular instances. On the contrary, both judicially[4] and extra-judicially, it has been recognised that because the powers of the Law Office are constitutionally upheld, they are absolute and cannot be compromised by common legislation: "A law, either pre-existing the Constitution or enacted thereafter, cannot validly alter or abridge the powers of the Attorney General conferred on him by the Constitution" (Artemis 1989, p. 4033).

Furthermore, as was stated in Chap. 3, the Constitution grants to the Office of the Attorney General an independent rather than a political status. The Attorney General is appointed, serves and can only be removed under the same conditions as the Judges of the Supreme Court, and his Office is not subject to any Ministry. Moreover, unlike the other independent office-holders (e.g. the Auditor General of the Republic and the Governor of the Central Bank), the Attorney General is not even obliged to submit an annual report to the President on the activities of his Office. Therefore, at least theoretically, he can formulate his prosecution policy totally independently of the Executive:

> '(The Attorney General) alone prescribes prosecution policy and supervises its implementation. It is important to appreciate that the executive has no authority in the matter. If, for example, the Ministry of Justice would wish to promote a policy decision for first-time drug users not to be prosecuted, the most the Minister can do is to make a suggestion to this effect to the Attorney General. However, it is for the Attorney General to make the decision'. (Malachtou-Pamballi 2005, p. 486)

Additionally, the courts have on many occasions been at pains to stress that the Attorney General's discretion is absolute and not reviewable. It has been repeatedly

[2]The questions of whether there is such a policy, which is this, and how it is actualised, are issues that will be raised in later sections of this chapter.

[3]As, for example, it is the case in England and Wales where the CPS is obligated by statutory legislation to publish a code with the criteria by which they exercise their prosecutorial discretion.

[4]E.g. The Police v. Athienitis (1983) 2 C.L.R. 223.

stated[5] that "it is the exclusive right of the Attorney General to represent the public interest" (The Police v. Athienitis 1983 2 C.L.R. 223) and that "the Attorney General in exercising his discretionary power is not to be subject to the direction or control of any other person or authority".[6]

Regarding the first issue of this section, what is concluded from the above is that the formulation of the prosecution policy is considered as falling within the absolute jurisdiction of the Attorney General without any limitations posed by statutory legislation and without sharing power with any other governmental department such as the Ministry of Justice.

Turning now to the second issue, namely the question of whether the Law Office is empowered to define or influence the prosecution policy of the rest of the prosecuting authorities: It was extensively discussed in Chap. 4 that the Attorney General's relationship with the police (as well as with other prosecuting authorities) is not only limited to his constitutional obligations and powers to oversee and control all prosecutions. The Police Law[7] clearly acknowledges that the police discharge their functions regarding prosecutions under the *superintendence* of the Attorney General and, based on that, it is accepted that the Attorney General could, if he wishes, define police prosecution policies.[8]

Consequently, the Attorney General's Office might not be obliged (or appear ready) to take the decision for prosecution in each and every case; nevertheless, it seems to be the institution responsible (or the institution that possesses the power) for the formulation of the overall prosecutorial policy in the system.

6.2 The Attorney Generals' Policies

In this section, an analysis of the way the Law Office have approached the broad discretion they enjoy in the formulation of their prosecutorial policy through time will be attempted. Have they developed any specific criteria by which decisions to prosecute should be made? Have they publicly announced them? Have these criteria/policies been consistent through the succession of different Attorney

---

[5]Xenophontos v. The Republic 3 SCCC 89, In Re Ttooulias (1984) 1 C.L.R. 885, Attorney General v. Ioannidi (1993) 2 C.L.R. 377, Attorney General v. Andrianou (1995) 1 C.L.R. 486.

[6]This was also particularly stressed by all the Attorney Generals; for instance: "When exercising this power (the power to carry out prosecutions or entering a *nolle prosequi*), the Attorney General is enjoying an absolute discretion and he is not subject to the directions of any authority; however, he is acting always in the public interest" (Tornaritis 1974, p. 18).

[7]And similar provisions in Laws that give to other Government Departments the right to prosecute. For example, Law 82/67 s.176(1) provides: "Prosecutions against this Law ... are referred to as custom prosecutions and are made subject to any direction of the Attorney General of the Republic".

[8]See Chap. 4 for further reflection on this matter.

Generals? These are some of the issues that will be raised here in an effort to examine how the great latitude afforded to the Attorney General has materialised.

6.2.1 Policies and Approach to Discretion

The examination of relevant circulars in the Law Office and some limited press releases, and the interviews with the serving and the former Attorney Generals revealed that the Law Office for many years have not developed a comprehensive and publicly announced policy which defines *a priori* how their prosecutorial discretion has been exercised. There has never been a code for prosecutors in Cyprus or any kind of public document which would explain the Attorney Generals' policy or state in a detailed way the criteria which should be applied in prosecutorial decisions. However, in the past, there have been some releases to the press explaining some prosecution practices or particular decisions and some statements by some of the Attorney Generals stating their broad philosophy regarding prosecutions.

The official rhetoric used by all the Attorney Generals to articulate their prosecutorial discretion has placed emphasis on the quasi-judicial nature of their power and their independent status. In this way, they have implied that a detailed specification of the criteria by which they exercise their discretion is not well suited to the judicial nature of their duties, nor is it essential, given their independent status:

> 'The Attorney General executes his prosecutorial discretion according to the public interest ... In doing so, he acts in a *quasi-judicial way* ... Like judges, he cannot publicly declare *a priori* his policies in detail ... The only criterion should be that his decisions should do justice'. (Interview with Mr Triantafyllides) (emphasis added)

> 'The Attorney General in Cyprus may not be a member of the Court as prosecutors are in most continental jurisdictions. However, his prosecutorial decisions are of a *quasi-judicial* nature'. (Tornaritis 1974, p. 18)

There has also been an emphasis on the virtues of individualised justice and the incapability to predefine very specific policies:

> 'Every case is unique. The danger in the publication of guidelines is that they can never include every eventuality. And the inescapable result would be that cases would arise which appear to come under a certain guideline, but this guideline will not be followed because of their specific circumstances ... and then everyone would protest and criticise us ... '. (Interview with Mr Triantafyllides)

The impression that is also given by the views of some of the Attorney Generals is that this "mystery" that surrounds the Law Office and the broad nature that characterises their powers are regarded as essential in order to retain respect and the symbolic role that they play in the prosecution process:

> 'The Attorney General enjoys enormous discretion and he should promote this picture so that everyone realises his powers and his role in the system. You cannot be on TV all the

> time explaining your policies and apologising for them. In the end you will lose respect... '. (Interview with Mr Triantafyllides)

> 'The Attorney General must engender by his attitude wonder, authority, and awe in order to be respected... '. (Interview with Mr Nikitas)[9]

The above comments are also directly related to the approach of each Attorney General to openness and accountability. Although none of the Attorney Generals has ever advocated a detailed a priori publication of their policies, not all of them have approached openness and the "public relations" game with the same attitude. Mr Triantafyllides and Mr Nikitas apparently took the view that political and procedural independence were best safeguarded by maintaining a low profile, whereas during Mr Markides' tenure of the office, a more open approach, as far as the work of the Law Office was concerned, was adopted. He used to appear regularly in Parliament giving some explanation about the Office's policies and performance and he was more open to the press and publicity in an effort to explain the functions of his Office and the way some decisions were made.[10]

So far in this section, the approach of successive Attorney Generals towards mainly the *publication* of any detailed policy has been discussed. However, were there any indications of a certain policy inside the Law Office, even if this had not been published or pronounced publicly? What were the trends that each Attorney General appeared to follow regarding (even broad) criteria for prosecutions?

All Attorney Generals argued directly or indirectly that although they used to promote individualised justice, they adopted a certain broad approach to prosecutions which was known to all Law Officers. Even if that was not explicitly expressed or stated in a written form, the small size of the Law Office was regarded as a guarantee of "shared knowledge":

> 'The Office was small. There was everyday contact with the Law Officers and therefore, my approach was well known'. (Interview with Mr Triantafyllides)

> 'We have policies and criteria on various issues (as far as prosecutions are concerned). They may not be publicised but Law Officers are aware of these policies and they do apply them ... In the past, I have also issued internal circulars ... they are just not codified'. (Interview with Mr Markides)

> 'Internal circulars are useful ... However, the Law Office is a small place and no one could convincingly argue that he does not know my policies and my views'. (Interview with Mr Nikitas)

---

[9] Mr Nikitas published a couple of circulars, as will be shown later. However, this was only to state that there was no need for the specification of certain criteria by which discretion to refrain from prosecution should be exercised, because he would only do so in very exceptional cases.

[10] All the Attorney Generals appeared in Parliament from time to time but not equally as frequently or with the same attitude. For example, Mr Tornaritis (see Tornaritis 1975, 1983c; and Memorandum G.E. 7/1969, dated 20/04/1975) furiously denied that he was obliged to explain to the Parliament the use of *nolle prosequi* in certain cases (indeed, theoretically, the Attorney General is not obliged to do so), whereas Mr Markides used to present to the Parliament at the end of the year a catalogue detailing the numbers of *nolle prosequis* he entered. See the concluding chapter for a brief discussion on the issues of public accountability and openness.

During *Mr Tornaritis' tenure*, the approach adopted towards the criteria by which prosecution decisions should be made evoked the corresponding approach adopted in Britain by Attorney Generals in the 1950s. Mr Tornaritis, in various talks, internal circulars[11] or articles,[12] repeatedly referred to Sir Hartley Shawcross's talk of 1951:[13]

> 'In deciding whether or not to prosecute in a particular case, a consideration of the repercussion on his personal political fortunes ... was altogether excluded. Apart from that, the Attorney General may have regard to a variety of considerations, all of whom leading to the final question *whether a prosecution would be in the public interest*'. (emphasis added)

The public interest appeared to be the dominant consideration; and the Attorney General as the "repository of public conscience" (Tornaritis 1974, p. 18) and the "arbiter of the public interest" (Tornaritis 1975, p. 4) was entrusted with the duty to take into account a variety of factors.[14] Mr Tornaritis, partly citing Sir Hartley Shawcross,[15] Sir John Simon[16] and Sir Theobald Mathew,[17] was referring to the effect that a prosecution, successful or not, would have upon public morale or order, issues of public policy, issues of national or international concern, the effect of the prosecution on the administration of law, the penalty that was likely to be imposed (if it was only a nominal penalty, a prosecution may be better avoided), the reaction of public opinion, humanitarian considerations, etc.

Studying the first documents written by Mr Tornaritis it appeared that (following the tradition of that period in Britain[18]) evidential considerations were regarded as one of many considerations that ought to be taken into account and were not clearly separated from the rest:

---

[11] Circular G.E. 7/1969, dated 22/01/1969.

[12] Tornaritis (1975, 1983a, c, 1985).

[13] H.C. Debates, Vol. 483, cols. 679-90, January 1951.

[14] "It is the Attorney General, applying his judicial mind, who has to be the sole judge of those (public interest) considerations" (Tornaritis 1985, p. 1745, partly citing Edwards 1964).

[15] H.C. Debates, Vol. 483, cols. 679–690, January 1951.

[16] H.C. Debates Vol. 2105–6, December 1925.

[17] Sir Theobald Mathew was the Director of Public Prosecutions in England and Wales from 1944 to 1964.

[18] As Mansfield and Peay (1987, pp. 30–31) report, referring to the parliamentary speech of Lord Shawcross in 1951, the common law tradition historically did not separate the evidential assessment of a case from the public interest one as neatly as is the case currently. Instead, public interest was regarded as the dominant consideration, while evidential sufficiency was considered as one aspect of the public interest assessment. Of course, as Lord Shawcross stated, the public interest would never demand "to put a man on trial ... when the evidence is insufficient to justify his conviction, or even to call upon him for an explanation". Nevertheless, these days, common law systems tend to separate in theory evidential considerations from "public interest" considerations but most of the time they embody in what they call the evidential assessment of a case, additional considerations which might be better included in the public interest limb of their evaluation.

> 'The Attorney General may have regard to a variety of considerations ... Usually it is merely a *question of evidence*; in other cases, *wider* considerations than that are involved'. (Tornaritis' Circular 22/01/1969, p. 2)[19] (emphasis added)

Later,[20] frequent reference was also made to the criteria for prosecutions that Glanville Williams advocated in his writings.[21] Although sufficiency of evidence was stated as the first question to be decided, a rather flexible approach to this issue was adopted which afforded again the latitude to take into account other considerations when deciding to prosecute an apparently "weak case":

> 'Since the enforcement authorities do not prosecute in the case of every crime which comes to their notice but they exercise discretion, the *first question* to be decided is whether there is sufficient evidence to warrant a prosecution. But it is also important to consider whether the prosecution is likely to succeed. It would not be a good thing for the administration of justice if prosecutions were undertaken without any possibility of success. Though there may be *special reasons* for launching a prosecution in what appears to be a *weak case* when the accused is definitely morally blameable and there is a serious legal point to be argued ... '. (Tornaritis 1985, p. 1745)

The same spirit and approach towards prosecution decisions was sustained during *Mr Triantafyllides' tenure*. His philosophy and arguments regarding prosecutions run along the same broad lines:

> 'The Attorney General should be guided by the *public interest* when deciding whether to prosecute. He has the final word ... he should balance the various considerations ... '. (Interview with Mr Triantafyllides)

During his tenure, there was strong criticism, especially from parts of the press, that he was making very frequent use of his prerogative to enter a *nolle prosequi*, as well as his power to refrain from prosecutions. As a result, he was forced to release a series of statements[22] to the press explaining the reasons why he refrained from prosecutions especially in some widely publicised and relatively serious cases. In those statements, some of the factors that Mr Triantafyllides took into account when deciding whether to prosecute can be identified: the seriousness of the offence, the fact that the defendant has put right the loss or harm caused, the victim's wishes, the defendant's remorse, etc. It is remarkable that again evidential sufficiency or the likelihood of conviction was referred to as one in a series of many factors that were considered.

Apart from the above releases, which were merely issued in order to explain specific decisions, Mr Triantafyllides issued another more general statement[23] explaining his approach to prosecutions. There are a number of interesting conclusions that can be drawn from this statement that illuminate Mr Triantafyllides' policies:

---

[19] Again citing Sir Shawcross's talk.

[20] Tornaritis (1984) and Tornaritis (1985).

[21] Especially in his article "Discretion in Prosecuting" (Williams 1956).

[22] Press releases G.E. 61/85/IV, dated 05/10/1993, G.E. 61/85/IV, dated 18/11/1993, G.E. 61/85/IV, dated 23/11/1993 and G.E. 61/85/IV, dated 15/12/1993.

[23] Mr Triantafyllides' Statement G.E 7/69/3, dated 02/12/1993.

(a) He considered the power to discontinue or refrain from prosecutions to be a power that can be used *regularly* and not only on very rare occasions.[24] However, he stressed that this was a power exclusively exercised by the Attorney General himself:

> 'The power to discontinue prosecutions is *regularly* and not rarely exercised whenever this is necessary, and it is an essential supplement to the power to institute prosecutions'. (Statement G.E. 7/69/3, dated 02/12/1993, p. 1)

(b) He stressed once again that the criterion on which the decision to prosecute must be taken is the public interest. He specified that public interest reasons for not prosecuting could be factors related to the *national interest* or the *interests of the society*, to the *special circumstances of the defendant* or the *victim*, as well as factors which concern the *progress of specific criminal proceedings*. He particularly stressed the consideration of *humanitarian reasons* associated with the defendant and the exclusion of any political or discriminatory influences.
(c) He made clear that the prosecutorial discretion of the Attorney General, as well as the policies he followed, were not subject to the control of any authority and, therefore, he was not obliged to explain publicly his decisions in every case. However, he declared that whenever it was judged wise, he would publicise the reasons for a specific decision so that the public received information about cases that might create doubts.

Although *Mr Markides* argued in favour of individualised justice as his predecessors did, he also stressed the importance of the principle of equal treatment.[25] That is why he considered it necessary to issue certain internal circulars regarding some categories of cases. These concerned mainly either cases for which a great number of requests for the discontinuance of prosecutions were received (and thus, it was felt that certain criteria must be established so that a common approach was ensured), or cases for which there was a particular sensitivity and the Attorney General wished to promote a very specific policy. More specifically, circulars were issued for:

(a) *Traffic offences by juveniles*
There is a relatively high rate of these offences (especially the offence of driving a motorcycle without licence) committed by juveniles in Cyprus. The Attorney General, after a meeting at the Law Office with the Assistant Chief of the Police, a representative of the Traffic Department of the Police, and a Social Services representative, issued a circular[26] stating that: "The first time that a juvenile committed such an offence, he would not be prosecuted. Instead, he would be cautioned in the presence of his parents and he would be warned that if the same offence was committed again, he would be prosecuted for both offences". Furthermore, the circular stated that requests from the defendants for

[24] See below the exactly opposite approach adopted by Mr Nikitas in his circular.

[25] Interview with Mr Markides on 15/05/2002.

[26] Circular G.E. 124/73/2B, dated 26/06/1997. This was issued to replace of a previous Circular G.E. 124/73/2A dated 03/05/1996.

the discontinuance of such criminal proceedings would be regularly denied unless extremely special circumstances argued to the contrary.

(b) *Traffic accidents which cause damages and/or minor injuries*
There was a circular[27] stating that prosecutions would not be instituted (or they would be discontinued if instituted) for such traffic offences provided that (1) there was a statement by the victim declaring that he did not want to proceed, (2) there was evidence that the damages had been restored and the victim had been compensated and (3) there were no previous convictions against the defendant for similar offences.

(c) *Domestic violence offences*
There was a particular sensitivity for these cases at the Law Office[28] during Mr Markides' tenure. Meetings were arranged between the police, Law Officers and Social Services at the Law Office dealing with serious cases of domestic violence. Since 1998, according to a circular from the Attorney General, the general policy was to prosecute such cases even if the victim did not wish to do so.

Furthermore, even if there were not written circulars regarding these issues, Mr Markides argued that he had a specific policy for some other types of offences as well:

(d) *Abortion*
The Attorney General argued that they had never instituted proceedings for abortion and they were not planning to do so in the future.[29] He confirmed that the reason that that offence had not yet been decriminalised was mainly the strong negative reaction of the Orthodox Church of Cyprus.

(e) *Libel/slander*
Mr Markides also stated that prosecutions for libel were not instituted either:[30]

> 'I believe that the specific legal provision is not suited to the current circumstances and the principles of freedom of expression.[31] We never prosecute journalists because they express their opinions, even if they do so in a strong way. Anyway, we believe that enough protection against this offence is provided by civil law'. (Interview with Mr Markides)

---

[27] Circular G.E. 50(B)/87/N.35/3, dated 23/12/1996.

[28] As was shown in Chap. 4, these cases are necessarily sent to the Law Office as a result of specific directions by the Attorney General. There is a team of Law Officers assigned with the duty to examine such cases. Furthermore, all officers of the Government Departments (police officers, social workers, doctors, etc.) to whose attention comes a case of domestic violence have an obligation to submit a report within seven days to the Attorney General.

[29] Interview with Mr Markides (15/05/2002). See also Discussions in Parliament on 25/09/2001, reported in the newspaper "Phileleftheros" on 26/09/2001.

[30] Contrary to this approach, Mr Triantafyllides, during his tenure, instituted prosecutions against journalists on a couple of occasions for which he was heavily criticised (see, for instance, articles in the newspaper "Alithia" on 29/04/94 and 10/07/94)

[31] There are numerous unworkable and antiquated provisions still exist in the Cyprus criminal code. Both the Attorney General and the Deputy Attorney General stated in their interviews that they refrained from carrying out prosecutions based on them.

(f) Contrary to the last two categories, there were some offences for which the Attorney General categorically argued that they were always prosecuted once there was sufficient evidence. These were: offences concerning the use of violence by the police against suspects, the employment of illegal immigrants, illegal hunting, and violence against animals.

All of the above concerned *specific* policies that Mr Markides adopted towards certain categories of offences. However, which were the criteria that he argued he applied more generally? Mr Markides was the first Attorney General to make a clearer separate reference to the evidential sufficiency criterion:

> 'The rule is that there is sufficient evidence for a case to be sent to court when there is a *prima facie* case ... when a court will be justified in finding a case to answer'. (Interview with Mr Markides)

Although it appeared that he adopted a very strict evidential criterion, later in his reflection of public interest reasons that might argue against prosecutions, there were also considerations regarding the reliability or the availability of evidence. Consequently, he appeared to take the view that although, as a rule, when there was a *prima facie* case, prosecution ought to be instituted, he accepted that other considerations – including the credibility, reliability or availability of evidence – might justify a non-prosecution decision or a decision to discontinue a prosecution:[32]

> 'The public interest requires, as a rule, that when there is sufficient evidence (*prima facie* case), a case must be prosecuted ... (For the opposite to occur) there must be some special reasons which argue for non-prosecution or discontinuance of prosecution. These reasons could be related to the security of the state; they could be related to the evidence available ... sometimes you can see that it is definite that the defendant will be acquitted either because the quality of the evidence is not good enough, or because witnesses may become unavailable ... in that case, the public interest says that a person should not be dragged through the courts; another reason could be the unnecessary harm that would be caused by a prosecution; for example, in the case of a drug user who, by the time of the trial, had managed 'to stay clean'; also, when the defendant has already been punished enough for his offence'.[33] (Interview with Mr Markides)

More generally, during Mr Markides' tenure, there were the first indications that more complete documents setting out prosecution criteria and policies might not be regarded as totally undesirable or inconsistent with the broad discretion that the Law Office enjoyed. For example, the Deputy Attorney General[34] issued a circular[35] to all prosecutors in which he declared that the Rules formulated by the International Association of Prosecutors, as well as the Recommendation of the Council of Europe (2000) 19 regarding principles for prosecutors, should be adopted and followed. Furthermore, he indicated his interest in the formulation of

[32]Note the similarity with the approach advocated by Mansfield and Peay (1987).

[33]He specifically referred to tax offences.

[34]The Deputy Attorney General was the immediate supervisor of all Law Officers regarding prosecutions.

[35]Circular G.E. 65/1993/3, dated 12/07/2002.

a code stating the principles on which a prosecution should be carried out or discontinued. He issued a circular[36] to all Law Officers asking for proposals and suggestions and attached to it samples of similar codes adopted in other countries.[37]

When *Mr Nikitas* was appointed to the office, he adopted a very different philosophy from his predecessors regarding his prosecutorial policy. Contrary to the emphasis that all the former Attorney Generals had placed on their very broad discretion regarding the decision to prosecute or not, Mr Nikitas, right from the beginning, underlined that:

> '... the Attorney General cannot replace the courts in a case ... The judges of a case are, and will always be, the courts and the members of the courts ...'[38]

His approach was characterised by a great respect for the judicial power (which could be partly explained by the fact that before his appointment, he was a Supreme Court Judge) and the values associated with a public trial. He strongly believed that the public interest was served by sending cases to courts and that the Attorney General should not try to usurp courts' powers by diverting cases on a regular basis:

> 'The public interest requires that all cases where there is enough evidence should be sent to the court. A public trial guarantees the rights of the defendants, and the court is the only judge of a crime. Here (at the Law Office), decisions are inevitably taken behind closed doors'. (Interview with Mr Nikitas)

Mr Nikitas strongly believed that neither the Attorney General nor the police had the right to filter cases out of the system due to mitigating factors concerning the defendant, apart from very extreme occasions.[39] He argued that all the relevant factors could be taken into consideration by the judge and any mitigating factors could be reflected in the verdict or the penalty:

> 'Even for minor cases you cannot argue that because they are minor, they should not be sent to court. If the law provides for a minor offence, it means that there is a distraction of the public order ... Maybe it should be decriminalised ... In addition, if there are mitigating factors, these can be taken into account in court ... Of course, if there is a terminal illness, for example, I will not prosecute ... but this is an exception. You cannot refrain from prosecutions on a regular basis. This is important for deterrence, as well as for retaining the trust of the public in justice'. (Interview with Mr Nikitas)

It is striking that his approach and the justification he offered for it were identical to the legality systems' philosophy.[40]

---

[36] Circular G.E. 41(K)/1947, dated 23/01/2003.

[37] This effort did not produce any results as, a few months after this circular, a new Attorney General (Mr Nikitas) was appointed, following the resignation of Mr Markides, with a totally different philosophy on prosecutions.

[38] Circular G.E. 41(K)/1947, dated 11/06/2003, p. 2.

[39] This was his approach even for juvenile offenders. See Announcement G.E.124/73/2, dated 11/03/2004.

[40] See Chap. 2.

In his circulars and public announcements he repeatedly stated that by sending all cases where there is enough evidence to court the principle of equality is safeguarded. The principle that all individuals should be treated equally according to law was an axiom constantly found in his written statements.[41]

Furthermore, Mr Nikitas on several occasions criticised his predecessors for the frequent use they made of their power to enter *nolle prosequis* or discontinue criminal cases. In a circular[42] he issued soon after he was appointed,[43] he clarified that this specific prerogative would be used rarely and exceptionally.[44] Although acknowledging that the Constitution entrusted the Attorney General with the power to discontinue cases or refrain from prosecutions whenever he judges that the public interest so requires, he argued that "the public interest requires the prosecution and the punishment of every criminal". Therefore, he continued, "the entering of a *nolle prosequi* will be used in exceptional cases and the reasons for doing so would be explained in court so that it can be demonstrated that the public interest so required in those specific cases".[45] In general, Mr Nikitas appeared to introduce an approach which advocated the restriction of the Attorney General's discretion.[46]

6.2.2 Police Prosecutorial Discretion

> 'Since diversion is a dispositive function, it is appropriate that it be fulfilled by a quasi-judicial official such as the crown prosecutor and not by someone whose principal task is the investigation and prevention of crime'. (Ashworth and Redmayne 2005, p. 206)

As shown earlier, theoretically the Attorney General is empowered to define the prosecution policy of the rest of the prosecuting authorities, especially the police, who according to the Police Law, discharge their functions regarding prosecutions under his *superintendence*. The question is whether and how successive Attorney Generals have realised this theoretical potential.

---

[41] See, for example Announcement G.E 93/1984/Y142, dated 19/10/2004 and Announcement G.E 40/82/II, dated 20/09/2004.

[42] Circular G.E. 41(K)/1947, dated 11/06/2003.

[43] This circular was also publicly announced.

[44] During the first months of his tenure, every request by defendants asking him either to enter a *nolle prosequi* or review a police decision for prosecution was either refused or returned unanswered. Inevitably, these requests dramatically reduced (see Chap. 4).

[45] Circular G.E. 41(K)/1947, dated 11/06/2003, p. 2.

[46] However, it seems that nowadays the previous philosophy regarding prosecutions is once again applied since, following the recent resignation of Mr Nikitas, Mr Clerides, the Deputy Attorney General responsible for prosecutions under Mr Markides' tenure, was appointed to the office. See also Footnote 71 in Chap. 4.

Since there was not a detailed and comprehensive policy providing even for their own prosecutorial decisions, it could not be expected that such a policy would have been issued for the police. However, all the Attorney Generals agreed that the harmonisation of police policies with the approach adopted by each Attorney General was achieved by:

(a) The close contact they had on an everyday basis with police prosecution authorities
(b) The notification of any internal circulars issued in the Law Office to the police as well
(c) The specification of certain categories of cases that should be forwarded to the Law Office so that the Law Office exclusively take prosecutorial decisions regarding them[47]
(d) The ex posterior review and overruling of police decisions especially after requests by the defendants or the victims[48]

Nevertheless, the most important means by which police prosecutorial policy was controlled had been the direction of all the Attorney Generals – which was, however, more forcefully applied by Mr Markides – according to which all cases that the police wished to filter out of the system ought to be forwarded to the Law Office. In Cyprus, most debates have always been centred on the frequency with which cases are filtered out of the system rather than on the possibility that weak or divertable cases are forwarded to the courts.

All Attorney Generals regarded diversionary decisions as *their* responsibility. Regardless of the approach that each one adopted to the frequency that cases could be diverted from courts, all appeared to agree that these decisions were the *exclusive* responsibility of the Law Office:

> 'The rule that the police should apply is to prosecute unless the Attorney General directs otherwise'. (Interview with Mr Triantafyllides)

> 'The power to refrain from prosecutions belongs to the Attorney General. The police *must* forward to the Law Office all cases for which there is a suggestion not to prosecute'. (Interview with Mr Markides)

> 'Only the Attorney General should decide that a case should not go to court ... and this ought to occur very rarely'. (Interview with Mr Nikitas)

The Attorney Generals accepted that the Law Office was not able to take every prosecution decision. However, by adopting the approach that the police were obliged to prosecute as a rule and forward to the Law Office all cases that they wished to filter out of the system, they demanded that any diversionary action should be carried out by the Attorney General. This contributed to the central

[47] See Chap. 4.

[48] See Chap. 4. Prosecutors serving in the Police Prosecution Departments stated: "a specific decision by the Attorney General to overrule a police decision serves as a guidance for future similar cases" (Interview with the head of the Central PPD). Similar statements were made by the heads of the PPD in Limassol and Nicosia.

control of any depositary actions (which admittedly are the most important prosecutorial decisions[49]) by a limited number of officials, a philosophy advocated by a legality system approach.[50]

6.2.3 Concluding Remarks

Closing this section on the prosecutorial policies and approach to discretion that successive Attorney Generals in Cyprus have adopted, some general conclusions can be drawn:

Firstly, all the Attorney Generals, with the exception of Mr Nikitas, were comfortable with the idea of their broad discretion in formulating prosecution policies. They emphasised the need for flexible and responsible decision-making by an independent official with a quasi-judicial status, entrusted with the duty to take into account various considerations, all of which made up the general public interest.

Secondly, they largely refrained from spelling out detailed criteria for their decision- making, although their general approach and specific policies for certain categories of cases were publicly announced. However, as time passed, especially during Mr Markides' tenure, a more positive approach to the formulation of more specific policies had been adopted without, however, extending to the level of formulating a comprehensive and detailed policy for all prosecutions.

Thirdly, all the Attorney Generals argued that even if it was not always published, a certain approach to prosecutions always existed and its consistent application in the Law Office was guaranteed by the small size of the service.

Finally, the theory had always been that prosecution was the rule and diversion from prosecution was an exception (regardless of how extensive or limited the use of this exception was, according to each Attorney General's philosophy) and, furthermore, that diversionary decisions were the exclusive responsibility of the Law Office. As a result, the central control of the prosecutorial policy regarding all prosecutions was (at least theoretically) achieved.

6.3 Ideology

> 'When there is widespread agreement among decision-makers, and when decision-makers have the same values and the same background and the same skills, discretion is likely to seem most desirable'. (Schauer 2005, p. 9)

[49] See Ashworth and Redmayne (2005, Chaps. 1, 2, 6 and 7) and Sanders and Young (1994, Chap. 6).

[50] See Chap. 2.

In this section, the approach of the Law Officers themselves towards their prosecutorial discretion will be examined. An analysis will be attempted of the way Law Officers understand and materialise the broad discretion afforded to the Law Office to formulate criteria and practices for prosecution decisions. How do they approach prosecution decisions? What do they aspire to promote? Which are the values and principles that they consider to be guarantees for the wise use of their discretion (Sect. 6.3.1)? And, more specifically, what do they consider important in their decision-making (Sect. 6.3.2)?

6.3.1 General Approach to Discretion and Decision-making – Values that Law Officers Aspire To

6.3.1.1 Flexible Decision-Making – No Strict Guidelines

Through discussions and interviews with the Law Officers, I realised that the absence of any declared policy or criteria on which their prosecutorial discretion was exercised was not regarded as a drawback. Law Officers, in their great majority, emphasised the need for flexible and responsible decision making in the pursuit of their various purposes and responsibilities regarding prosecutions. This approach reflected a certain way of thinking which was cultivated over the years in the Law Office, as shown in the previous section:

> 'You have to be flexible when you are dealing with real-life cases ... Your judgment should be guided by the law, but very often the solution to a problem cannot be found within the law ... Therefore, you are obliged to reach outside the letter of the law and take into account a variety of considerations'. (Law Officer 09)

This philosophy also explained their reserved approach towards strict guidelines that would provide for the way they should exercise their prosecutorial discretion. There was a fear that rigid rules would hamper their ability to be flexible, and also scepticism that guidelines could ever be useful in practice:

> 'Written guidelines would be inflexible. This has always been the philosophy of common law. That's why, for so many years, there were no written laws'. (Law Officer 05)

> 'There is no recipe ... I don't think that we should have guidelines ... Every case is unique; it has its own peculiarities; there are no formulae in criminal cases ... This does not mean that you can say x today and y tomorrow on the same issue ... We never do this ...'. (Law Officer 07)

> 'Guidelines would not be useful ... Each case is different ... Guidelines could not include every singularity of each case and therefore, eventually, they would not be just or useful ...'. (Law Officer 18)

> 'You cannot set rules and guidelines ... Can you say, for example, that age is a factor which advocates against prosecutions? But what will happen in the case of a rape? Guidelines cannot provide for everything and thus, are not useful. This is mere philology ...'. (Law Officer 09)

Some Law Officers were less absolute in their responses and specified some occasions and circumstances under which guidelines could be useful:

> 'It depends on how guidelines are defined ... They can be useless if they are very broad or if they don't take into consideration the complexity of real-life cases. They can be helpful only if they are carefully defined, explicit and provide for specific cases ...'. (Law Officer 04)

> 'Specific criteria would be useful for minor cases for which, every day, we receive numerous requests for discontinuance (and entering of *nolle prosequis*). If there were specific criteria for those cases, we would save a lot of time; and defendants would probably not send so many requests, if they knew a priori that their cases were not included in those criteria'. (Law Officer 12)

> 'Guidelines could help to a limited extent ... Things are not black or white ... There are some clear cases, but there are other cases with complicated circumstances ... which cannot be predicted a priori and included in the guidelines ...'. (Law Officer 15)

6.3.1.2 Individualised Decision-Making

Directly connected to their ideas on flexibility in decision-making was the fact that individualised justice was regarded by all Law Officers as the ideal that ought to be respected and aspired to, and guide their prosecutorial decisions:

> 'We should be sensitive to the singularities of each particular case ... We ought to take into account the facts and circumstances of each individual case before deciding whether or not to initiate a prosecution, and if we do, what charges and mode of trial should be chosen ...'. (Law Officer 02)

> 'We should be guided by the public interest when deciding whether to prosecute in each case. What do we mean by public interest? You cannot make an exhaustive list; not even an indicative one. There are so many considerations that you have to take into account ... You can define public interest in *each case* depending on the specific circumstances. You can say this is what the public interest demands in this particular case ...'. (Law Officer 05)

> 'Each case should be dealt with on its own merit. A strict formula could never be sufficient as a guide to good prosecuting. The ideal is to always have the time to look deeper into the particular circumstances of a case and reach the best solution'. (Law Officer 09)

Some of the Law Officers readily admitted that such an approach to decision-making could not be possible in all categories of cases.[51] What was still important, though, was the fact that the values of individualised justice constituted what they regarded as the measure of their success. Failure to measure up to these ideals was considered by most of the Law Officers as a compromise to what was regarded as *good prosecuting*.

[51] See Sect. 6.4.

6.3.1.3 The Law Officers' Status as Guarantee for Consistent and Fair Decisions

Although Law Officers emphasised the need for flexible and adaptable decision-making, they themselves acknowledged the dangers that a very broad discretion could entail. Therefore, the emphasis on individualised justice did not ignore the ideal of consistency, but rather assumed that it would be maintained mainly through the personal competence and professional standards of the Attorney General and his staff attorneys:

> 'A person of the highest ethical and legal status is appointed to the office of the Attorney General... Based on that, it is considered that he can interpret the public interest rationally'. (Law Officer 06)

> 'The Attorney General represents and interprets the public interest according to our Constitution. The guarantee for the right and just interpretation of the public interest is the independence, integrity, high esteem and reputation of the Attorney General himself'. (Law Officer 05)

> 'Control of our decisions is exercised by the courts, which judge the cases we send to them ... Security is also, and most importantly, provided by the ethos and the qualifications that a person should have in order to be appointed to the office'. (Law Officer 09)[52]

The Attorney General as an independent official with a high status and guarantees of neutrality, entrusted by the Constitution to act in the public interest, was a powerful image in Law Officers' ideology and was reflected in the views of *their* status as well. Therefore, Law Officers believed that by virtue of their independence and their qualifications, they could be trusted to perceive the best solution to each prosecutorial dilemma, even when they were not constrained by rigid written rules. The representation of public interest and the "ministry of justice approach" to prosecutions were recurring themes in their description of their role and prosecutorial decision-making:

> 'I never use the word 'prosecution authority' ... I prefer to say that we are the representatives of the public ...'. (Law Officer 06)

> 'We have no vested interest in the cases ... We are part of the administration of justice'. (Law Officer 12)

> 'We represent the public interest; therefore, we represent the people, the security of society, the rule of law, the interests of the victims and the interests of the defendants ... We have to be fair to the defendant and secure his rights, but we also have to secure the interests of the victim ... Every decision we take has to take all of these into account'. (Law Officer 05)

---

[52]However, a couple of Law Officers argued that the publication of their policy would be an additional control of their power:

> 'It would be useful to have written criteria ... It would be good to have them published as well. The better way to exercise control of a power is to have transparency ... Furthermore, the public has the right to know ...'. (Law Officer 19)

6.3.1.4 "Shared Ethos": The Attorney General Balances Possible Differences

Furthermore, the fact that the Attorney General's Office has traditionally been a relatively small office, and the number of Officers dealing with prosecutions limited, strengthened even more the idea of a "shared ethos" within the Law Office:

> 'We get to know the approach to prosecutions through experience and everyday contact with the Attorney General ... We are a small office and the approach towards prosecutorial decision making is a common one'. (Law Officer 10)

> 'Although we don't have detailed written criteria by which we exercise our prosecutorial powers, in practice we have developed criteria which guide our decisions ... A small number of Officers are dealing with prosecutions. Thus, we discuss cases with each other, exchange opinions and generally follow a similar approach'. (Law Officer 02)

Moreover, they all agreed that all crucial decisions were taken by the Attorney General (or the Deputy Attorney General) himself, and therefore, the absence of a detailed set of guidelines was not a major shortcoming:

> 'We all know the way of thinking and the policy of the Attorney General and anyway, every crucial decision is taken by him personally'. (Law Officer 06)

There was a widespread perception among the Law Officers that when a controversial problem occurred, the solution was given by the Attorney General himself. They argued that the balance of different interests in each difficult case was a task that was achieved by the Attorney General guided by the public interest:

> 'Whenever there is a doubt in a particular case, we ask the Attorney General ... especially for serious cases, where different considerations advocate different solutions ...'. (Law Officer 13)

> 'When there is an important issue, we always ask the Attorney General for directions. Especially the decision on the discontinuance of a prosecution is strictly controlled by him personally'. (Law Officer 14)

Some Law Officers were particularly emphatic in stating that the discretion regarding prosecutions was vested in the Attorney Generals and their role was only to assist him in exercising that discretion, which at all times remained his:[53]

> 'The constitution entrusts the Attorney General with the responsibility for prosecutions and with broad discretion in performing his duties. We are applying *his* policy and ought to follow *his* directions'. (Law Officer 03)

However, most Law Officers admitted that they themselves enjoyed a considerable degree of discretion:

> 'We exercise a discretion that is vested in the Attorney General ... We are supervised while executing our powers. However, the Attorney General allows us discretion ... the crucial thing is to know when you should ask for direction'. (Law Officer 19)

---

[53] At times, there was the impression that by denying that they were applying their own discretion, they were allowed to keep a distance from potentially bad decisions.

6.3.2 *Specific Considerations in Law Officers' Decision-Making*

> 'In which direction does the public interest lie? Crown prosecutors are often engaged, either explicitly or implicitly, in a balancing exercise between considerations of evidential sufficiency, culpability, law enforcement and recourse management'. (Ashworth 1987, p. 596)

Despite their support for individualised decision-making and their scepticism towards strict written guidelines, Law Officers, when prompted, were ready to offer a series of factors that they usually took into account when making decisions on prosecutions. In this subsection, a closer examination of those more specific considerations, which arguably preoccupied their decision-making on whether and how to prosecute, will be attempted.

6.3.2.1 Complexity of Considerations – Sophisticated Way of Thinking

Before referring to the specific considerations that Law Officers cited as factors they used to take into account, there are some preliminary remarks that ought to be mentioned:

Firstly, Law Officers appeared to be deeply conscious of the inherent complexity that a prosecutorial decision usually entailed and the vast variety of considerations that had to be calculated. In their responses they did not refer only to factors related to the offence, the defendant or the victim. They also referred to considerations related to the resources of the Office, the credibility and efficiency of the system, the reaction of the public, implications for other criminal justice agencies, etc.[54] Their reflection on prosecutorial decision-making, especially when they were talking about specific cases, indicated a sophisticated train of thought which did not try to avoid apparent dilemmas and conflicting interests in the process. In the words of one Law Officer:

> 'Conflicting demands are not always easy to reconcile in practice. Delicate judgments about complex considerations are often needed . . .'. (Law Officer 02)

They also acknowledged the different sub-decisions that a prosecution decision used to involve: choice of charges, mode of trial, possible prosecution of the co-accused, etc. Moreover, they recognised the need for a *continuous review* of their decisions as the cases proceed:

> 'Circumstances change all the time . . . You have to be able to react and change or modify your decision as the case proceeds'. (Law Officer 09)

---

[54]Factors that prosecutors in other jurisdictions often avoid admitting but which they surely consider in practice. See, for example, Fionda (1995, p. 229): "In England and Wales . . . such considerations are still regarded with a certain distaste and cause jurisprudential anguish at what are seen as unjustifiable reasons for compromising the course of justice, and for informalising the legal process".

> 'Witnesses could change their mind, evidence could be discredited, the defendant might offer a guilty plea ... Our decisions are modified all the time'. (Law Officer 04)

However, what Law Officers failed or appeared reluctant to recognise was that in order to be able to resolve contradictions between different interests and reach the right solution, you might need to set some principles and priorities beforehand. As was shown above, they argued that the balance of different interests in each case was a task that was achieved by the Attorney General himself guided by the public interest.

6.3.2.2 The Rule Is to Prosecute: Extensive Exceptions

Secondly, Law Officers argued that the starting point in their decisions on prosecutions was that criminal cases should go to court when there was a *prima facie* case. They agreed that there should be a presupposition that where there was a breach of criminal law, the offender should be subject to prosecution, but, at the same time, they admitted that beyond this point there were many exceptions, based on a variety of considerations:

> 'You start with the theory that, as a rule, the public interest requires that a case should go to court'. (Law Officer 03)

> 'As a rule, cases should go to court. This is, of course, a rule with many exceptions, but we have to start from this basis so that we do not appear to be appropriating the powers of the legislature and those of the court'. (Law Officer 09)

In addition, they asserted that this rule also contributed to the better control of their discretion by the Attorney General:

> 'The Attorney General, at times, may exercise a looser control over our decisions to send cases to court ... maybe it is because this is regarded as the rule and, anyway, the courts will eventually judge our decisions ... However, he is very thorough with our decisions not to prosecute or to discontinue a prosecution'. (Law Office 14)

6.3.2.3 Evidential Considerations

Law Officers, in their initial responses, appeared to follow a long-standing tradition in the Law Office[55] that did not clearly separate evidential from other – public interest – considerations. In their reflections of what criteria were used when deciding whether or not (and also how) to prosecute, matters that could be characterised as evidential issues were mixed with a variety of other factors.

However, this proved to be a hasty conclusion to a superficial analysis of their responses. Law Officers did mix evidential with other issues, but only on a

[55] See earlier in this chapter the successive Attorney Generals' policies and criteria for prosecutions.

secondary level of their arguments. They firstly clarified that a *prima facie* case was the minimum evidential limit that should be reached so that a case could be sent to court and when that was satisfied, the rule was to prosecute. On a secondary level, though, issues of reliability, credibility and availability of evidence were mixed with other public interest considerations in order to decide whether a case should be prosecuted.[56]

However, even the definition of a *prima facie* case they offered was not as strict as it might sound but it rather afforded weighing of the evidence. They used definitions similar to the 1962 Practice Note which is also the test applied by Cyprus Courts at half-time submissions:[57] "When the evidence adduced by the prosecution ... is so manifestly unreliable that no reasonable tribunal could safely convict on it".[58] Cyprus Courts adopt the position that in order to require the accused to make his defence, the prosecution evidence must be credited, at least provisionally, as reliable. In the same way, when Law Officers argued that there should be at least a *prima facie* case in order for a case to be sent to court, by this most of them meant "enough provisionally reliable evidence":

> A: Sufficient evidence means admissible and relevant evidence which proves all the essential elements of the offence.
> Q: Do you examine the reliability of the evidence?
> A: When evidence is obviously so unreliable that no court would accept it, we do not prosecute. (Law Officer 02)

Most Law Officers, though, readily accepted that although a *prima facie* case (even the broader definition of it) was a minimum, very often it was not enough. They offered some examples where a higher evidential test should apply:

> 'It is very dangerous to send people to court based only on evidence the reliability of which is in serious question ... particularly with some specific categories of crime, people can be stigmatised very badly ... (we are a small society) we should be very careful ... it is not always easy to send people to courts ...'. (Law Officer 02)

> 'I admit that in some economic crime cases – those on the borderline – we apply a higher evidential criterion ... The victim could be better protected by civil action in most of these cases ... So it is better to go to court when there is a clear possibility of winning the case, otherwise a lot of time is wasted'. (Law Officer 03)

Some, but not all, Law Officers[59] also admitted that the mode of trial was another reason which might argue for "evidence of a better quality":

---

[56]This was the approach of Mr Markides himself. See earlier Mr Markides' responses in his interview.

[57]See Azinas and Another v. The Police (1981) 2 C.L.R. 133 and Attorney General v. Christodoulou (1990) 2 C.L.R. 133.

[58](1962) 1 All E R 448.

[59]See in Sect. 6.4 that practice showed that the mode of the trial is indeed a serious influential factor in the level of evidence required.

'Cases in front of Assize Courts take a lot of time and resources . . . You should think twice before you send a case there when the quality of evidence is not of a certain standard'. (Law Officer 01)

They also remarked that as the case proceeded, a constant review of the evidence ought to be carried out, which might lead to the discontinuance of a case. Law Officers usually referred to the chance they had to meet with witnesses before the trial. For Assize Court cases, after the committal, there was a practice followed by the Law Officers of seeing the main witnesses before they testified in court. They argued that this constituted a chance to check the quality of the evidence and possibly discontinue the case or modify the charges.

More generally, Law Officers appeared to take the view that in cases where they had the chance to have a personal and more complete view of the case – e.g. in cases where they were involved in investigations or in serious cases where meetings with victims, witnesses and experts were arranged – and therefore, it was possible and more justifiable to check the quality of evidence, a higher evidential criterion was somehow automatically involved in their judgments.

6.3.2.4 Public Interest Considerations

'What do we mean by "public interest"? You cannot make an exhaustive list, not even an indicative one. There are so many considerations . . . No one 'dares' to specify this term . . .'. (Law Officer 05)

'You have to consider everything . . . seriousness, resources, time, personal circumstances, the effect on the public . . .'. (Law Officer 19)

As shown earlier, Law Officers appeared to acknowledge the variety of considerations that a prosecution decision should entail. Before detailing various other issues that they took into account, all Law Officers referred to the specific policies for particular categories of cases that the serving Attorney General determined.[60] They were, therefore, aware of, and alert to, cases for which specific choices had been clearly made by the Attorney General.

More generally, most of the other considerations which they cited were expressed in a negative form as considerations that could advocate towards non-prosecution.[61] These were:

Factors Related to the Defendant

All Law Officers appeared sensitive to the personal circumstances of the defendants and argued that, especially in minor cases, these could lead to a decision for no

[60] See Mr Markides' specific policies earlier in this chapter.

[61] This is consistent with their view – mentioned earlier – that prosecution is the rule and non-prosecutions are the exceptions.

prosecution; while in more serious cases, they could lead to the choice of a lesser charge. Age, health reasons, family circumstances, absence of prior criminal record, disproportionate consequences of a prosecution for the defendant's future, and remorse were some of the factors detailed:

> 'Prosecution decisions should be humane and take into consideration personal factors as well ... We do not apply mathematical formulas and we cannot close our eyes to such factors'. (Law Officer 05)

Taking such factors into account was regarded as part of the "individualised justice approach" that they argued they promoted.

Factors Related to the Victim

Law Officers cited the wishes of the victim as an influential factor in their prosecutorial decision. They clarified that these were not always followed, as they sometimes needed to be balanced with other interests or concerns.[62] However, they were particularly influential in specific types of offences like sexual offences and such minor offences as common assaults, affrays, etc. Law Officers argued that they ought to be sensitive towards victims' views in some types of offences and meetings with them were often essential in order to discuss their wishes. They also referred to the need to save vulnerable victims from testifying in court as a reason to accept a plea to a lesser charge.

Issues of "Wider Public Interest"

Law Officers also referred to issues of "national or international concern", which might advocate against prosecutions:

> 'In the past, we had a case – not a very serious one – concerning two (reference to the nationality of the offenders). Their government demanded they be left free to return to their country. We were in danger of a diplomatic incident, as during this particular period, our relations with that country were in crisis. We could not risk such a serious crisis by insisting on prosecution. That was one of those exceptional cases where national interests prevailed'. (Law Officer 09)

Factors Related to the Offence

The triviality of an offence was also mentioned as a potential reason to refrain from prosecutions but most of the time in connection with other factors like the wishes of

[62]For example, in domestic violence cases the policy is to prosecute cases, even if the victim wishes otherwise.

the victim, the payment of possible damages caused by the offence, etc. Law Officers clarified that even minor offences ought to be sent to courts when there were certain reasons:

> 'Even some minor offences should always be sent to court ... For example, when there is an increase in this particular form of criminality ... or when we want *to promote a certain policy*: e.g. we always prosecute the owners of night clubs in tourist areas for regulatory offence regarding the running of their business, even if this would only result in a nominal penalty ... it is because we want to send the message that services relating to our tourism industry should maintain good and quality standards'. (Law Officer 03)

> 'Some offences, although appearing relatively minor, *if commonly committed*, should be sent to courts'. (Law Officer 19)

"Specific Choices"

Law Officers also admitted to some considerations that, at first sight, might appear unjustifiable. As they explained, though, these were choices that prosecutors had to make as the result of a balancing exercise between conflicting interests. Most of them referred to the choice of not prosecuting some co-defendants in exchange for their testimony against others, but there was a particular Law Officer who also cited the necessity of sometimes "letting off" police informants for minor crimes. They emphasised, though, that these were sensitive decisions that only the Attorney General himself could take after careful consideration:

> 'For example, in a case of a series of frauds and abuse of power by a senior public servant, we decided not to prosecute his accomplices because this was the only way to convince them to testify against him. We considered it to be more important to convict the public official, even if this meant that others would go unpunished ... We did not have any other choice'. (Law Officer 01)

> 'Let's say, for example, that a police informant commits a very minor offence ... and this person is at the heart of the crime (she refers to a certain area known for its high criminality) ... he provides police with invaluable information that cannot be obtained otherwise ... You cannot risk loosing him (as an informant) because he committed a very minor offence ... I do not claim that you should allow a serious crime not to be prosecuted ... but there is a balance of interests that should be struck'. (Law Officer 09)

It could be argued that Law Officers' willingness to admit to the existence of such considerations showed an approach that did not attempt to deny obvious dilemmas in the prosecution process. Rather, they tried to face them by acknowledging their sensitivity and accepting that the only one responsible for finding the right solution each time was the Attorney General.

Resources/Workload/Time

Law Officers appeared to consider their limited resources, as well as the resources of other criminal justice agencies (mainly courts), as a factor that they inevitably ought to take into account:

We don't have unlimited resources and unlimited time. Therefore, we cannot take decisions regardless of these considerations. (Law Officer 01)

They seemed to acknowledge that a possible backlog of the system would lead to major injustices and therefore, sometimes, less than ideal decisions ought to be taken in order to avoid just that.

Plea negotiation was regarded by some Law Officers as one of the legitimate ways to deal with time pressures and save resources:

> 'If, by accepting a plea, justice is done, then saving court's time, witnesses' time and our time is very important'. (Law Officer 09)

> 'Sometimes it is a good way to handle the case. Why waste five months in court when you could get a guilty plea to the next lower charge available? You save time and money, you have a conviction, and justice is done'. (Law Officer 01)

> 'The acceptance of a plea is a pragmatic choice in terms of efficiency and serves the public interest. However, pleas would be refused if . . . they do not reflect the seriousness of the incident at all'. (Law Officer 05)

The general attitude tended to be that the plea should reflect the criminality of the offence and not affect the sentence too greatly. Most of the Law Officers, though, admitted that they would not insist on the defendant being tried on the most serious charge, even when they thought it would be justified, if accepting a plea to a lesser offence or fewer offences would avoid the time and effort involved in running a trial in court.

6.3.2.5 Concluding Remarks

Summarising, it could be stated that Law Officers, reflecting on their prosecution decisions, placed emphasis on the need for *flexible and responsible decision-making* and *individualised justice*. The emphasis did not necessarily ignore the ideal of consistency, but rather assumed that it would be maintained through the personal competence, professional standards and guarantees of neutrality and independence of the Attorney General and his staff attorneys. Failure to measure up to the ideals of individualised justice was considered by most of the Law Officers as a failure of "good prosecuting", which sometimes was inevitable for some categories of offences.

More specifically, Law Officers appeared to be genuinely aware of the inherent complexity of prosecutorial decisions and the vast variety of considerations that ought to be calculated each time. In their responses, they did not refer only to factors related to the defendant, the victim or the offence. They also referred to considerations related to the resources of the Office, the credibility and efficiency of the system, the reaction of the public, implications for other criminal justice agencies, etc. Their reflection on prosecutorial decision-making indicated a sophisticated way of thinking, which attempted to solve even the most "sensitive" dilemmas and conflicting interests in the process. Generally, they regarded it as the role of the Law Office to try and balance conflicting interests in the prosecution process and interpret the public interest in each case.

6.4 Practice

In this section, a more empirical approach to both the way prosecutorial decisions are carried out in the Law Office and the factors that are considered regarding them will be attempted. This undertaking will mainly draw on the results of the examination of cases that was carried out in the Law Office, as well as on the conclusions drawn from the observation period spent there.

Several empirical studies have emphasised the illusion policy-makers may promote that a catalogue of criteria for prosecution decision-making could be automatically translated into practice, ignoring the multiplicity of conflicting values and aims in the process. In the previous sections, it was shown that the situation in Cyprus has been the reverse. Successive Attorney Generals, and the Law Officers themselves, were deeply conscious of the variety of concerns involved in prosecutions, and for many years have declared the inherent fallibility of an a priori specification of criteria for prosecutions. They rather adhered to the values of individualised justice through a small number of officials, with guarantees of neutrality and independence, empowered to do justice in each case. One of the purposes of this section will be to examine the extent to which the practice lives up to this ideal. Theory suggests that Law Officers have many advantages/powers in the pursuit of this ideal (e.g. involvement in investigations, as shown in the previous chapter, additional information from other sources, meetings with witnesses). Do they make use of these powers in all cases? Additionally, which are the factors which practice shows that they affect their prosecutorial decisions? And how closely do they correspond to their theoretical reflection on this issue? Which other circumstances exert influence on their decision-making? These are the main issues that this section will touch upon which broadly correspond to two questions: (a) In which *way* are prosecutorial decisions carried out in practice, and (b) which *specific factors* are considered regarding them?

As shown in Chap. 4, the Law Office's workload is extremely varied not only in the type of cases involved, but also regarding the stages that different cases reach the Office and the reasons that they are sent there. For systematic reasons, prosecution decisions will be examined separately for each of the categories of cases that the Law Office is dealing with. In this way, differences between categories of cases will be illustrated more easily.

6.4.1 Review and Prosecution of Indictable Cases (and Complex/ Sensitive Summary Cases)

As was shown elsewhere, these cases were considered as the core of the Law Office workload. The fact that they were the sole responsibility of the Attorney General and were continually under the immediate control of the Law Office meant that *questions regarding all aspects of the cases were being raised* (considerations of evidence and public interest, level of charges, etc.), and also that Law Officers' decisions regarding them could be re-examined or modified as they proceeded.

6.4.1.1 The Way that Prosecutorial Decisions Were Carried Out

It was very obvious from the beginning of the fieldwork that this part of the Attorney General's Office workload was distinct from the rest, in the sense that it was given considerably fuller consideration, time and resources.

Information on which decisions were made concerning these cases was not exclusively obtained from the police investigation file. On many occasions, as discussed more extensively in Chap. 5, Law Officers were also involved in the investigative stage and therefore had a more complete view of the cases from their early stages. The defence was also very active in providing the Law Office with alternative stories about the facts of the cases. Furthermore, for cases where an initial positive decision for prosecution was made, there was the chance for prosecutors to collect even more information and assess the quality of the evidence at a later stage. After the committal proceedings, there was a practice followed by the Law Officers to see the main witnesses before testifying in court.[63] This was justified theoretically in terms of clarifying inconsistencies or refreshing their memories but in practice, it extended to far more than that. Such a practice was giving them the chance to judge the "quality" and the "sufficiency" of the evidence.[64] As a result, their decisions in various cases were altered or modified (e.g. they dropped some charges or modified some others, or they decided to accept a plea to a lesser offence because of the vulnerability of the witness):

> Case CP: Rape/indecent assaults – Although police were confirming victims' willingness and desire to testify in court, after a meeting with the victims, the Law Officer began to consider the possibility of accepting the defence's offer of a plea of guilty to a lesser charge. 'Victims were so terrified by the thought of testifying in court that I am not sure whether they could cope with the procedure, or whether further harm would be caused.' (Law Officer 01)

> Case AR: Possession of drugs with intent to supply – The case was committed for trial before the Assize Court. The Law Officer confirmed 'the instinct he had that something was wrong with this case' when he had the chance to meet the under-cover agent of the police before the opening of the trial. 'After a couple of questions, I realised that he was lying about certain things. I confronted him and he told me the truth.' A *nolle prosequi* was entered.

---

[63] See Block et al. (1993, p. 106) describing the absence of such a practice in England and Wales: "There is little or no contact between the CPS and prosecution witnesses in the run-up to trial, this being currently a police function. Closer liaison between the CPS and witnesses and victims would enable some assessment to be made as to the latter's willingness, likelihood and ability to testify, and to some kind of track of them to be kept between committal and trial".

[64] Furthermore, quite often, consultations were arranged with expert witnesses such as forensic scientists or doctors so they could explain to Law Officers their statements and clarify complex points of their evidence.

More generally, it was observed that decisions regarding these cases were *under a continuous review*. Law Officers were expected to review the decision to prosecute in the light of emerging developments affecting both the quality and/or availability of the evidence and other public interest considerations. Such common developments were:

(a) Evidential problems appearing after the beginning of the trial: e.g. a main witness refused to testify, the main witness changed the testimony in court or left the country.
(b) The accused had already been convicted of another offence and sentenced to many years of imprisonment.
(c) A guilty plea was entered to some of the charges and the rest of the charges were discontinued (plea bargaining).
(d) Victim's wishes: Extreme circumstances. E.g.:

Case JE: A case of rape – The offender was the ex-boyfriend of the victim. While at the beginning she was willing to testify, later on, she sent a letter to the Attorney General stating that she did not wish to testify and she was going to marry the offender. The Attorney General initially refused the entering of a *nolle prosequi* but after a *personal meeting* he had with the victim and her advocate and the insistence of the victim that further harm was going to be caused, he changed his opinion).

6.4.1.2 Specific Factors that Were Considered

The analysis of these cases resulted in some general conclusions about the considerations that would influence decision-making:

Firstly, regarding the evidence required for such cases, it could be said that there were conflicting interests at stake suggesting different levels of evidence. On one hand, the seriousness of the offences advocated for the prosecution of cases even if there was only a *prima facie* case. On the other hand, though, the resources required for a trial in front of the Assize Court, and the fact that serious allegations were potentially damaging to the reputation of an innocent person, advocated for a higher level of evidence. Law Officers appeared to adopt a higher level of evidence in cases where they had personal knowledge of the quality of the evidence (e.g. due to their involvement in investigations) and as far as the rest of the cases were concerned, as the cases proceeded and more information was obtained, initial decisions could be overruled or modified. It should be noted here that a specific category of cases for which a higher level of evidence was usually required (even from the beginning) was economic offences for which civil action could be instituted.

Secondly, it was generally difficult for a very serious case not to be prosecuted at all, based only on "public interest" considerations. Public interest considerations for these cases would rather justify a suggestion for a trial before a District Court or a prosecution for a lesser charge.

However, Law Officers did refrain from (or discontinue) prosecutions in a number of these cases based on a variety of considerations. These were:

(a) Extreme personal circumstances:

E.g.: Case JE (see p. 173)

(b) When the case was only technically regarded as an indictable offence due to the level of its seriousness (The circumstances of the offences would normally argue for a suggestion for a summary trial) and there were, additionally, extra mitigating factors relating to the accused.

E.g.: Case NC – A case of forgery of a cheque of £50 (because of the amount of money involved, this case would be normally tried in front of a District Court instead of an Assize Court). The accused suffered from a psychological disorder. There was a relevant report from the Social Services confirming that.

6.4.2 Choice of Mode of Trial for Indictable Offences

This category of cases primarily provided important information on the criteria that Law Officers were employing in the choice of mode of trial for indictable offences. As explained elsewhere, in the Cyprus Legal System, there are no "triable either way" offences. There are summary offences[65] tried by the District Courts, and indictable offences tried either by the Assize Courts or by the District Courts, provided that the Attorney General consents to that mode of trial. Thus, by law,[66] the Attorney General may choose the mode of trial of every indictable offence.

6.4.2.1 The Way that Prosecutorial Decisions Were Carried Out

The first and most important question being addressed in those cases was "What mode of trial is appropriate for this case?" Or even more specifically, "Would the special circumstances of the case justify a summary trial, even though it concerns crimes punishable with a penalty that exceeds five years?"

The *information* on which decisions were made was mainly the investigation file. Law Officers themselves admitted (and were observed to do so) that, most of the time, in those cases they would only read the summary report prepared by the investigator; they only read witnesses' statements, or other documents, when they found something unusual or unclear in the summary, or when the police requested their advice on particular aspects of the case (apart from the determination of the mode of trial). A more careful study of those files, though, revealed that the police

---

[65] Offences punishable with a term of imprisonment not exceeding five years and/or a fine not exceeding £5,000.

[66] Court of Justice Law 1960, s.24.2.

did often ask questions or request directions about various issues in the case. As a result, in some cases the Law Officers, besides granting consent for the summary trial of indictable offences, were also giving advice/directions on any other offences included in the same criminal file, or general advice about the handling of the case in court (see, e.g. a drug case where the Law Officer called the expert in order to clarify a point in his statement and accordingly he gave a direction to the police on how to handle the case in Court).[67] It was also found that for some of those cases, the advice of the Law Office was sought during the investigation of the offence mainly via telephone communication between the investigator and the Law Officer.

Additional information from other sources which might influence the choice of the mode of trial was provided only in cases for which an Assize Court trial was selected and, thus, they were kept in the Law Office and were handled by Law Officers. In those cases information from the defence for, e.g. mitigating circumstances relating to the defendant, or a later check of the quality of the evidence by the Law Officer himself handling the case (for example, after meeting with witnesses or after a more thorough study of the criminal file), led, in a number of cases, to an alteration of the initial decision. As a result, and depending on the stage of the process, the case was either remitted to the District Court[68] or a *nolle prosequi* was entered and another prosecution was instituted in the District Court.

6.4.2.2 Specific Factors that Were Considered

Based on the analysis of these cases, the following factors appeared to influence the selection of the mode of trial:

(a) *The seriousness of the offence*:
For many categories of offences in which the question of the choice of trial was raised, the maximum sentence in Law was very high and there were no predefined subcategories (e.g. the maximum sentence in Law for forgery of a cheque of £15 is the same as for forgery of a cheque of £150,000!). Therefore, the seriousness of each particular case and the perceived appropriate sentence was the main factor that was observed to influence the choice of the forum of the trial. This was determined by, for example, the value of the goods stolen in a burglary, the amount and type of drugs in drug cases, the injury suffered by the victim in offences against the person.

---

[67] In 28 cases (43%) out of 65 that were included in this category in my sample, the Law Officers dealt with other issues besides the determination of the mode of trial, and in 21 of them that occurred after the police prompting.

[68] According to s.155(b) of Criminal Procedure Law, during the period between the completion of committal proceedings and the beginning of the trial in the Assize Court, the Attorney General has the power to remit a case to the District Court.

(b) *The particular circumstances surrounding the criminal incident*:
These were mainly the intention/motive behind an offence (a very common factor for the offence of carrying a firearm[69]), the gross provocation by the victim and the time that had passed since the commission of the offence.
(c) *Mitigating factors relating to the defendant*:
The most common ones were the young age of the defendant or the old age of a defendant with no prior record, special personal or family circumstances, and health reasons.
(d) *Burden of work*:
The choice of the mode of trial in some cases was substantially influenced by the pressures of the workload that Law Officers were dealing with. The choice of an Assize Court trial had the inevitable consequence that the case would stay at the Law Office to be handled by a Law Officer. Therefore, in some cases it was clearly stated that "due to the heavy workload that the Office is facing at the moment, it is judged that this case can be tried in a District Court". It has to be noted though, that most of these cases could be characterised as borderline cases for which either decision could be justified.[70]
(e) *Legal complexity of the case*:
This reason advocated towards the choice of an Assize Court trial in cases for which, if based only on the prediction of the sentence likely to be imposed, a District Court trial might be chosen. Law Officers preferred to keep a couple of cases in the Assize Court which were particularly complex or in which evidential difficulties were likely to arise. The Deputy Attorney General commented:

> Assize Court is undoubtedly a better forum for the trial of difficult cases, as Judges are more experienced and a Law Officer would deal with them in Court. This way, we have the chance to keep a close eye on them.

(f) *Publicity (media coverage)*:
For similar reasons, it was preferred that another borderline case was kept in the Assize Court. Widespread publicity and media coverage advocated towards an Assize Court trial.
(g) *Evidential reasons*:
Questions about the credibility of the victim/witness and the circumstances under which the offence was committed were reasons for some cases to be tried in the District Courts. The words of a Law Officer explaining his choice in a particular case were illuminating:

> 'It is not possible for all cases to be tried before the Assize Court; therefore, if you have to choose, you will not send cases where there are serious doubts about the credibility of the witnesses or the victim ... Of course, you cannot drop a case mainly based on the

[69] This mainly concerned cases relating to the carrying of a firearm for hunting without a licence or during the period that hunting is not permitted.

[70] However, Law Officers themselves admitted that in particularly busy period even cases that could be characterised as rather clear Assize Court cases could be sent to District Courts (Interviews with Law Officers).

credibility of the witness – this is a matter for the Court – so you send it to the District Court, where at least not so many resources are wasted'. (Law Officer 01)

6.4.3 Categories of Cases that the Attorney General Specifically Directs to Be Forwarded to the Law Office

These categories included offences where the Attorney General was of the opinion that particular attention was required, or were "cases that might reveal important considerations of public policy" and, therefore, it was judged that it would be better that the decision for prosecution was taken by the Law Office. As shown in Chap. 4, these were domestic violence cases, offences committed by juveniles and corruption by public officers' cases/"consent" cases.

The main question regarding these cases was *whether the public interest required a prosecution*, taking into consideration the specific policy of the Law Office relating on these categories of offences.

6.4.3.1 The Way that Prosecutorial Decisions Were Carried Out

Information for most of these cases (especially for juvenile and domestic violence cases) was secured from additional sources other than the police. More specifically:

(a) *For juvenile cases*:
There was a special procedure followed for this category of cases. There were committees comprised of representatives of the Police Constables and of Social Services for each district, responsible for reviewing all juvenile cases. The Social Services would prepare a report on each juvenile, giving details about his/her background, family circumstances, character, etc. The committees' suggestions for the proper disposal of the cases and a review of the Social Services' report were forwarded to the Attorney General's Office with the relevant criminal file. The Law Officers usually accepted the committees' suggestions.

(b) *For domestic violence cases*:
As shown in Chap. 4, since 1998, according to Circular G.E. 50(C)/1992/N.42 by Mr Markides, all officers of Government Departments (police officers, social workers, doctors, etc.) to whose attention came a case of domestic violence had an obligation to submit a report within seven days to the Attorney General. A *team of Law Officers* examined the reports and gave directions. Until 2000, all criminal files were forwarded to the Law Office after the police investigations and Law Officers decided whether to prosecute or not. Due to the large amount of files arriving at the Office, the police were directed to send only those cases in which *they decided not to prosecute or they were not sure whether they should prosecute*.

There was a declared policy that these cases should be prosecuted unless very special circumstances advocated for the opposite. Even when the victims withdrew their complaints, the procedure followed was to send the case to the Court and if the victims still did not wish to testify, a *nolle prosequi* was entered.

Furthermore, there was close cooperation between the Social Services and the Law Officers' team dealing with these cases. In very serious cases, meetings were arranged between the police, Law Officers and Social Services even during the investigations.[71]

6.4.3.2 Specific Factors that Were Considered

(a) *For juvenile cases*: As a rule, the suggestion of the special commission mentioned above was adopted. This was usually a suggestion for no prosecution unless the case concerned a particularly serious crime or "the juvenile showed a persistent criminal behaviour".
(b) *For domestic violence cases*: As mentioned above, the rule for these cases was in favour of prosecution unless very special circumstances advocated for the opposite.
(c) *For corruption by public officers' cases*: If there was sufficient evidence, it was regarded that the public interest required the prosecution of these cases. This category represented a good example where specific choices had to be made about the prosecution or not of all co-defendants. Where there was not enough independent evidence, Law Officers would prosecute the public official and offer immunity from prosecution to his co-defendants in order to ensure that they would testify in court against him.

6.4.4 Review of Summary Cases

As was shown earlier, although summary cases were usually dealt with by Police Prosecution Departments, the police were obliged to forward to the Law Office cases in which they suggested that a prosecution was not required due to public interest factors or regarding which they were not sure whether there was enough evidence for prosecution. Thus, in these cases, the Law Office had to decide *whether diversion from prosecution was justified.*

---

[71] There was a particular sensitivity for domestic violence offences at the Law Office. They admitted that the police attitude towards these cases until recently had not been the proper one. I even observed a number of short, educational sessions about the handling of these cases, organised by the Law Officer in charge, in which police officers, Social Service Officers and Law Officers participated.

6.4.4.1 The Way that Prosecutorial Decisions Were Carried Out

The *information* on which these decisions were made was mainly the investigation file. Law Officers were observed to adopt a more pragmatic attitude towards this aspect of their work, which advanced standardisation rather than individualised justice. It was observed that the extent to which a case would be thoroughly reviewed depended on the workload that the Law Officer had to deal with regarding the rest of the cases.[72] In very minor cases, they were only looking for some standard information in every case which could be routinely and quickly checked: e.g. in minor assault cases, a letter from the victim that he did not want to proceed; in minor drug possession cases, confirmation from the police that the defendant was a first offender.[73] However, they appeared to be alert to unusual cases of this category that might demand a more careful consideration (e.g. a case against a well-known journalist, cases of carrying arms to terrorise, a case of extortion by a police officer).

It was also observed that the opinion of the police, although not always adopted, was given considerable weight. There was the underlying presupposition, especially by some Law Officers, that these were police cases and, therefore, the views of the police ought to be seriously considered.

6.4.4.2 Specific Factors that Were Considered

Questions of evidence were not usually disassociated from other considerations and, therefore, the overall question that was raised in these cases was whether a certain case could be justifiably filtered out of the system. Factors that contributed towards a positive answer to this question were:[74]

(a) The triviality of the offence in connection with other factors such as remorse/apology, etc.
(b) Mitigating factors related to the defendant, such as no prior criminal record, good character/law-abiding citizen, health reasons, difficult family circumstances, commission of the offence under enormous stress, the offender has already been punished, remorse/apology, payment of the damages. Especially in minor drug cases (concerning use and possession of illegal drugs), the rule

[72]Blumberg (1967), in his classic work on the criminal justice system, argues that the most common reason for criminal justice officials deviating from their ideological and professional commitments is the intolerably large caseloads they have to deal with.

[73]Especially during very busy days, or days that Law Officers had also to appear in court, these cases were dealt with quickly and sometimes casually. A Law Officer admitted:

> 'When I don't have to be at court all day, I have the time to examine these cases carefully, communicate with the investigator, ask for clarification, etc. Also, when I have time, I prefer to read witnesses' statements instead of relying on the police summary. However, I admit that next week when I will be in court most of the time, things will be different'. (Law Officer 01)

[74]These were almost identical with the factors on which *nolle prosequis* were granted.

was that a prosecution was not instituted for the first offence, in order to give defendants "a second chance".

(c) Withdrawal of the victim's complaint mainly in cases concerning common assaults, affrays, negligent acts, etc.
(d) Misleading information from, or acts by, the responsible authority or a later obtaining of a relevant licence (mainly for regulatory offences).
(e) "The accused assisted the police in the past with the investigation of other offences": There were a couple of minor cases concerning police informants in which the police made the suggestion to refrain from prosecution.
(f) Evidential reasons: these might concern (1) problems in establishing even a *prima facie* case but also (2) problems with the availability or the credibility of the evidence which, in combination with the (lack of) seriousness of the case, advocated towards a non-prosecution decision.

It has to be remarked that for cases where it was decided not to prosecute mainly for reasons under categories (b) and (c), Law Officers would direct that the files should remain "open" for a defined period of time. If during that time the accused did not commit another offence, then the file was closed.

Factors that contributed towards a negative answer to the request or suggestion by the police to refrain from prosecution were:

(a) A specific policy of the Attorney General to prosecute all offences coming under a certain category.
(b) The nature of the offence:

- *Offences that involved carrying arms*:

Case CJ: A case of threatening violence and carrying arms to terrorise – Despite the withdrawal of the complaint, the apology of the accused, the fact that the accused was a first offender, the commission of the offence under enormous stress and the police suggestion that prosecution would cause problems in family relations (the victim was the son and the accused was the father), the Law Officer directed to prosecute because "the settlement of a dispute carrying arms is unacceptable and extremely dangerous". (See in comparison Case KJ on p. 182).

Case CF: Another case of carrying arms to terrorise – The Police suggested no prosecution as the accused had very serious family problems and suffered from a psychological disorder. The Law Officer refused as "the accused could be a danger to himself as well as to the public, and prosecution is necessary in order to be deprived of the license to carry a weapon".

- *Offences concerning "sensitive issues" for which a possible non-prosecution could create the impression of being "let off"*:

Case CH: A case of extortion by a police officer – The police had serious doubts about the victim's credibility and suggested that the case be dealt with using disciplinary measures/procedures. The Law Officer directed prosecution: "The credibility of the witnesses is a matter for the Court. Cases involving public servants should be sent to the Court in order for the accusation of letting off public servants to be avoided".

(c) The prior criminal record of the accused.

6.4.5 *Requests to Enter a Nolle Prosequi* or to Review Police Decisions

This category of cases concerned the consideration of requests submitted to the Attorney General by defendants asking him to exercise his power to terminate criminal proceedings (or, to a lesser extent, to review a decision for prosecution before a charge is preferred in court). They concerned mainly summary offences handled by the Police Prosecution Departments and a small number of prosecutions by other Government Departments. What Law Officers were called upon to decide in these cases was *whether a prosecution should be discontinued.*

6.4.5.1 The Way that Prosecutorial Decisions Were Carried Out

There was a *special procedure* followed regarding this aspect of the Law Office's workload, in which eleven Law Officers were employed.[75] It is noticeable that among them were Officers who were not dealing with criminal cases systematically. Every week a different Law Officer was responsible for dealing with all requests that reached the Law Office. This special procedure was adopted due to the numerous requests that were reaching the Law Office, as well as in an effort to increase objectivity in the handling of these cases.

The *information* on which decisions were taken was received from both the defence and the police. Defendants, in their requests, used to state the facts of the case and various reasons why they asked for the discontinuance of the prosecution. Most of them were based on *public interest factors* (e.g. health reasons, remorse, disproportionate consequences of a possible conviction, oppressiveness in prosecution, reconciliation between offender and victim), but a number of them were based on *evidential reasons* (total absence of evidence, unreliable evidence, abuse of process by the police). For each request, the Law Officer responsible would send a fax to the Police Prosecution Department dealing with the case, in which he/she informed them of the request (forwarding a copy of the letter) and asking their opinion. The PPD would reply stating the facts of the case and the reasons why a discontinuance was justified or not. For some cases (6% of my sample), the Law Officer asked the PPD to forward to the Law Office the whole criminal file.

This is one of the categories of the Law Office's workload for which Law Officers had to meet the Attorney General personally and make their suggestions on them, since it was regarded that only the Attorney General himself could take these decisions. It was observed that this procedure was generally followed, but Law Officers stated that in very busy periods the Attorney General was asking them to forward to him only the cases in which there was a positive suggestion for the entering of a *nolle prosequi*. This was another indication that in theory prosecution

[75] See Appendix 1.

was the rule and the power not to prosecute or discontinue a prosecution was an exception that had to be controlled more tightly – even within the Law Office. Mr Markides issued a circular on that directed to all Law Officers, firmly stating that especially decisions to discontinue a prosecution ought to be taken *exclusively* by him.[76] Nevertheless, in the great majority of cases, the Attorney General would accept the Law Officers' suggestions.[77]

In many of the cases, the Law Office agreed with the PPD's suggestion, which was often positive.[78] However, there were cases for which there was disagreement and the Law Office's decision prevailed. In my sample, there was disagreement in 15% of the cases. The most common reasons for disagreement were: (a) a certain policy of the Law Office regarding some categories of offences, or (b) a different evaluation of some public interest factors.

In some of these cases the Attorney General set conditions on his entering of a *nolle prosequi*: e.g. (a) the accused must pay the damages, (b) he must pay the costs of the trial up to that point, (c) a *nolle prosequi* will be entered to certain charges if the accused plead guilty to the remainder, and (d) if the accused commits another offence in a defined period of time, the prosecution for this offence will be re-instituted.

6.4.5.2 Specific Factors that Were Considered

The main reasons for requests being granted were mainly:

(a) The triviality of the offence: These requests concerned mainly minor offences such as motoring offences, minor drug offences, public insults, common assaults, affrays, regulatory offences, etc.[79]
(b) Mitigating factors related to the defendant such as: no prior criminal record, good character/law-abiding citizen, health reasons, the offender had already been punished (e.g. in a traffic accident, the responsible person had been seriously injured), remorse/apology, payment of the damages, difficult family circumstances and commission of the offence under enormous stress. E.g.:

> Case KJ: A case of threatening violence and carrying arms to terrorise – A 17 year old was the accused and his father was the victim. There was a withdrawal of the complaint, the apology of the accused and the fact that the accused was a first offender. Moreover, the offence was committed under enormous stress after a series of family problems caused by the father.

---

[76]Circular G.E. 74/72/7, dated 02/05/2001.

[77]In 2000, 46.4% of the requests were granted while 53.6% were rejected; in 2001, 44.7% were granted and 55.3% rejected. In my sample, 47% were granted and 53% were rejected.

[78]In many of these cases, it was clear that police wanted the discontinuance of the case even independently of the defendant's request.

[79]See Chap. 4 for a detailed catalogue of these cases.

(c) Withdrawal of the victim's complaint (which was usually accompanied by his unwillingness to testify in court after his reconciliation with the offender), mainly in cases concerning common assaults, affrays, negligent acts, etc.
(d) Misleading information or acts by the responsible authority or the later securing of a relevant licence: mainly for regulatory offences.
(e) Weakness of evidence.

The main reasons for requests being rejected were mainly:

(a) The seriousness of the offence.
(b) A repeated behaviour/prior record.
(c) A need for deterrence in particular categories of cases due to the increase of criminality concerning these offences.
(d) The inherent dangerousness of the offence, despite the actual consequences of the offence.
(e) The victim's wishes to proceed with prosecution.
(f) The fact that the trial was already at a late stage and a possible discontinuance would constitute intervention in courts' jurisdiction.
(g) There was a declared policy of the Attorney General on particular categories of cases[80] (e.g. motoring offences by juveniles, domestic violence offences, unlawful employment of immigrants).

6.4.6 Concluding Remarks

There are a number of general conclusions that can be drawn from the analysis of Law Officers' decisions in the above cases:

It was observed that Law Officers would make a genuine effort to adhere to the values of individualised justice which they advocated in the theoretical reflections of their decision-making. However, due to the pressures of their workload, this type of decision-making was not always possible for all categories of cases. When Law Officers had to make a choice, cases concerning indictable offences were their priority. For the rest, Law Officers appeared not to always have the same time and information needed for a detailed and reflective decision.

The rest of the cases that usually attracted more careful consideration than the others were cases for which there was a specific/explicit policy on them, cases for which the defence appeared particularly active in providing information, and cases that were subject to media exposition. More generally, all decisions concerning non-prosecution or a discontinuance of prosecution were regarded as exceptions (regardless of their number) and were more carefully approached (and more tightly controlled) than positive decisions for prosecutions.

[80] See the Attorney General's specific policies in Sect. 6.2.

The factors that were usually considered in prosecutorial decisions were broadly those that Law Officers referred to in their theoretical reflections (mitigating factors related to the defendants, the seriousness of the case, victim's wishes, availability of resources). What was noticeable was that specific and declared policies of the Attorney General regarding particular cases were almost without exception followed and were one of the most powerful reasons that the Law Office might disagree with police suggestions in specific cases. This would suggest that carefully drafted guidelines *do* make a difference on some occasions after all.

6.5 Summary

The Cyprus prosecution system appears to adhere to the *opportunity principle* and to the values of individualised justice through a small number of officials (in the Law Office), who are empowered to do justice in each case. It also seems to combine characteristics that are associated with both the legality and the opportunity-based systems.

The Constitution entrusts the Attorney General with a very *broad discretion* regarding prosecutions, while it ensures guarantees for his neutrality, independence and "ministry of justice" status. The formulation of the overall prosecution policy is considered as within his absolute jurisdiction *without any limitations* posed by statutory legislation (e.g. the publication of his policy) and without the sharing of this power with any other government department.

Successive Attorney Generals largely refrained from spelling out detailed criteria for their decision-making, although their general approach and their specific policies on certain categories of cases were publicly announced. They all emphasised the need for *flexible and responsible decision-making* by an independent official with *quasi-judicial status*, entrusted with the duty to take into account various considerations, all of which made up the *general public interest*. All the Attorney Generals argued that even if it was not always published, a certain approach to prosecutions had always existed and its consistent application in the Law Office was guaranteed by the small size of the office. Furthermore, due to their approach of regarding prosecutions as the rule and diversion from prosecutions as both the *exception* (regardless of how extensive use of this exception could be made) and the *exclusive responsibility* of the Law Office, a *central control* of the prosecutorial policy regarding all prosecutions was achieved.

Law Officers too, reflecting on their prosecution decisions, placed emphasis on the need for flexible and responsible decision-making and *individualised justice*. They did not ignore the ideal of consistency but they believed that by virtue of their independence, qualifications and *shared ethos*, they could be trusted to perceive the best solution to each prosecutorial dilemma even when they were not constrained by rigid written rules. The representation of public interest and the "*ministry of justice approach*" to prosecutions were recurring themes in the description of their role and prosecutorial decision-making.

More specifically, Law Officers appeared to be genuinely aware of the inherent *complexity* that prosecutorial decisions usually entailed and the vast variety of considerations that ought to be calculated each time. In their responses, they did not only refer to factors related to the defendant, the victim or the offence. They also referred to considerations related to the resources of the Office, the credibility and efficiency of the system, the reaction of the public, implications for other criminal justice agencies, etc. Their reflection on prosecutorial decision-making indicated a *sophisticated way of thinking*, which did not attempt to avoid "sensitive" dilemmas and conflicting interests in the process.

In practice, it was observed that Law Officers were trying to incorporate into their decision making the values of individualised justice that they advocated in theory (e.g. varied sources of information, continuous review of the cases). However, this type of decision-making was not always possible for all categories of cases, mainly due to their heavy workload. When they had to make a choice, cases concerning indictable offences were their priority. For the rest, Law Officers appeared to not always have the same time and information needed for a detailed and deliberate decision. Nevertheless, other cases that usually attracted more careful consideration, apart from the very serious cases, were those for which there was a specific/explicit policy, those for which the defence appeared particularly active in providing information, and those that were subject to media exposure. More generally, all the decisions that concerned a non-prosecution or a discontinuance of prosecution were regarded as exceptions and were more carefully approached and more tightly controlled than positive decisions for prosecutions.

Specific factors that were usually considered in prosecutorial decisions were: the seriousness of the case, mitigating factors related to the defendant, the victim's wishes, the availability of resources, specific and declared policies of the Attorney General regarding particular categories of cases, etc. As far as questions of evidence were concerned, once Law Officers had clarified that a *prima facie* case was established, on a secondary level, issues of reliability, credibility and availability of evidence were mixed with other public interest considerations in order to decide whether a case should be prosecuted:

> '(R)ules can be evaluated in a decision-theoretic way. A strongly rule-based environment is prone to those errors that will be made when a faithful and accurate application of the rules will poorly serve a rule's background justification. And a strongly discretionary environment is prone to the errors that will be made when decision-makers of limited judgment, limited experience, limited wisdom, or simply limited time directly apply background justifications, but apply them incorrectly. Thus, one type of error – the error that comes when rules are avoided – is the error of empowering poor decision-makers to exercise too much discretion. And the other type of error – the error that comes when rules are the dominant form of decision-making – is the error that is the consequence of hampering and constraining wise and experienced decision-makers by rigid rules'. (Schauer 2005, p. 7)

Chapter 7
Recapitulation and Conclusions

> 'The Attorney General is entrusted with the *ultimate responsibility* for, and *control* of, prosecutions'. (Tornaritis 1969, p. 2)

The objective of this book has been to explore the role of the Cyprus Attorney General's Office in prosecutions, an enterprise neglected so far on both the theoretical and the empirical level. In the preceding chapters the findings of my research have been set out, focusing on the workload of the Law Office and its relationship with the police, the role it acquires during investigations and its role in the formulation and application of prosecution policies and principles. In this concluding chapter, all the findings will be drawn together and further discussed, so that the role of the Attorney General's Office in prosecutions can be elucidated and more profoundly understood. Some preliminary observations on several potentially weak points in the system will be exposed and implications for further research and reform proposals will also be considered.

7.1 Law and Rhetoric

> 'If we are to make sense of this chaotic picture, we will have to look beyond official criminal justice rhetoric to the reality of criminal justice practice – whilst also recognising the sense in which the rhetoric is a part of the reality.' (Lacey 1994, p. 33)

The prime characteristics of the legal provisions regarding the Attorney General's role in prosecutions are their broad nature and the great latitude they afford to the post-holder in the specification and use of his powers. As was shown in Chaps. 3 and 4, the prosecution system in Cyprus is not prescribed or fully set out in any single document. It is grounded in the Constitution and in some sections of statute law, but many of its aspects are implied or left to the Attorney General to define. The rhetoric developed on prosecutions in Cyprus after 1960, is characterised by the affirmation on any given opportunity of the supremacy of the Attorney General

D. Kyprianou, *The Role of the Cyprus Attorney General's Office in Prosecutions: Rhetoric, Ideology and Practice*,
DOI 10.1007/978-3-642-01921-0_7, © Springer-Verlag Berlin Heidelberg 2010

over all the other actors involved in prosecutions which was never combined, however, with a profound appraisal of his exact role in the process.

7.1.1 The Law Office's Constitutional Position, Workload and Relationship with the Police

The Constitution, although preserving the right to private prosecution, and consequently the right of other agencies to prosecute, recognises the Attorney General as the head of the prosecution system who is entitled to intervene in, control and supervise any prosecution. Therefore, the Constitution does not give the monopoly of instituting criminal proceedings to the Attorney General; neither does it define his intervention in each and every prosecution as obligatory. It does declare, however, his right to exercise a retrospective control over all prosecutions through his potential intervention ("take over, continue, discontinue"), besides his right to institute his own proceedings ("institute").

It was observed in previous chapters that the rhetoric which has been developed over time has placed great emphasis on the symbolism and the potential of the power of the Attorney General rather than on the everyday execution of his prosecutorial function. The limited discussions on the role of the Attorney General focus upon the word "control" which signifies more oversight and accountability rather than minute direction. It is repeatedly asserted that "the Attorney General is entrusted with the ultimate responsibility for, and control of, prosecutions" (Tornaritis 1969, p. 2), but it is also repeatedly deduced that his direct involvement is not expected in every prosecution.

Therefore, apart from specific categories of cases for which the Law Office has acquired *exclusive* responsibility by statutory provisions (the Assize Court cases and the "consent prosecutions"), it is regarded as the Attorney General's absolute discretion to choose which other types of cases he wishes to deal with. Nevertheless, there is a general expectation by all actors in the system that certain categories of cases would always be included in the Law Office's workload: complex and "sensitive" cases, cases that concern constitutional or novel legal issues, cases that involve public officers or "important public persons", etc.

The police – as well as a number of other agencies – also have the right to institute criminal proceedings in the interests of law enforcement. However, Article 19 of the Police Law clearly states that the police discharge their functions regarding prosecutions under the superintendence of the Attorney General. Although there is some confusion in the discussions concerning the justification of the relationship between the police and the Law Office, as was discussed in detail in Chap. 4, it has been argued that it is on this special provision of Police Law that the more direct relationship between the police and the Law Office is based. Article 19 formally recognises the Attorney General as the *immediate* supervisor of the police and, therefore, entitled to exert *direct* control over police decisions regarding both individual cases and also matters of general policy. It consequently constitutes a further step that enables the Attorney General not only to confine himself to an ex posterior control or supervision of police decisions (permissible by the constitutional provisions) but also to give compulsory directions to the police and to control their everyday functions regarding prosecutions. It is based on this statutory provision that the Attorney General is entitled to order the police not to charge anyone, as well as the right to order them to do so contrary to their will.

7.1.2 The Attorney General's Role During Investigations

As was shown in Chap. 5, the specific provision of the Police Law (Cap. 285, Art. 19) and also the general constitutional relationship between the police and the Law Office, formally place the investigation of crimes by the former under the instructions of the latter. Therefore, the Attorney General is entrusted with a role in investigations on top of his other functions relating to prosecutions.

The law does not give the Attorney General – and, thus, the Law Officers – *direct* investigatory powers. As a result, the Law Officers themselves are not empowered to undertake any specific investigative actions such as interrogating witnesses and suspects or collecting any other evidence. However, they are empowered to intervene during investigations and/or require further information and to cause the investigation by the police of any matter they consider important.

Moreover, it has been demonstrated that the legal text does not make the Attorney General's intervention in investigations obligatory. It does not set out specific duties and responsibilities for the Law Office during the investigation period; neither does it associate the legality of the investigation with the authorisation or the final control of the Attorney General. What it does ensure, though, is the theoretical potential and power of the Attorney General to act in such a way if he chooses to do so.

Nevertheless, apart from the general position that places the police under the control of the Law Office during investigations, a series of legislative provisions has been gradually introduced which either confer on the Attorney General a *direct* investigatory power, or directly connect the legality of some investigations to the oversight and final control of the Law Office. These legislative provisions seek to ensure the *obligatory* (and not just discretionary) involvement of the Law Office in investigations, especially in areas where either coercive measures could be used or sensitive/complex issues may arise.

7.1.3 The Attorney General's Role in the Formulation of Prosecutorial Policies

It has been shown that the Cyprus prosecution system, given its common law origins, adheres to the opportunity principle. There has never been an unavoidable obligation placed by law on the prosecuting authorities to institute proceedings for all offences that come to their notice. Therefore, it is accepted that the prosecuting authorities enjoy a certain amount of discretion in deciding whether or not to institute criminal proceedings and, thus, to develop the policies by which this discretion is exercised.

The discussion about the Attorney General's role in the formulation of prosecutorial policies has been centered on two themes: the first is the extent of the discretion that is allowed to the Law Office to formulate its own policies regarding prosecutions, and the second is the role that the Law Office has to play in the formulation of the *overall* prosecution policy of the jurisdiction and, thus, the question of whether the Law Office is empowered to define the prosecution policies of the rest of the prosecuting authorities.

The Constitution entrusts the Attorney General with a broad discretion regarding his prosecutorial decisions, without imposing any terms or conditions on the execution of this power. Neither the Constitution nor statutory legislation oblige the Attorney General to declare publicly the principles upon which he acts in exercising his discretion in prosecuting; neither do they oblige him to give reasons for his decisions in particular instances. On the contrary, both judicially and extra-judicially, it has been recognised that because the powers of the Law Office are constitutionally upheld, they are absolute and cannot be compromised by common legislation.

Additionally, the Constitution grants to the Law Office an independent rather than a political status. The Attorney General is appointed, serves, and can only be removed under the same conditions as the Judges of the Supreme Court, and his Office is not subject to any Ministry. Therefore, in theory, he can formulate his prosecution policy totally independently of the Executive. Furthermore, the courts have on many occasions declared that the Attorney General's discretion is absolute and not reviewable.

Therefore, regarding the first aspect of the Attorney General's role under this section, it has been established by now that the Attorney General is considered as the official who is exclusively responsible for the formulation of the prosecution policy of the Law Office, without sharing power with any other government department such as the Ministry of Justice, or being constrained by statutory legislation.

Turning now to the second aspect of the Attorney General's role in this area: It has been extensively discussed in this book that the Attorney General's relationship with the police is not only limited to his constitutional obligations and powers to oversee and control all prosecutions. The Police Law (as well as similar provisions in Laws that give the right to prosecute to other Government Departments) clearly acknowledges that the police discharge their functions regarding prosecutions under the *superintendence* of the Attorney General. Based on this, it is accepted that the Attorney General could, if he wishes, define police prosecution policies. Consequently, the Attorney General's Office might not be obliged or appear ready to take the decision for prosecution in each and every case; nevertheless, as has been argued in this book, it appears to be the institution responsible (and the institution that possesses the power) for the formulation of the overall prosecutorial policy in the jurisdiction.

7.2 The Attorney Generals' Policies

> 'However much care is taken in the formulation of the powers associated with the respective offices, there is little doubt that the experience, standing and personalities of the people occupying these positions... have to be carefully assessed, if a realistic picture is to be gained of the day to day administration of justice'. (Edwards 1989, p. 101)

Given the very broad legal provisions and the great discretion that is afforded to the Attorney General to specify his powers regarding prosecutions, this study regarded as essential the need to examine how successive office-holders themselves have interpreted their role and chosen to utilise their broad discretion over time.

A general conclusion that can be drawn is that successive Attorney Generals have been comfortable with the broad nature of their role and the fact that they have acquired complete freedom of action to define and pursue their tasks. The impression is given that the mystique that surrounds the Law Office and the excessive latitude that characterises its powers have been regarded as essential in order to retain its symbolic role in the prosecution process. However, as time passed, a slight tendency can be observed – caused by the approach of particular office-holders – towards a greater specification of the role of the Law Office in prosecutions.

The second general conclusion that can be drawn is that the involvement of the Law Office in prosecutions has progressively become both more active and more extensive. This is again attributable to the choices of certain office-holders, as well as to a series of other reasons that advocated towards such an expansion.

7.2.1 Policies Regarding the Law Office's Workload and Relationship with the Police

As has been shown, the theory had always been that the Attorney General would be entitled to intervene in any case but enjoyed the discretion to choose the categories of cases that he wished to deal with. In the past, there was less expectation of the Attorney General to be involved in cases other than the most serious ones and there grew also a tendency by some office-holders to reserve their involvement for only the most exceptional cases. Over time, the involvement of the Law Office in various categories of cases became greater, and its control over the police became more effective. It has been argued in this book that the personality and the choices of each Attorney General constituted some of the most significant factors that shaped the Law Office's workload.

Mr Tornaritis placed emphasis on the *control function* of the Attorney General over the prosecution system rather than on the everyday involvement of his Office in every prosecution case. He underlined the symbolic role of the Attorney General in the system and his potential to intervene whenever necessary. The institution of criminal prosecutions on behalf of the Law Office – apart from the Assize Court cases – during that period was not very usual. Mr Tornaritis did not establish a proactive policy on the type of cases that the police were required to forward to the Law Office, nor did he set up procedures for systematic contacts with the police regarding the cases that they used to deal with. However, he did manage to impose his status as the ultimate prosecuting authority. It is interesting to note that, since that period, the police have regarded themselves as being part of a chain of command headed by the Attorney General in relation to prosecutions.

The passing of the Public Prosecutors Law 8/1989 marked the beginning of the tenure of Mr Triantafyllides as Attorney General. That Law, although full of uncertainties and not giving extra powers to the Law Office, appeared to signal a new era in the philosophy of the relationship between the police and the Law Office. It was the beginning of a closer relationship between them (during his tenure, the police sought his directions more frequently than before, and he intervened on many occasions in cases that did not belong to his regular "Assize Court" workload) and it provided the reaffirmation that the Attorney General was the undoubted supervisory authority. In spite of this, Mr Triantafyllides, like his predecessor, refrained from defining specific directions as to which cases he wished to deal with and from setting comprehensive requirements on the police to report specific cases. He strongly believed that interpersonal dynamics was the crucial factor that would enable him to exercise control over the police, and that classifying categories of cases or defining guidelines would somehow compromise his broad powers to deal with whatever he chose.

During Mr Markides' tenure at the office, his approach and the way he interpreted his role, together with a combination of other factors, advocated the extension of the Law Office's workload in terms of both the variety and the volume of cases that they were dealing with. Mr Markides followed a more structured approach to the workload of his Office, systematised his communication with the police, introducing a series of measures towards that direction and, for the first time, he defined in writing some specific categories of cases that the police should forward to the Law Office. These included offences for which he was of the opinion that particular attention was required or were "cases that might reveal important considerations of public policy". Nevertheless, he admitted that the involvement of the Law Office in every case was not possible, but he appeared confident that the theoretical potential of the Law Office to intervene influenced both the police to send problematic cases to the Law Office and also the victims/defendants to ask for the Law Office's intervention when necessary.

Mr Nikitas did not find it necessary to give explicit directions to the police or the public prosecutors concerning the cases that they should forward to the Law Office. He appeared more preoccupied with the establishment of solid principles on which cases should be decided rather than with which cases reached his Office. Although he appeared very strict and detailed regarding prosecution criteria, he did not seem to pay the same attention to which cases his Office was, and should be, dealing with.

Mr Nikitas argued that the Law Office's workload did not change significantly from that under his predecessor, but there are indications that his more general views on the criteria that should be applied in prosecution decisions influenced the workload of the Law Office.

7.2.2 Policies Regarding the Law Office's Investigatory Role

It has been demonstrated that the law in the majority of cases does not make the involvement of the Law Office in investigation obligatory. Once again, the extent and the way that these powers are used are left open to the Attorney General to define. This research revealed that the Law Office for many years hardly developed any *active* or at least publicly pronounced policy on investigations in practice. Successive Attorney Generals preferred to deal with cases on an *ad hoc* basis instead of formulating a deliberate and comprehensive policy regarding all investigations.

However, it appeared not to be unusual for all the Attorney Generals to direct the police to initiate investigations regarding particular incidents or request information regarding ongoing investigations. This mainly concerned cases that created media attention and publicity or cases of particular sensitivity or complexity that came to the attention of the Law Office. The impression that was given from the content of the correspondence between the police and the Attorney General was that the police had always regarded themselves – at least theoretically – as absolutely bound by an instruction from the Law Office, at least concerning those serious or high-profile cases. This generally cooperative relationship between the Law Office and the police may also be attributed to the fact that in general, apart from those special cases, the succeeding Attorney Generals did not appear to promote or declare a very interventionist policy towards the police investigative role.

Summarising the philosophy of all the Attorney Generals towards their role in investigation, it can be said that: (a) they all declared their theoretical potential to intervene in every stage of the investigations, but they were cautious not to claim that this was a regular job for their Office to be carried out on a systematic basis; (b) they talked more about legal advice rather than supervision of investigations apart from specific categories of cases ("sensitive cases", cases involving public figures, allegations against police officers) when they chose to use a more authoritative terminology; and (c) they clearly considered it as their duty to thoroughly examine the evidence and order further inquiries if required, during the stage that a case was forwarded to the Law Office for a prosecution decision to be taken.

7.2.3 Formulation of Prosecutorial Policies

All the Attorney Generals, with the exception of Mr Nikitas, strongly promoted their broad discretion in prosecution decisions. The official rhetoric used by all of them to articulate their prosecutorial discretion has placed emphasis on the quasi-judicial nature of their power and their independent status. In this way, they implied that a detailed specification of the criteria by which they exercise their discretion was not well suited to the judicial nature of their duties, nor was it essential, given their independent status. Furthermore, they praised the virtues of individualised justice and they emphasised the need for flexible and responsible decision-making by an independent official, entrusted with the duty to take into account various considerations that make up the general public interest.

This research revealed that successive Attorney Generals, for many years, had not developed a *comprehensive* and publicly pronounced policy which defined *a priori* how their prosecutorial discretion ought to be exercised. They largely refrained from spelling out detailed criteria for their decision-making (e.g. there has never been a prosecution code in Cyprus), although their general approach and their specific policies on certain categories of cases were publicly announced. However, over the years, and especially during Mr Markides' tenure, a more positive approach towards the formulation of more specific policies had been adopted without, however, extending to the level of formulating a comprehensive and detailed policy for all prosecutions. Nevertheless, all the Attorney Generals argued that, even if it was not always published, a certain approach to prosecutions always existed and its consistent application in the Law Office was guaranteed by the small size of the service.

It was evident that apart from the common characteristics observed relating to their prosecutorial discretion, each Attorney General adopted his own prosecution policy. The most striking difference in prosecution policies was observed between the approach of Mr Triantafyllides and that of Mr Nikitas. Mr Triantafyllides considered the power to discontinue or refrain from prosecutions on public interest reasons as a power that can be used *regularly* and not only on very rare occasions. He stressed, though, that this was a power exclusively exercised by the Attorney General himself. On the other hand, Mr Nikitas strongly believed that the Attorney General should not filter cases out of the system due to mitigating factors concerning the defendant, apart from on very extreme occasions. He argued that the public interest was served by sending cases to court and the Attorney General should not try to usurp courts' powers by diverting cases on a regular basis. In general, Mr Nikitas, contrary to all his predecessors, appeared to introduce an approach which advocated the restriction of the Attorney General's discretion.

As shown earlier, theoretically, the Attorney General is empowered to define the prosecution policy of the rest of the prosecuting authorities, especially the police who, according to the Police Law, discharge their functions regarding prosecutions under his *superintendence*. The question is whether and how successive Attorney Generals have realised this theoretical potential. All the Attorney Generals agreed that the harmonisation of police policies with the approach adopted by each Attorney General was achieved by (a) the close contact they had on an everyday basis with police prosecution authorities, (b) the notification to the police of any internal circulars issued in the Law Office, (c) the specification of certain categories of cases that should be forwarded to the Law Office so that the Law Office exclusively take prosecutorial decisions regarding them, and (d) the ex posterior review and overruling of police decisions, especially after requests by the defendants or the victims.

Nevertheless, the most important means by which the police prosecutorial policy was controlled had been the directive of all the Attorney Generals (which was, however, more forcefully applied by Mr Markides) according to which all cases that the police wished to filter out of the system ought to be forwarded to the Law Office. All the AGs regarded diversion from prosecutions as the *exclusive responsibility* of the Law Office (regardless of the approach that each office-holder adopted to the frequency with which cases could be diverted from courts). Therefore, they ensured a central control of any depositary actions, which admittedly are the most important prosecutorial decisions and, thus, a central control of the overall prosecutorial policy in the jurisdiction.

7.3 Ideology

A further objective of this research has been to uncover the ideology that characterises the Law Officers' approach to their prosecutorial role. In order to get a fuller picture of the role that the Law Office plays in prosecutions, it was considered important to gain an appreciation of Law Officers' own understanding and attitudes towards their functions which, presumably, also infuse and influence their practices.

7.3.1 The Law Officers' Approach to Their Workload and Relationship with the Police

As far as their attitude to the Law Office's workload was concerned, Law Officers declared categorically the ultimate responsibility of their Office to control and oversee all prosecutions in the jurisdiction. Although they theoretically accepted that the Law Office could also deal with minor cases, they considered the most serious cases as the core of the Law Office's workload. Regarding the rest of the cases, it was obvious from Law Officers' accounts that exceptional, complex or sensitive cases were regarded as "Law Office material", in contrast to ordinary or run-of-the-mill cases.

The rhetorical position that the Attorney General was also responsible for the cases which the police were dealing with was emphatically adopted by the Law Officers. However, the way they reflected on it (especially the justifications they offered for the Law Office–Police relationship) was characterised by the same contradictions as the rhetoric itself, and probably was a result of this.

Law Officers realised that they could not exercise everyday control in all "police" cases mainly due to resource issues and, therefore, they focused on their "control function" and their ability to intervene when necessary. Furthermore, they accepted that there was a considerable degree of flexibility regarding police reporting procedures, although the serving Attorney General (Mr Markides) was far more specific in his directions than his predecessors. They acknowledged that this allowed the police a wide discretion, but they appeared confident that if something really important needed their attention, there were sufficient mechanisms in place to find out.

7.3.2 The Law Officers' Approach to Their Role in Investigations

The Law Officers' approach to their role in investigations reflected the consistent policies that successive Attorney Generals had promoted over time. They regarded their involvement in investigations more as a *power* rather than a duty and, although they considered it as extremely beneficial, they acknowledged that due to their heavy workload it could not be particularly extensive. Therefore, it was inevitably limited to those cases that were complex or difficult, or those where police chose to ask for their advice.

They appeared to consider investigations as predominantly a police job and their role usually as complementary, providing essential legal knowledge in the investigative process. They talked more about legal advice rather than supervision of investigations, apart from specific categories of cases ("sensitive cases", cases involving public figures, allegations against police officers) when, like their superiors, they chose to use a more imposing terminology. In general, they emphasised the good cooperation and trust that ought to characterise their relations with the police so that police investigators were encouraged to seek their assistance when needed.

Law Officers appeared to separate the stages during which they could intervene in the main investigative stage before a complete file was formed, and the stage when a case was forwarded to the Law Office for a prosecution decision to be taken. At that latter stage, Law Officers appeared to consider it as their *duty* to thoroughly examine the evidence and order other lines of inquiry or further information, if that was required.

7.3.3 The Law Officers' Approach to Prosecutorial Discretion and Decision-making

Law Officers, reflecting on their prosecution decisions, placed emphasis on the need for flexible and responsible decision-making. Directly connected to their ideas on flexibility in decision-making was the fact that individualised justice was regarded by all Law Officers as the ideal that ought to be respected and aspired to, and ought to guide their prosecutorial decisions. Failure to measure up to this ideal was considered by most Law Officers as a compromise to what was regarded as *good prosecuting*.

Their approach to prosecutorial decision making did not ignore the ideal of consistency but they believed that by virtue of their independence, qualifications and *shared ethos*, they could be trusted to perceive the best solution to each prosecutorial dilemma, even when they were not constrained by rigid written rules. The representation of public interest and the "ministry of justice approach" to prosecutions were recurring themes in the description of their role and prosecutorial decision-making. The Attorney General as an independent official with a high status and guarantees of neutrality, entrusted by the Constitution to act in the public interest, was a powerful image within Law Officers' ideology and was reflected in the views of *their* status as well. Nevertheless, they all agreed that all of the crucial decisions in the Law Office were taken by the Attorney General himself and, therefore, the absence of a detailed set of guidelines was not a major shortcoming.

More specifically, Law Officers appeared to be genuinely aware of the inherent *complexity* that prosecutorial decisions usually entailed and the vast variety of considerations that ought to be addressed each time. When prompted, they were ready to offer a series of factors that they usually took into account when making prosecution decisions. They did not only refer to factors related to the defendant, the victim or the offence, but they also referred to considerations related to the resources of the Office, the credibility and efficiency of the system, the reaction of the public, implications for other criminal justice agencies, etc. Moreover, they recognised the need for a *continuous review* of their decisions as the cases proceeded. Their reflection on prosecutorial decision-making indicated a *sophisticated way of thinking*, which did not attempt to avoid taking into consideration "sensitive" dilemmas and conflicting interests in the process.

7.4 Practice

> '"practice" (is) a relatively structured field of action of agents or groups of agents, which can only be understood in terms of the assumptions, values, goals, and interpretive frames which inform the agents' actions and infuse the surrounding context in which those actions take place'. (Lacey 1994, p. 31)

The last objective of this research has been to explore the *practices* developed in the Law Office when discharging their prosecutorial functions and, thus, to provide a first insight into their actual day-to-day activity regarding prosecutions.

7.4.1 Workload of the Law Office

In practice, it was observed that the workload of the Attorney General's Office was incredibly diverse and multifarious. It included an interesting mixture of not only high-profile cases and complex and "sensitive" ones, but also minor and *prima facie* run-of-the-mill cases which used to reach the Law Office for a variety of reasons.

Apart from those that they were required by law to deal with (Assize Court and "consent" cases), the Law Office also dealt with categories of cases that the Attorney General had clearly specified *a priori* or chosen *ad hoc*, cases for which the police requested advice or directions, as well as cases for which other agents in the process – usually the defendants – asked for the Law Office's intervention, usually in order to overrule a police decision. Cases that the police wished to filter out of the system, mainly on public interest grounds, and those for which the entering of a *nolle prosequi* or discontinuance was requested were observed to constitute a very crucial part of the Law Office's workload.

As shown earlier, although the serving Attorney General had been more specific than his predecessors in defining categories of cases that ought to be forwarded to the Law Office, he had not fully utilised his powers. As a result, apart from specific categories of cases, the police were left to judge semi-autonomously what was important and problematic enough to be sent to the Law Office. However, the fact that there was a strong consensus on the matter of principle – namely that the Attorney General was the ultimate authority in prosecutions and had the authority to give directions regarding *all* prosecutions – appeared to inform the practices of all the actors in the system. Victims and defendants quite often used to request the Law Office's intervention in cases that did not regularly belong to their workload and the police practices appeared to be influenced by this theoretical potential.

7.4.2 The Law Office's Role in Investigation

In practice it was observed that there were three stages during which the Attorney General's Office could exert its powers regarding the investigation of, and the collection of information for, a case. The Attorney General could order the *initiation* of investigations; he could intervene *during* the conduct of investigations; and he could also order *further investigations* after the file of a case was forwarded to the Office for a decision to prosecute or not.

The Law Office used to order the instigation of investigations in cases of particularly serious crimes or crimes that created publicity. What usually caused the exercise of this Attorney General's power was the receipt of information that a certain incident had occurred and usually was not properly investigated by the police, or the media coverage of an event that contained allegations of a crime. Moreover, it was also observed that the Attorney General sometimes used to set priorities as to the initiation or the process of investigations of particular serious cases (usually when exceptional public outcry was present and speedy investigation was crucial).

During investigations, Law Officers used to provide extensive legal advice to the police, usually when the police sought such advice, but sometimes because Law Officers themselves judged that due to the sensitivity of a case, they ought to intervene. Regarding the latter cases, supervision and directions were far more comprehensive and there was a sense that Law Officers and the Attorney General himself were actually leading the investigation. Concerning the rest of the cases, there was no formal structure to facilitate the Law Office's involvement in police operations from the beginning. However, it was observed that there was a well-developed culture that was encouraging the police officers to seek the Attorney General's advice regularly. Police investigators usually asked for Law Officers' directions concerning disputed points of law, regarding the collection of evidence with special investigative techniques, and they used to seek Law Officers' assistance when wishing to obtain judicial authorisation for their activities.

During the stage that a file was forwarded to the Law Office for a prosecution decision to be made, Law Officers used to order further inquiries and additional evidence quite regularly. It is true that this approach was not adopted for all cases with the same vigilance. It is equally true that, very often, their directions for further investigations concerned only clarification of details or correction of internal inconsistencies which had for some reason been overlooked by the police. However, it was not rare for Law Officers to order new lines of inquiry in various cases or to challenge the "police construction of a case". That usually occurred when the defence provided them with alternative information or drew their attention to possible misuse of police powers and suspicious police practices.

7.4.3 Prosecutorial Decision-making Within the Law Office

In practice, it was observed that Law Officers used to make a genuine effort to adhere to the values of individualised justice which they advocated in the theoretical reflections of their decision-making (e.g. varied sources of information, continuous review of the cases). Due to the pressures of their workload, however, this type of decision-making was not adopted for all categories of cases with the same vigilance. Cases concerning indictable offences appeared to be the Law Office's priority. For the rest, Law Officers were observed not to have always the same time and information needed for a detailed and deliberate decision.

Other cases that usually attracted more careful consideration, apart from the very serious cases, were those regarding which the Attorney General adopted a specific policy, those where the defence appeared particularly active in providing information, and those that were subject to media exposure. More generally, all decisions concerning non-prosecution or a discontinuance of prosecution were regarded as exceptions and were more carefully approached and more tightly controlled than positive decisions for prosecutions.

The factors that were usually considered in prosecutorial decisions were broadly those that Law Officers referred to in their theoretical reflections: mitigating factors related to the defendants, the seriousness of the case, the victim's wishes, the availability of resources, etc. What was noticeable was that the Attorney General's specific and declared policies regarding particular cases were almost without exception followed and were one of the most powerful reasons why the Law Office might disagree with the police suggestions in specific cases. Based on that, it could be assumed that carefully drafted guidelines *did* make a difference, on some occasions, after all. As far as questions of evidence were concerned, once Law Officers had clarified that a *prima* facie case was established, on a secondary level, issues of reliability, credibility and availability of evidence were mixed with other public interest considerations in order to decide whether a case ought to be prosecuted.

7.5 Choices of the Cyprus Prosecution System and Functions of the Attorney General's Office

As shown in Chap. 2, the main questions that have troubled most prosecution systems over time centred on three crucial dichotomies:

(a) Systematic v. Unsystematic approach to prosecutions
(b) Prosecutors' power to direct investigations v. Complete separation of the investigative and the prosecutorial stages
(c) Legality v. Expediency principle

The choices that prosecution systems have adopted regarding these issues have traditionally and at large defined their characterisation as adversarial or inquisitorial systems. However, as was also demonstrated, these dichotomies have progressively eroded not only in practice but also in the legislations providing for prosecutorial arrangements. Nevertheless, even today, certain existing characteristics of prosecution systems can be traced back to their different origins and convey their different philosophies. In this section, in the light of the aforementioned findings of my research, the answers that the Cyprus prosecution system has provided for these questions will be briefly exposed, highlighting the special position that the Attorney General's Office occupies in them.

Cyprus prosecutorial arrangements make up a system which reflects the influence of the English legal model during its early development, but one which has been refined according to local needs and has also incorporated numerous characteristics associated with the inquisitorial rather than the adversarial tradition. This system seems to represent a compromise between common law's traditional unsystematic approach to prosecutions and the continental European tradition which requires prosecutions in general to be structured and controlled by an independent public official responsible for all of them. On the one hand, it retains the right to private prosecutions and, consequently, the right of various other agencies – most crucially the police – to carry out a significant number of prosecutions, according to the original common law tradition. On the other hand, however, it entrusts to an independent, quasi-judicial official (the Attorney General) the ultimate responsibility for, and control of, all prosecutions, in line with the continental tradition, besides giving him the monopoly of the most serious prosecutions; and it places the police under the superintendence and immediate directions of the Law Office, denying them the complete independence that they used to enjoy in common law jurisdictions.

In common law jurisdictions, investigations have been traditionally regarded as the preserve of the police, contrary to the pure continental tradition which has placed prosecutors in charge of the investigative as well as the post-investigative stages. In Cyprus, the Attorney General is empowered to intervene in investigations, like his counterparts in inquisitorial jurisdictions. In spite of this, his intervention is nor obligatory, nor does his authorisation or final control constitute a prerequisite for the legality of the investigations. In theory, as well as in practice, the Law Office's involvement in investigations is not regarded as an everyday activity, which would substitute the role of the police, but as a complementary function and, more importantly, as a theoretical potential that allows for the overall control of police actions during the investigative stage.

As far as prosecutorial discretion is concerned, the Cyprus prosecution system, again, seems to combine characteristics that are associated with both the legality and the opportunity-based systems. The Constitution entrusts the Attorney General with a very *broad discretion* regarding prosecutions (following the opportunity principle), while it guarantees his neutrality, independence and *quasi-judicial* status (following the continental tradition). Furthermore, this unlimited discretion only refers to a small number of officials in the Law Office. Due to the Attorney Generals' policy to regard prosecutions as the rule and diversion from prosecutions as both the *exception* (regardless of how extensive use of this exception could be made) and the *exclusive responsibility* of the Law Office, a *central and strict control* of non-prosecution decisions is achieved (contrary to the situation in common law jurisdictions, where most non-prosecution decisions are still made by a relatively large number of police officers and, thus, are difficult to control).

In light of the above remarks, combined with the findings of my research, it can be said that the main functions that the Law Office has been observed to fulfil within the Cyprus prosecution system appear to be as follows:

(a) *Prosecution of serious crime and exceptional cases*
The Law Office is the *exclusively* responsible service for dealing with the prosecution of the most serious cases, together with those that are regarded as exceptional, complex, sensitive or in need for particular attention by the serving Attorney General.

(b) *Control and oversight of all prosecutions in the jurisdiction*
The Attorney General serves as the head of the prosecution system and exercises overall control and supervision of all prosecutions carried out in the jurisdiction, even when he is not closely and systematically dealing with all of them. These powers, and also the theoretical potential to intervene dynamically in the bulk of criminal prosecutions, form very crucial aspects of his role and appear to influence the practices of all prosecuting agencies (especially the police) in the system.

(c) *Formulation of prosecutorial policies – Central control of diversionary decisions*
The Attorney General determines and formulates the prosecution policy of his Office, as well as the overall prosecution policy in the jurisdiction. Furthermore, he provides a central and relatively tight control of all diversionary decisions.

(d) *Ultimate control of the investigative stage*
The Attorney General orders the initiation of investigations in serious cases, when the police fail to act appropriately, and offers valuable legal advice to the police during investigations. By ordering further inquiries and taking into account alternative information, usually provided by the defence, he provides an obstacle to the absolute control of the investigative stage by the police and enhances confidence in the integrity of investigations.

(e) *Review forum*
One of the most crucial functions that the Law Office appears to perform is that it serves as a forum of appeal where all prosecutorial actions (or inaction) of other prosecuting agencies in the system can be reviewed. The public ask for the Law Office's intervention when investigations are not carried out properly, or are not carried out at all; they require the Law Office's intervention in cases that usually do not belong to its workload, when they judge that they are not being handled properly by the police; and they apply for a review or overturn of police prosecutorial decisions.

In addition to the aforementioned functions that the Law Office carries out, there are at least a couple of others that it could theoretically serve, but appears reluctant to do so. These are (a) the systematic involvement in, and handling of, all prosecutions, and (b) the regular intervention in all investigations. This book has demonstrated that the rhetoric regarding the Attorney General's role in prosecutions, combined with the choices of successive office-holders, as well as structural and attitudinal factors within the Law Office, advocate against this approach.

7.6 Critique and Implications for Further Research and Reform Proposals

> 'Is it possible to make prescriptions about a practice unless we understand how it works? Are our explanatory interpretations of criminal justice practices really untainted by our normative commitments?' (Lacey 1994, p. 24)

The purpose of this book has been to develop our knowledge and understanding of the role of the Attorney General's Office in prosecutions. This study did not set out to criticise this role or to compare it to an ideal model; neither did it aim to propose reforms to the current system. It is believed that there are two prerequisites that should be fulfilled *prior* to an attempt to criticise a given phenomenon and provide proposals for possible reforms: (a) the existing situation should be explored and profoundly understood, and (b) normative questions about "how the situation ought to be" should be extensively discussed and answered.[1]

[1] See Lacey (1992, pp. 380–388).

My research has aimed to offer insight into the first of these issues. Obviously, more empirical studies on decision-making within the Law Office would be useful. Furthermore, studies on the role that Law Officers play at the trial stage[2] and specific research on the role of other agencies in prosecutions are also required. However, apart from these, it is equally important to reflect on questions concerning the *appropriate* role for the Attorney General in prosecutions, and the *justified* criteria and principles upon which he should carry out this role; an enterprise that this research only indirectly has touched upon. Nevertheless, Lacey (1994) maintains that these two broad research approaches inevitably interact with each other. Normative reflection about the proper role of prosecution agencies provides the lenses through which the current situation is viewed and, conversely, more descriptive or empirical research approaches inform the theoretical discussion of the appropriate role and functions of a prosecuting agency and throw light on possible difficulties in realising this role.

It is only in this context that some observations on several potentially weak points regarding the current role of the Attorney General's Office in prosecutions will be exposed here. They can only serve as preliminary remarks in a future discussion about possible reforms of the system:

(a) The Attorney General in Cyprus enjoys a very broad discretion in the specification and use of his powers regarding prosecutions. Although there are important guarantees for his independence and objectivity, and this research indicated a high level of trust with which the Law Office is surrounded, these are very wide powers to be left to a single person to define and an enormous discretion to be left without any form of control.

(b) The Law Office appears to adopt a very reserved attitude towards openness and accountability. Some office-holders in the past have taken the view that their independence and quasi-judicial status are best safeguarded by maintaining a certain mystique relating to the execution of their powers. However, the Law Office performs one of the key functions of the state and, especially in the absence of any other forms of control (judicial or legislative), openness and transparency in the execution of its role ensures a form of accountability and a greater understanding by the public of the Law Office's functions. Although, lately, there have been positive steps towards the publication of the Law Office's prosecutorial policies, there are still further steps to be taken in this direction.

(c) Related to the above point is the following remark: It has been observed that the representation of the public interest is a core aspect of the Attorney General's role and one that largely justifies his wide powers and responsibilities. It is emphasised that the Attorney General is the only responsible official to define the public interest in prosecutions, balancing in each case the different interests at stake. However, Sanders (1988a, p. 40) points out that "even the

[2] This research has focused on the pre-trial stage of prosecutions and considered the role of the Law Office during the trial stage only indirectly.

existence let alone the content of one universal 'public interest' is far from self evident. If any concept of public interest is to have legitimacy, it must be based on specific, clearly articulated and publicly debated values".

(d) The formulation of guidelines, even within the Law Office, has been regarded for years as unnecessary. The fact that the Attorney General's Office has traditionally been a small Office and the number of Officers dealing with prosecutions a limited one has cultivated firstly the idea of a "shared ethos" within the Law Office and secondly the assumption that all crucial decisions are taken by the Attorney General himself. It is true that, as Schauer (2005, p. 9) remarks, "when there is widespread agreement among decision-makers, and when decision-makers have the same values and the same background and the same skills, discretion is likely to seem most desirable".[3] However, although generally Law Officers appeared to hold similar views on the crucial issues of prosecutions, and a relatively tight control of important decisions by the Attorney General was indeed observed within the Law Office, there were indications that this was starting to change as the workload of criminal cases was increasing and the Law Office was expanding. The words of a Senior Law Officer are illuminating:

> 'We used to be a very small and tight team . . . 15 years ago, the news that a new counsel was appointed to the office was big news. The Attorney General would introduce him to the rest of us one by one . . . Nowadays, the Office is expanding dangerously . . . We will reach a point where we will not know each other'. (Senior Law Officer 14)

(e) Successive Attorney Generals have always feared that the specification of their powers would result in their restriction. That is why, with the exception of Mr Markides, they largely refrained from specifying the categories of cases that they would deal with, and from setting specific prosecution policies. This research has demonstrated that this fear is false. On the contrary, where predetermined categories of cases were set, the Law Office's role in prosecutions appeared more active and its intervention became more systematic. Furthermore, it was observed that where specific policies were in place, instead of limiting Law Officers' discretion, they formed one of the most powerful factors in not unquestioningly endorsing other agencies' decisions. Therefore, this indicates that what successive Attorney Generals feared as limiting their powers could instead result in the potential for an even more proactive and wider role in the prosecution process. Related to this is the assumption that the need to formulate guidelines may be an incentive to successive Attorney Generals to think more thoroughly and critically about the objectives to be attained and the policies to be followed regarding prosecutions.

[3] Schauer (2005, p. 9) continues "And that is perhaps why the common law, a far more discretionary approach to legal decision-making than the civil law, arose at a time when it was widely believed that English judges, by virtue of their training and background, could be trusted to perceive the best solution to a legal problem even when they were not constrained by rigid written rules".

(f) Finally, the Attorney General's Office, as explained in Chap. 3, functions both as the Legal Service of the Government as well as the Office of Public Prosecutions. Consequently, its workload apart from responsibilities concerning the criminal prosecutions also includes a considerable and diverse body of other duties. All post-holders have admitted that this inevitably exerts some influence on the volume of criminal cases that the Law Office can deal with. Therefore, the creation of a separate service responsible for prosecutions or the reorganisation of the Attorney General's Office are some issues that should not be excluded from discussions about possible reforms of the system.

7.7 Concluding Remarks

The central purpose of this book has been to provide a more profound understanding of the role of the Cyprus Attorney General's Office in prosecutions, an undertaking lamentably neglected so far. On a more general level, though, it is hoped that this study has also shed light on the choices of the Cyprus prosecution system in some of the most debatable issues regarding prosecutions in many jurisdictions. Questions concerning the desirability of prosecutors and police having a more clearly hierarchical constitutional relationship; the giving of direct investigatory functions to prosecutors; the retention by the police of the power to filter cases out of the system without any control from the prosecuting authorities; and the institution responsible for formulating the prosecution policy in the jurisdiction have constituted the most controversial topics of discussion among academics and practitioners and are still included in the reform agenda of various commissions. The choices of the Cyprus prosecution system – a system initially based on the original British model which, however, has developed and been modified through time – have been exposed, always in the light of the pivotal position that the Law Office occupies in them.

This research has demonstrated that, in Cyprus, the Attorney General's role in prosecutions is impressively wide and multifarious. There are enough indications that it will, most probably, be further extended in the future. The examples of other jurisdictions show a growing role for prosecutors who are called to deal with new challenges in the criminal justice system. Moreover, in Cyprus, recently enacted legislative provisions add new duties to the already broad powers and responsibilities of the Law Office.[4] Therefore, a wide scale appraisal of the Attorney General's role, combined with an empirically informed reflection on his appropriate functions in the system, is more urgent than ever. It is hoped that this research has provided the foundation for such a discussion, as it has offered an

[4]See, for example, in Chap. 5, the various Laws that provide for his obligatory intervention in investigations.

insight into the rhetoric, ideology and practices involved regarding the role of the Attorney General's Office in prosecutions. Moreover, since it constitutes the first research study being carried out in the previously closed environment of the Law Office, it is anticipated that it may open some windows for further research on this topic.

Appendix 1
Research Strategies and Methodology

> 'The importance of the methodology is that it provides a sense of vision, where it is that the analyst wants to go with the research. The techniques and procedures (method), on the other hand, furnish the means for bringing that vision into reality ... Just as painters need both techniques and visions to bring their novel images to life on canvas, analysts need techniques to help them see beyond the ordinary and to arrive at new understandings of social life'. (Strauss and Corbin 1998, p. 8)

In this chapter the *vision* of my research and the *means* by which I brought it about will be detailed. This research on the role of the Attorney General's Office in prosecutions has been an *exploratory* study which drew on data gathered using a variety of mainly *qualitative* methods. The influences on the choice of my research strategies and the specific methodology will be explained in the *first part* of this chapter, followed by an explanation of the necessity of two broad research strategies. In the *second part*, my first research strategy (fieldwork in the AG's Office) will be developed starting from the description of the process of negotiating access to the AG's Office and the pre-fieldwork period I spent there; these will be followed by an account of the three different techniques of data collection (observation, documentary survey and semi-structured interviews) I employed. In the *third part*, my second research strategy including a documentary analysis of internal circulars, press releases, memoranda, etc., issued by the succeeding AGs, as well as interviews with the AGs themselves, will be presented followed by the development of an argument about the reliability and validity of the research and the approach I adopted for the data analysis (*fourth part*).

Research Strategies

Exploratory Research

Stebbins (2001, p. 6) argues that researchers who want to explore effectively a given phenomenon for which they have little or no scientific knowledge "must approach it with two special orientations: flexibility in looking for data and open-mindedness about where to find them". In the case of my research, the lack of any prior scientific knowledge or research, which would provide some information or suggest theories about the role of the Attorney General's Office in prosecutions, dictated the choice of an *exploratory study* instead of a theory-testing strategy and a *flexible methodology*. In Cyprus there is not a single *empirical* study about the criminal prosecution system (or aspects of it) and only a handful of studies on other areas of the criminal justice system in general.[1] *Theoretical* studies about criminal justice issues have also been very limited and most of them are confined to the mere description of legal provisions or the review of the case law.[2] More specifically, there is no definitive work on the structure of the Cyprus criminal prosecution process and the system has not been the subject of a detailed and systematic review by any state agency. The only relatively comprehensive description of the various functions of the Attorney General's Office dates back to 1974.[3]

The dearth of any theoretical or empirical work on criminal prosecutions is largely the reflection of the limited legal or socio-legal research of any kind in Cyprus. The greatest volume of research in other countries emanates from academe. The absence of a Law School at the University of Cyprus for many years has imposed obvious difficulties to academic research.[4] In addition to that, the tendency of practitioners to rely on English, and increasingly also on Greek, French and American textbooks or Law Reviews for their everyday practice derived from their educational background, discourages any studies focused exclusively on the Cyprus System, which could reveal the singularities or any special features of the System.

Qualitative Study: Influences on the Choice of Study

The Research Question

Strauss and Corbin (1998, p. 36) observe that "some problem areas clearly suggest one form of research, over another . . .; an investigator should be true to the problem at hand". The research question to a large degree determines the most appropriate method. The purpose of this research was to explore the role of the Attorney General's Office in the Cyprus prosecution system. As much mystery surrounded this area, the idea was to contribute insight and understanding of the constitutional position of the Law Office, its workload and the functions it is called to fulfil.

Other research studies about prosecution arrangements in organisations such as the DPP's Office and the CPS, as well as studies about prosecution systems in

[1] See Kapardis (1983, 2002) and Ministry of Justice and Public Order, Republic of Cyprus (2004).

[2] Most of these articles are published in the Cyprus Law Review and in the Cyprus Law Tribune.

[3] Loucaides (1974) "The Office of the Attorney General of the Republic of Cyprus".

[4] A Law Department has been recently established at the University of Cyprus.

general,[5] have demonstrated the advantages of more *qualitative* approaches in order to fully understand the complex interaction of formal and informal influences, organisational constraints, shared ideologies and procedural requirements involved in the operation of a prosecution agency (as indeed in any criminal justice agency).[6] The questions that such studies seek to answer are not amenable to any rigidly structured methods preferred by a quantitative approach; rather they demand the richness and the wealth of information of data generated by more intensive research methods.

Furthermore, a qualitative approach for my methodology was better suited to the exploratory design of this research. There is a widespread tendency to view quantitative research as being suited to the confirmation and rejection of theoretical prepositions and hypothesis. By contrast, qualitative research is depicted as placing emphasis on the discovery of the novel and unfamiliar, which its more unstructured approach to data gathering deemed to facilitate (Bryman 1984). This connection of quantitative/qualitative with confirmation/discovery should not be read as a hard and fast principle.[7] However, it is widely accepted that the constant interchange between theory and data, the "discovery-based" approach in which "there is a development, refinement and perhaps even reformulation of research ideas in accordance with what is discovered as fieldwork continues" (Jupp 1989, p. 58), is a methodological characteristic more closely associated with the ethnographic tradition.

The Research Perspective

Whilst the choice of method is primarily determined by the research question, it also involves some more general assumptions about the nature of the social world being studied. It has been advocated that research techniques are of high theoretical relevance, and can no longer be viewed as "atheoretical tools". The research methods represent lines of action taken towards the empirical world, while each theory demands and produces a special view of the research act (Denzin 1978). It is, therefore, admitted that the sociological approach informing this research project influenced, the selection of the methodology, at least to some extent.

Positivism or naturalism could not represent the theoretical standpoint for my research enterprise. Positivism assumes that methods of natural sciences could and should be unproblematically applied to the social world and that human behaviour should be studied within a deterministic framework. However, social sciences are not the same as natural sciences, essentially because their subjects are human beings who can attribute meanings to the situations in which they are placed,

[5] See *inter alia* Mansfield and Peay (1987), McConville et al. (1991), Fionda (1995) and Hodgson (2005).

[6] See Lacey (1994).

[7] As Bryman (1988) himself argues elsewhere.

and may therefore react to and possibly alter those situations.[8] Hammersley and Atkinson (1995) point out that both positivism and naturalism neglect social research's fundamental reflexivity: the fact that we are part of the social world we study, and there is no escape from reliance on common sense knowledge and methods of investigation.

By contrast, closer to my assumption about the nature of social reality is the view that the social world should be seen "as something which is continuously under social construction via social interactions by the participants themselves rather than as some external, objective and ill-constraining reality ..." (Jupp 1989, p. 29). According to this paradigm, it is important to gain access to the "actors' viewpoint", as well as to the structures within which they operate, in order to understand the way in which the criminal justice system is constructed. However, I do not agree that this is sufficient. It is also important not to neglect the analysis about the legal status of the criminal justice agencies that are studied, their formal powers and the rhetoric that is being developed about their legitimacy and operation. I agree with Lacey (1994) that research on criminal justice agencies have to take into account all of these factors since rhetoric (alongside a number of other things) forms a part of the reality.

Two Broad Research Studies

This conveniently brings me to the reasons I decided to integrate two research strategies for my research. As stated earlier, this study sought to explore the role of the Attorney General's Office in prosecutions. Originally, it was intended to provide an "in-depth" description of the working of the Law Office as far as prosecutions are concerned and penetrate the operational philosophy of an agency which much mystery surrounds. In order to achieve this, it was judged essential to attempt to get behind the public life of the Law Office and perhaps reveal a rich and "concealed underlife" (Bryman 1989, p. 142). It was, therefore, inevitable to immerse myself fully in the process of prosecution and the everyday life of the Office, as access to organisational culture cannot be obtained through methods employed at a distance.[9] Consequently, it was decided to conduct a fieldwork period in the Law Office including a variety of methods.

However, during the pre-fieldwork period, I realised that the exploration of the current situation in the Law Office mainly by an ethnographic approach could only give a partial and incomplete picture of the role of the Law Office in prosecutions. A study of the rhetoric that has been developed over time regarding the functions of the Law Office was also essential, since legal provisions in this area have remained limited and vague over the years and sometimes caused contradictory

[8] See Bottoms (2000) and Giddens (1984).

[9] See Crompton and Jones (1988).

interpretations. Furthermore, these broad statutory provisions, as mentioned before, allowed the holders of the Office a particularly extended discretion in defining their role in the system. Therefore, since that much appeared to depend on the particular office-holders, I thought that it would be very interesting to explore how successive Attorney Generals approach their role. That would place my research also into a historical context and, consequently, make it possible to uncover and understand how the role of the Law Office has been formed, developed and possibly modified over time. Therefore, I decided to employ an additional research strategy which would respond to this additional objective of my study. That entailed a documentary analysis of internal circulars, press releases and documents that successive Attorney Generals who have served office since the establishment of the Cyprus Republic (1960) had issued. Additionally, it was supplemented by interviews carried out with three of those post-holders.[10]

First Research Strategy: The Fieldwork Study in the Attorney General's Office

Gaining Access

The Access Problem

Any kind of social research involves gaining access to data. It is not unusual to experience difficulties negotiating access to any research setting, but seeking access to an organisation may be particularly problematic: "A research project is an intrusion into the life of the institution to be studied. Research is a disturbance, and it disturbs routines, with no perceptible immediate or long-term pay off for the institutions and its members" (Flick 1998, p. 57). Researchers recall how tiresome it can be to negotiate access[11] and they report that this process takes time, months or in some cases years. Furthermore, they point out that "the researcher is dependent on the goodwill of organisation 'gatekeepers'. This dependency creates risks that are beyond the control of the researcher and which are difficult to predict or avoid" (Buchanan et al. 1988, p. 56). Therefore, they warn that from the very beginning, the research timetable must take into account the possibility that access may not be automatic and instant, but take time-consuming meetings and correspondence to achieve.

If gaining access generally in organisations is characterised as difficult, the same enterprise in relation to criminal justice agencies, most of the time, faces

[10]Mr Triantafyllides, Mr Markides and Mr Nikitas.

[11]E.g. see Baldwin (2000).

insurmountable obstacles. Certain features of them ensure that the difficulties in their case are particularly highlighted. As Jupp (1989) reports, the peculiarities of research on criminal justice derive from a number of facts: the "sensitive" nature of this area, the criticism levelled very often against the government for its policies,[12] the fact that on certain occasions information that researchers might wish to uncover is meant to be kept secret by gatekeepers, and the actuality that some areas of the system (e.g. prisons) are formally closed.

Negotiating Access

Having all the above in mind and being fully conscious of the obstacles that my undertaking might encounter, I decided to ask permission for conducting research at the Attorney General's Office.

Researchers differ in their opinions about the level within the organisation at which access should be sought. Crompton and Jones (1988) advocate that it is desirable to start negotiations at the top of the organisation. They argue that trying to secure access through a lower level may mean that much time is spent in negotiations only to be turned down at the last minute by those with the ultimate authority for such decisions.[13] In my case, I thought that it was more secure and less time consuming to ask permission directly from the head of the Office.

Having been informed that the Attorney General himself had a particularly heavy schedule during that period, initially I asked for a meeting with the Deputy Attorney General. Rather than "going on cold", I chose a more secure way by using as a contact a family friend who had worked in the past with him.[14] This first meeting could have been characterised as "exploratory" as I was aiming to explore the general possibility of conducting a study in the Law Office and assess the degree of the cooperation I could expect. Given the fact that no other empirical research had been carried out before in the Law Office, I was not sure how such a proposal would appear and be considered by those in charge of the Office. During that first meeting, I explained to the Deputy Attorney General my original research proposal and objectives in general terms. Subsequently, I asked permission to spend initially a period of time at the Law Office in order to test the general feasibility of carrying

[12]These policies, as Jupp (1989, p. 130) remarks, are inevitably underpinned by important political viewpoints about which there is often considerable dispute: "It is not surprising, therefore, that those who formulate such policies and those who activate them are sensitive to and often hostile towards those who appear to be questioning or undermining such policies and practices".

[13]However, other researchers (e.g. Buchanan et al. 1988) express some reservations about such a strategy, supporting that it is sometimes more advantageous to seek access through lower levels. It should be noted, though, that knowing who has the power to open up or block off access is not always straightforward and sometimes it becomes itself an important aspect of sociological knowledge about the organisation (Hammersley and Atkinson 1995).

[14]The use of friends, family and academic contacts is mentioned as a useful asset by a number of authors drawing on their own experience in negotiating access for research; see, e.g. Van Maanem and Kolb (1985) and Bryman (1988).

a study along the lines proposed and make the necessary modifications, as well as collect relevant material and information needed for the final research plan of my main fieldwork. To my surprise, he appeared enthusiastic with the idea and straight away granted me the permission I asked for, adopting an attitude which implied that "they had nothing to hide and they were willing to help".

After that meeting, I carried out several visits at the Office, during which I had discussions with key-personnel, collected some relevant documents and observed the actual workload of the Law Office. During that period, I also spent some time at two Police Prosecution Departments in order to get some initial information about their cooperation and dealings with the Law Office. After that, I had another meeting with the Deputy Attorney General to inform him about my final decision (if allowed) to carry out my research at the Law Office. I asked an official permission by a formal letter which was accompanied by a more detailed research proposal. He immediately replied that he was happy to allow me access to the Law Office and offered me any help they could reasonably give "without disturbing the proper everyday functioning of the Office". He finally, kindly asked me to provide him with a draft of my book or a report after the completion of my research, as "it would be valuable for the Office".

What surprised me more was that I was not asked to sign any research undertakings. The assurance of protecting confidentiality and guaranteeing anonymity in the formal letter by which I asked access was apparently sufficient for them. However, in order to be on the safe side and avoid problems subsequently, I thought that it would be wise to emphasise the fact that the results of my research would probably be published, not necessarily only in my thesis. That statement did not seem to alarm the Deputy Attorney General.

My explanation for this rather generous "treatment" was that more important than the fact that I was introduced by my contact as "a person who can be trusted", I was perceived to be a student who presented no danger. In addition to that, the lack of any tradition of similar empirical studies at the Law Office or any other criminal justice agency, at this stage, turned out to be an advantage. At least, it saved me from long hours of negotiation about the technicalities of a research undertaking.

However, I was fully aware that formal access is not something which can be taken for granted after it has been given, neither problems of access cease when entry has been established. Jupp (1989, p. 149) warns that "this continuous process of negotiating access does not end when one has successfully bypassed all those who have some formal power to prevent the research taking place. Arrival at the sources of data provides no guarantee that research work can begin".

Accessing a setting is far more than the granting or withholding of permission by the "gate keepers". It is widely acknowledged by researchers that another negotiation begins once you enter the field. The researchers need to capture the cooperation of the members of the organisation with whom they will have the most immediate contact: "Once research access to an organisation has been negotiated successfully, it then becomes necessary constantly to renegotiate access to the lives and experiences of the individual members of that organisation. "Getting on" with respondents is fundamental to the quantity and quality of data collected"

(Buchanan et al. 1988, p. 58). This point conveniently brings me to the value of the preparatory period of the research not only for building up rapport but also for a number of other issues.

Preparatory Period

> 'Until we enter the field, we do not know what questions to ask or how to ask them. In other words, the preconceived image we have of the settings and people we intend to study may be naïve, misleading, or downright false'. (Taylor and Bogdan 1998, p. 25)

It has been advocated, that in exploratory research the best move is "to get your feet wet", enter the field, gaining some intimacy with the situation and then decide on your specific research methods. Until you are actually engaged in the study, you can not be sure which of the lines you have in mind will be most fruitful (Taylor and Bogdan 1998). This made me realise the need for a preparatory period in order to facilitate the selection of the most suitable methods of data collection. This initial period proved to be of extreme value also in a number of other ways. Before describing how it assisted me in constructing my specific methodology, I will detail some other aspects of fieldwork it made me recognise and obstacles it helped me overcome.

Entering the Field: Establishing Rapport

The first days of the fieldwork were definitely the most difficult ones. Having a legal educational background and relevant working experience, a criminal justice agency did not seem a completely unfamiliar environment to me. Entering the field I might not have experienced a "cultural shock", as other researchers recall from their fieldwork; however, I was definitely preoccupied with the same silly-sounding but very "stressful questions": "who looks too busy to talk to me? Where can I sit without being in the way? Can I walk around? What can I do to avoid sticking out like a sore thumb? Who looks approachable?" (Taylor and Bogdan 1998, p. 45).

During the very first days, collecting data appeared to be secondary to getting to know the setting and the people. I discovered that just wandering around the corridors of the Office, the library, even the photocopy rooms brought with it numerous opportunities to be introduced to people, explaining why I was there, listen to informative conversations and slowly but steadily become a familiar figure in the Office.

During this period, I realised that the decisive battle of real access in the organisation was not fought at the top (that one, as I explained earlier, was not really a battle) but at the lower level of each Law Officer. I understood, early enough, that the permission of the Deputy Attorney General was not itself enough to achieve a sustained level of cooperation with the Law Officers. My effort was to make them understand the aim of my study and feel that they could contribute to it and then gain their trust dispelling notions of an obtrusive research approach. All the researchers highlight the importance of gaining the approval and establishing the trust of the "actual people researched". In practice, I recognised that this requires a constant and delicate negotiation but when achieved, it certainly makes life in the field much easier. Further on (arguing about the validity of my research), I will discuss why I think that I managed to establish such a relationship with most of the Law Officers.

Key Informants

Some people from the very beginning of this preparatory period seemed to be more willing to help than others. I was very lucky to have the support of a very respected and knowledgeable Law Officer who became, as Taylor and Bogdan (1998) would call him, my "key informant" at that stage. During the first days in the Office, he showed me around, introduced me to other Law Officers and he was also tipping me off about crucial information. However, although it was extremely helpful to have as an informal "sponsor" an "insider" of the setting, I had soon to acknowledge the danger of assuming that all informants shared the same perspective or had the same depth of knowledge as he had.[15] As the days passed, I started interacting with other Officers and broadening my sources of information.

Detecting the Most Suitable Methods of Data Collection

This initial period, besides teaching me how to act appropriately in the setting, helping to break the ice and establishing my identity as a trustworthy person, it was originally designed to assist me with selecting the most suitable methods of data collection. I spent more than three weeks at the Law Office doing virtually a bit of everything. I visited the offices of a number of Law Officers and discussed with them different aspects of their work. I also observed prosecutors handling criminal cases at various stages: e.g. reviewing criminal files sent to them by the police, preparing for court hearings, meeting police officers and prosecution witnesses, appearing at court, etc. That gave me a clearer picture of the procedures that were followed and enabled me to uncover some aspects of the working practices of the Law Office that previously were not apparent. What is more, I was provided with a better understanding of the Law Office's actual workload, which was not clearly defined anywhere causing confusion and only unclear speculations. This enabled me to detect the most suitable methods for data collection which could correspond to the diversity of the Law Office's workload and powers.

[15] See Van Maanen (1988).

Specific Methods of Data Collection

Subsequently, in this section, I will embark upon a detailed account of my methods of data collection after the exegesis of the multi-method approach I employed.

Multi-method Approach: Triangulation

> 'All methods have their strengths and weaknesses, better to ask what combination of strategies will be most adequate and most fruitful'. (Bulmer 1984, p. 32, original emphasis)

Researchers who advocate the use of one technique of data collection are criticised for excluding other research tools, which can produce different data useful for addressing the same research problem (Trow 1957). Most researchers now recognise the advantages of combining a variety of techniques and encourage a multi-method approach. Moreover, qualitative research itself is inherently multi-method in focus (Brewer and Hunter 1989). It is advocated, that the combination of multiple methods, empirical materials and perspectives in a single study is best understood as a strategy that adds rigor, breadth and depth to any investigation (Flick 1992).

Furthermore, the value of "across-method triangulation" (Denzin 1989), whereby the use of more than one method of data collection is employed, is that it balances the strengths and the weaknesses of differing methods. Besides having the benefit of producing a rich stream of data, triangulation assists in raising social scientists above particular biases that stem from single methodologies and provides some internal "quality control" for the research.

The preparatory period I spent at the Law Office was crucial for the adoption of a multi-method approach for my research. What I observed was that part of the prosecutors' work was written and file-based, part of it centred around the formal verbal exchanges in court and some of the particularly interesting issues were dealt with by means of informal chats and telephone conversations with the defence attorneys, the police and other prosecution agents as well as with colleagues. Moreover, the broad variety of duties that comprised the Law Office's workload entailed sufficiently wide-ranging aspects to require an equally wide-ranging selection of methods of collecting data. Therefore, in order to achieve a good coverage of prosecutorial practices and cover the breadth of prosecutorial work, I decided to combine *observation* and *informal discussions* with a *survey of documentary materials* (examination of criminal files) and *semi-structured interviews* (see Fig. 1). Many researchers advocate the combination of the above techniques and argue that data collected by each of them come to complement each other (Denzin 1989, Taylor and Bogdan 1998),[16] and, thus, enhance reliability and validity.

[16]Young (1996), acknowledging the complexity of studying especially discretionary power, advocates sensitive methodological strategies and a combination of methods. He points out that the decision maker being studied may be unwilling or unable to articulate the reasons why decisions are reached; therefore, interviews must be supplemented by other methods, such as the examination of records.

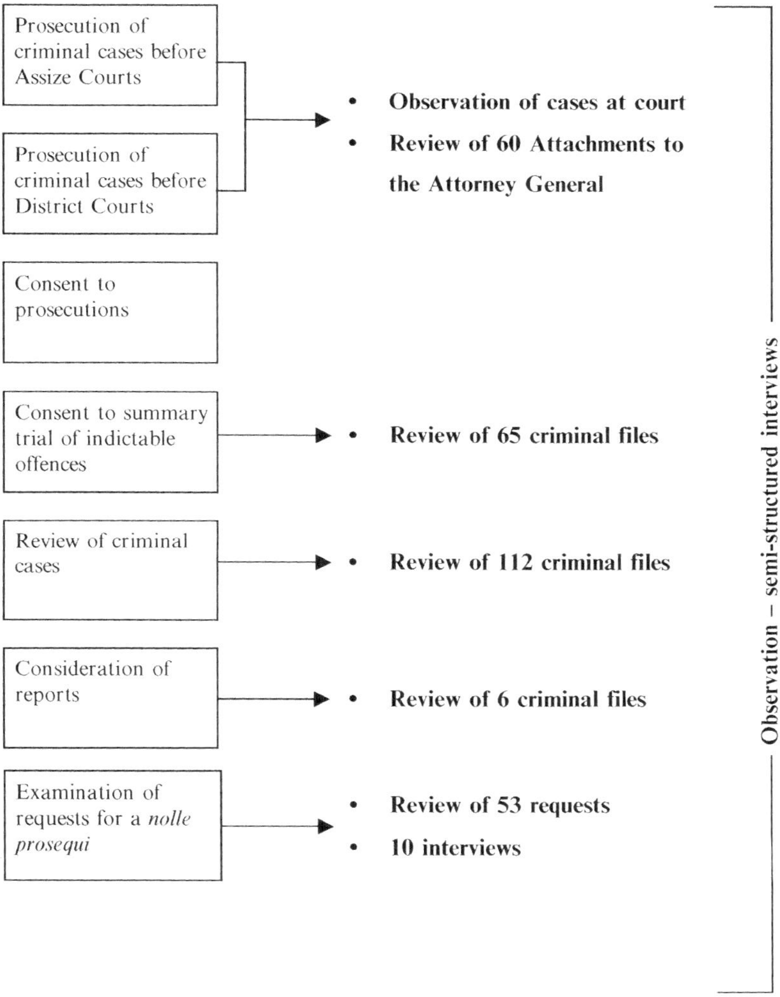

Fig. 1 The Law Office's workload and methods of data collection (Research Strategy I)

Methods of Data Collection

Observation

> 'One must immerse oneself in everyday reality – feel it, touch it, hear it and see it – in order to understand it'. (Kotarba and Fontana 1984, p. 6)

Observation was essential in giving a good overall understanding of the work of the Attorney General's Office and providing a framework for the rest of the research. It was an ongoing activity existing even in parallel with the use of the other techniques. This was expected, since the very concept of observation is defined by some researchers as a field strategy that simultaneously combines document analysis, interviews of respondents and informants, direct participation and observation and introspection (Denzin 1989 and Bogdan and Taylor 1998). One of the strengths of "direct observation"[17] is that it allows the researcher to look behind the formal aspects of organisational settings and to reveal the aspects of their everyday life.

I spent more than five months (including the pre-fieldwork period) at the Law Office on a daily basis during their working hours[18] trying to observe every aspect of their work and grasp their routine. Most of my time in the Office was devoted to reading files and having informal conversations with the Law Officers. It was not possible to have my own desk in an office but that proved to be an advantage rather than a drawback. The first option I had was sitting at the Library situated next to the Conference Room. While studying there, I had the opportunity to hold very interesting discussions with most of the Law Officers, who were frequently visiting the Library looking for Law Reviews and legal textbooks. I was also able to attend some meetings of Law Officers taking place at the Conference Room, about which I probably would not have found out if I were not in the right place at the right time. As a second option, I was sometimes allowed to examine criminal files at prosecutors' offices.[19] This enabled me to discuss with the prosecutors the decisions they had made in particular cases, while they were dealing with their office work. Being there, I was also able to listen to the prosecutors dictating correspondence, having telephone conversations and discussing cases with colleagues. Moreover, Law Officers were commenting on their work and were showing me other criminal files they were dealing with. I was often present when police officers or defence attorneys had meetings with the Law Officers to discuss about particular cases (or, occasionally, to investigate the possibility of an "informal plea-bargain"). These observations generated a considerable amount of information. I was keeping notes during the day and writing up fuller notes each evening.

In addition to the above, I often accompanied the Law Officers appearing in courts on behalf of the Attorney General.[20] There were about 15 Officers who

[17] I use the same term that Hodgson (2005, p. 10) uses to describe her field role agreeing with her that this term is preferable to the most commonly used "participant observation", "as it more accurately describes the role of the observer who remains a researcher, rather than a participant in the sense of contributing to the goals of the organisation under study".

[18] Law Office's working hours are: Monday to Friday 7:30–14:30 except from Thursday which are 7:30–14:30 and 15:00–18:00. These are also the working hours of Courts in Cyprus.

[19] Each Law Officer either has his/her own room or shares a room with another Law Officer.

[20] Most of the time, I was accompanying Law Officers at Assize Courts, where they usually appear and most of the cases I followed up to the end were Assize Court cases. I managed though, to observe a few cases at District Courts in order to have at least a flavour of this procedure. My limited time and the fact that I was working alone, inevitably forced me to choose the most important category of cases to focus on, without, however, totally ignoring the rest.

would exclusively or mostly deal with criminal cases at the Law Office.[21] During my fieldwork period I managed to accompany and observe nine of them at court. My initial intention was to follow a number of cases from the arrival of the criminal file at the Office up to the outcome of the trial through all their trial stages. The long period of time that intervenes between these two stages, various difficulties with the listing of cases and the very frequent adjournments made this impossible for a large number of cases. Eighteen cases were followed through their trial stages and provided me with valuable information, as well as offered me a fuller picture of the procedure, necessary to keep in mind while reviewing documentary evidence.[22] Although these cases were not enough for a proper analysis of the role of the Law Officers in *presenting cases* at court – my research anyway intended to focus more on the pre-trial role of the Attorney General – that aspect of my fieldwork was a precious experience in many ways. I was able to observe the Law Officers "at work" both in and outside the courtroom. Thus, for example, I was able to listen to discussions between police officers – usually the investigators of the offence – and prosecutors, which took place in private rooms before the court session began or to informal conversations between the prosecutors and the defence attorneys. Moreover, travelling to and from the court with the Law Officers provided an excellent opportunity for informal discussions because it was one of the few occasions when there were no competing demands for their time.

Examination of Documents

In order to put into context the data collected by observation and informal discussions and, thus, strengthen the database, examination of criminal files and other documentary materials was necessary.

Review of Criminal Files

As mentioned earlier, there is not a very clear distribution of criminal cases between the Attorney General's Office and the Police Prosecution Departments. In order to get a real sense of the extent of the Law Office's involvement in prosecutions, I had to explore how this was translated in everyday practice. My preliminary observations enabled me to sketch an outline of the Law Office's workload. There were,

---

[21] During Mr Markides' tenure, the Law Office was theoretically divided into various divisions (e.g. Civil Law, Administrative Law and Criminal Law divisions); see Chap. 4, Sect. 4.2.3. Although Law Officers did not *strictly* come under one of them, those 15 Law Officers were either exclusively or mostly dealing with prosecutions.

[22] Some of these cases had not been completed by the day I left the field. However, I was able to find out about their outcome from communication with the LO presenting them, after I left the field.

however, a number of questions to be answered: Which cases actually reach the Law Office, what type of cases are usually judged as "sensitive" or "complex", which are filtered out of the system, etc.? The right way to arrive in answers regarding these issues was (besides observing) by examining the files that were allocated to Law Officers and discover what type of cases they were concerning.

Every day, files concerning the review of criminal cases that were forwarded to the Attorney General's Office were allocated to six particular Law Officers. Although, as I stated earlier, there were 15 Law Officers dealing with criminal cases, only these six used to receive criminal files coming under this category of the Law Office's workload (if they could not manage all of them, they would distribute them to the rest of the Law Officers). In order to cover all types of cases reaching the Office and study the decision-making strategy adopted by each Law Officer, each week I would locate (with the precious help of the administrative staff), and then examine, all the files allocated to a different Law Officer. Although I used a rather flexible format, capable of responding to the particular characteristics of each category of cases, in so far as possible I recorded the same basic information from each file. I was making notes on the type of case and offences they were concerned, the reason they were referred to the Law Office and the information the police sent to the Law Office (e.g. the summary of evidence, the record of interviews, witness statements and confidential information). All papers with the information sent by the police were placed inside a file jacket upon which the Law Officers would record their opinion, directions or advice depending on the specific circumstances. Sometimes they wrote in some detail the reasons for their decisions, but on other occasions the comments were quite brief. However, in a later instance, the notes that were made were occasionally used as a basis for discussions in which prosecutors would elaborate on their reasons.

In total 183 files of this category were examined.[23] The selection procedure I employed (described above) ensured that in this sample all types of cases which usually reach the Law Office were represented. However, since the data to be drawn from my research methods were to be primarily qualitative and were not intended to be statistically representative, the size of the sample was not as critical as it would have been for an equivalent quantitative study. Nor was it necessary or even possible for the total number of files to be decided firmly in advance. Thus, the final sample size was the result of a balance between what would be manageable in the time available and what I conceived in practice to be large enough to produce sufficient material for the type of my study.[24]

[23] One hundred and eighteen of them concerned cases coming under category 4 of Law Office's workload and 65 cases under category 5 (see Fig. 1).

[24] It has to be noted, here, that a significant part of the Law Office's workload was not necessarily file-based. See, for example in Chap. 5, the cases for which the Law Office's advice was sought during the investigative stage: for serious cases, police investigators used to come to the Office in person and consult with the Law Officers. See also Footnote 74 in Chap. 4.

Examination of Requests for the Entering of Nolle Prosequi Submitted by Defendants

There was a special procedure followed regarding this aspect of the Law Office's workload, in which eleven Law Officers[25] were employed. Every week a different one was responsible to deal with all requests that reached the Law Office. Fifty-three requests for the entering of a *nolle prosequi* and the outcome of them were examined during my fieldwork period. In this sample I included an almost equal number of requests reviewed by each Law Officer. As with the files I reviewed, I did not predefine a certain number of requests which needed to be examined. In this case, the final size was less the result of time considerations than the effect of the "theoretical saturation", as Adler and Adler (1994) describe the point when the generic features of the new findings start to consistently replicate earlier ones.

Attachments to the Attorney General

Realising that I would not be able to follow many "live" cases concerning indictable offences through all their trial stages (see above), I decided to employ an additional method of exploring decision making regarding this category of cases. I was informed that after the completion of a case before an Assize Court, the Officer in charge sends to the Attorney General the decision of the Court accompanied with an *attachment* explaining how she/he handled the case and offering a critique of the outcome. Access to these attachments was relatively easy. I examined 60 attachments, which represented virtually almost all the attachments of cases finalised during 2001. I acknowledge the limitations involved in finding out about a case based on what is written afterwards. A written record of what has happened is never a full one and there is always the danger that some information could have been written so as to justify a decision rather than directly reflecting the actual basis on which the decision was made. Therefore, their purpose of and the possible bias within them were critically appraised and borne in mind throughout the analysis of the information collected from these documents. Although I had the opportunity to discuss some of these cases with the Law Officers, clarify issues and gain additional information about them, I have to note that few of these attachments were as detailed and thorough as I would wish and, therefore, they were only used as a supplementary source of data instead of a primary one.

Semi-structured Interviews

The advantages of interviews as a combined method of data collection with observation has been well documented (see, e.g. Hammersley and Atkinson 1995).

[25] Seven out of those eleven Law Officers were part of the group of Law Officers who were exclusively or mostly dealing with criminal cases in the Law Office, while for four of them criminal cases constituted only one of the various aspects of their work in the Office.

Therefore, besides everyday informal discussions, semi-structured interviews during the last period of my fieldwork were designed to clarify observed procedural details and to act as a method of preventing me from misinterpreting events or wrongly giving significance to observed situations. Apart from this "factual" sort of information, I was also particularly interested in eliciting from Law Officers their own views about their role in the prosecution system and about how they put this role into practice. Moreover, I wanted to gain an insight into their perceptions and philosophies about a variety of issues; for example, their approach to prosecutorial discretion, explanation of their own experiences in the system, their opinions and views on their relationship with the police, etc. Using Fionda's (1995, p. 4) words referring to her own empirical study, "(t)he interview technique lended itself particularly well to this project since prosecutors were able to give reflective and thoughtful explanations of their own experiences in the system as well as their opinions and views about current criminal policy in general".

Therefore, I carried out semi-structured interviews with 13 Law Officers (out of 15 LOs dealing with criminal cases[26]). The semi-structured form of interviewing was elected because it was more flexible and thus, suitable for the aims of my interviews (Bryman 1989). The interviews were conducted in the LOs' offices and they tended to last a couple of hours. I used an *aide-memoire*, which reminded me of the topics I wanted to cover, while I was giving the Law Officers latitude over what they wanted to say and how to say it. Written notes were taken during the interviews and these were later expanded to reflect the contents of the interviews as fully as possible. I made a conscious decision not to force them to accept a tape recorder as soon as I realised that they did not feel comfortable with the idea of being recorded and that could inhibit the openness of their responses. I felt that insisting on using a tape recorder while they were assuring me that "they will talk slowly and I could stop them anytime I wanted so I could write down everything" would emote unwanted suspicions and fears without making that much difference. The inability to use a tape recorder surely had some implications for my recording of the information; it was difficult to record the information verbatim although the field notes were as faithful to the original phrasing of comments as possible. However, it also had advantages; while writing down their responses, LOs had some time to think, clarify earlier remarks, add to earlier responses or refer to examples they could not recall previously. Moreover, in this way, the very time consuming process of transcribing the tapes was avoided.

Because of the distinct procedure that was followed regarding requests for a *nolle prosequi* and the special features that characterised this part of the Law Office workload, I conducted a separate series of interviews (10 interviews in total) with the responsible Law Officers, devoted exclusively on this aspect of their work. These interviews tended to last about 40 minutes.

[26]The other two were on leave for most of the time I spent at the Law Office.

In the last week of my fieldwork period I managed to interview apart from the Attorney General (see Sect. 3), the Deputy Attorney General.[27] The interview with the latter lasted about 2 hours and 30 minutes in total,[28] and I was allowed to use a tape recorder. This interview was extremely beneficial and informative, particularly regarding the policy of the Law Office as far as prosecutions are concerned and the relationships of the Law Office with other agents involved in the prosecution process.

In addition to these interviews, I carried out a semi-structured interview lasting 50 minutes with the head of the Police Prosecution Department in Nicosia and another one lasting almost an hour with the head of the Police Prosecution Department in Limassol. I also had the opportunity to hold briefer and more unstructured discussions with the Chief of the Cyprus Police and the head of the Central Police Prosecution Department as well as with three Defence Attorneys.[29] These interviews aimed to offer me an insight (limited I admit) into the relationship of the Law Office with other participants in the prosecution process from these participants' points of view and to provide possibly alternative understandings of the Attorney General's Office role. Moreover, the interviews with the Police Officers were valuable in supplying me with information about the cases that they usually forward to the Law Office and about the procedures which are followed for each category of cases. It has to be mentioned here that apart from these more formal interviews with these criminal justice agents, there were also other opportunities for me to hold valuable discussions with them, mainly with police officers (investigators) and defence lawyers when they were visiting the Law Office to discuss cases with the Law Officers or when appearing in Court.

Second Research Strategy: Documentary Analysis and Interviews with Post-holders

Attempting to place my research in a historical context and gather information of how succeeding Attorney Generals have approached their role and powers regarding prosecutions, two main methods of data collection were employed: a documentary analysis and interviews with post-holders. The advantages of using more than one method of data collection have been presented earlier in this chapter when discussing about the various methods I employed during my fieldwork study.

---

[27] I had the opportunity to hold informal discussions with the Deputy AG on several other occasions.

[28] The interview with the Deputy AG had to be interrupted after the first hour due to a tape-recorder problem (!); however, Mr Clerides kindly agreed to continue the interview the next day.

[29] These are three of the 11–13 Attorneys who are specialised in criminal cases in Cyprus and their selection was made on an opportunistic basis.

Documentary Analysis

My first step towards gaining information about how succeeding Attorney Generals have interpreted their powers was the search of any articles or books authored by them and published. I used the Supreme Court Library and the Law Office Library to locate such documents. Unfortunately, I discovered that only Mr Tornaritis authored a number of short monographs relevant to the role of the Law Office in prosecutions.[30]

My second step was to search *inside* the Law Office for internal circulars, press releases, memoranda or archival documents which were related to the prosecutorial role of the Law Office. I asked permission to access such documents and that was granted. With the assistance of one administrative officer, I discovered that most of these documents were kept under a series of files titled "Responsibilities of the Attorney General" which were chronologically kept. In these files a variety of materials were placed including all the pre-mentioned types of documents, albeit without separating them in well-defined and clear-cut categories. Therefore, I went through all of these files in order to discover what was relevant to my study. Studying these documents, I found out that there was a lot of cross-referencing to other Law Offices' files and, as a result, I tried to go through as many Law Office's files as it was possible to locate within the Law Office. Unfortunately, there were not many detailed documents authored by the Attorney Generals, but there was some interesting information in them which was sufficient to shed some light on the Attorney Generals' approach towards their role in prosecutions. The very fact that there was only limited written information on this issue even *within* the Law Office was another indication that the succeeding office-holders have been avoiding the – at least direct – specification of their broad powers.

Interviews with the Attorney Generals

Having completed the examination of documents, I proceeded to the second method of data collection: interviews with the post-holders themselves. This sought to gain a more *direct* view of how succeeding Attorney Generals translated their role over time and therefore, add to the information gathered by the documentary analysis:

> 'Elites need to be interviewed. The best way of finding out about people is talking to them. It cannot guarantee to secure the truth, especially from people well practised in the arts of discretion, but it is surely superior to any alternative ways of discovering what they believe or do'. (Crewe 1974, p. 43)[31]

---

[30] Nevertheless, after a newspaper search, I found a couple of interviews given by Mr Markides and one by Mr Triantafyllides in which they reflected *inter alia* on issues relevant to their prosecutorial role.

[31] Quoted in Malleson (1995, p. 69).

I firstly approached Mr Triantafyllides and asked him to give me an interview, explaining in brief the nature of my research study. He agreed and we arranged a meeting at his office a couple of weeks afterwards.[32] That interview lasted about one and a half hours and written notes were taken. While at the Law Office during my main fieldwork period, I also had the chance to interview Mr Markides.[33] His interview lasted about an hour and 15 minutes and I was allowed to use a tape recorder. Several months after the completion of my main fieldwork, Mr Markides resigned and Mr Nikitas was appointed to the office. To keep my research up to date, I decided to extend my research study so that *his* approach on the Law Office's prosecutorial role could also be covered. Therefore, I employed both of my methods of data collection (that I used for the other Attorney Generals) in order to cover Mr Nikitas' tenure as well. As far as the interview was concerned, I sent him an official letter asking to interview him and we arranged a meeting at his office for this purpose.[34] That interview lasted about an hour and 20 minutes. The semi-structured form of interviewing was elected for all three interviews because it was flexible enough to cover all the topics I wanted to, while at the same time it was giving the Attorney Generals latitude over what they wanted to say and how to say it.

I felt particularly privileged to be able to interview those three post-holders, given the well-known problems which researchers usually face when approaching elites for any kind of research.[35] I had a unique opportunity to gain first hand information about an area regarding which even indirect information had been very limited. At the same time, I fully acknowledge that the data collected especially concerning the tenures of the rest of the office-holders, apart from Mr Markides, are limited; they offer a restricted account of the *actual* working of the Office during those times (since they are not corroborated by direct observation as the data on Mr Markides' tenure are). Having said that, it has to be mentioned that the main purpose of this part of the research was not so much to produce a complete picture of the day-to-day life of the Office through time; it was predominantly to gather information of how succeeding Attorney Generals themselves have approached their role and powers regarding prosecutions.

Reliability, Validity and Data Analysis

The traditional criteria of methodological adequacy, validity and reliability were formulated and initially associated with the positivist paradigm. Positivists' obsession with objectivity, based on the assumption that everything in the universe can in

[32] Date of the interview: 01/02/2002.

[33] Date of the interview: 15/05/2002.

[34] Date of the interview: 11/01/2004.

[35] See Reiner (1992) and Hammersley and Atkinson (1995).

principle be explained in terms of causality, led them to insist on and emphasise the need for standardised and rigid procedures in order to gain validity and reliability for a research project. In response to the extreme positivist assumptions, some social sciences have tended to overreact by stressing the possibility of alternative interpretations of everything to the excluding of any effort to choose among them.[36] I do not support this extreme relativism but I do acknowledge that qualitative research is inherently more flexible and interpretivistic than other paradigms and therefore, it should be assessed in this context. However, this does not mean that qualitative researchers should be unconcerned about the accuracy of their data. "A qualitative study is not an impressionistic, off-the-cuff analysis based on a superficial look at a setting or people. It is a piece of systematic research conducted with demanding, though not necessarily standardised, procedures" (Taylor and Bogdan 1998, p. 9). Some concerns about the reliability and validity of my project and how I dealt with them follow here.

Reliability

A criticism levelled especially against observational research is that it lacks reliability. "(W)ithout statistical analysis to confirm the significance of observed patterns or trends, researchers cannot ensure that their findings are real and not merely the effects of chance" (Adler and Adler 1994, p. 381).[37] Direct observers need to consider the impact of their own views on the research because any interpretation of subjective meaning will inevitably incorporate the researcher's own perceptions and experience (Dawe 1973). There is no guarantee that if another researcher entered the same research setting, he/she would perceive things in the same way or record the same things. However, it has been argued that the reliability of ethnographic research should not be measured by the ability of another researcher to replicate findings (Hammersley 1990). The fact that research is inevitably affected by the researcher's own values means that it is important for researchers to be value aware:

> 'There is no neutral Archimedean point from which objective data can be collected: the researcher always influences the social interactions that constitute the data. All one can do is seek to be reflectively aware of this and interpret material in the light of the probable biases'. (Reiner 2000, p. 221)

Nevertheless, it has been advocated that the researcher's views are less likely to influence ethnographic research than research carried out using more structured methods, because the ethnographer does not have rigid hypotheses that he/she wants to test (Becker 1970b). The researcher enters the field with "foreshadowed

[36] For a critic of both extremes, see Kirk and Miller (1986).

[37] See also Denzin (1989).

problems" but should be responsive to what she finds (Hammersley and Atkinson 1995). In my research, I did not have any firm preconception about what I might find in the Law Office, because little was actually known about that organisation; therefore, it would be justified to argue that the probability of observer bias might have been reduced. Moreover, as Hutter (1988) remarks, it is difficult for the researcher to record the deviant when the subjects engage in quite routinised behaviour and the researcher is in contact with them for some time, as in my case.

Validity

In a qualitative study, the researchers need to be watchful about some issues that could weaken their data and employ some tactics which validate and increase confidence in the findings of their research (Miles and Huberman 1994):

Checking for Researcher's Effects

More crucially than in other cases, researchers who do direct observation need to address the effect their presence may have had on the research subjects, when considering the issue of validity. While negotiating my field role with the Law Officers – my research subjects–, I was aware of the significance of convincing them that I was not "important". Becker (1970a) has commented that the researcher is not normally as important to the research subjects as what they are doing at the moment of observation. However, difficulties may arise if the researcher is perceived to be important, for example if informants believe that he/she knows someone whose opinion of them matter. As I secured access to the Law Office from the top, I had to convince them about my real research purposes and establish a relation of trust. In every occasion I was stressing that I was not reporting to superiors nor discussing with colleagues the behaviour or comments made by individual prosecutors. I also assured the Law Officers that their anonymity would be protected in any publication based on the research. The impression I got was that I was perceived as a student who presented "no danger". There were occasions, especially in the first days, where I was fed the "official line". As time passed though, generally the Law Officers did appear to trust me and instead of the "official line" they more often told me that "we are supposed to do this, but sometimes we do that". They very often made "off the record" comments and discussed some of their colleagues in unfavourable terms, signs which by themselves indicated a level of trust. Especially at the initial stages, besides being not threatening, the student definition offered me the opportunity to appear quite credible in the "ignorant and inexperienced" role and encouraged Law Officers to be explicit about what they were doing and clarify ambiguous comments.

Checking for Representativeness

Representativeness in qualitative research does not represent what exactly the same term does in quantitative studies. It was not a purpose of my study to analyse a strictly statistical representative sample of cases. However, the small size of the Law Office and the long period I spent there[38] allowed me to cover almost all aspects of prosecution practices and types of cases, as well as to observe virtually all the Law Officers working at the Office. This gives me some confidence to argue that I reported what normally occurs in the setting and formed a full picture of its workload.

Getting Feedback from the Informants

As Miles and Huberman (1994, p. 275) point out "(o)ne of the most logical sources of corroboration is the people you have talked with and watched. After all, an alert and observant actor in the setting is bound to know more than the researcher ever will about the realities under investigation". During my fieldwork, building up a very good rapport with the Law Officers enabled me to seek clarification for certain findings. That occurred more often during the last period of the fieldwork, when research findings began to take shape and the danger of introducing bias by feeding information back was less possible.

Data Analysis

Denzin and Lincoln (1994, p. 14) remark that "qualitative research is endlessly creative and interpretive. The researcher does not just leave the field with mountains of empirical material and then easily write up his or her findings". Especially in an exploratory study, there is a constant interaction between research design, data collection and analysis.

I did not go into the field to test a particular well-formulated hypothesis; in this research the findings came from the data. My approach of analysis is an articulation of analytic induction and grounded theory (Glasser and Strauss 1967), which essentially requires the making of constant comparisons between analytic categories identified by a careful reading and coding of the data. For example, as I discussed earlier, after some data collection through observation during my initial period of fieldwork, I was able to generate the various categories of the Law Office workload and then undertake further data collection in order to refine or expand my first impressions.

[38] The fieldwork period lasted for about 5 months: the pre-fieldwork period for almost three weeks and the main fieldwork period for more than 4 months.

Concluding Remarks

The findings of this research were set out and discussed in the previous chapters. Derived from data collected by a blend of methods, they have been arguably more valid and reliable than they could have been if drawn from one source alone. These data, gathered by "watching, asking and examining" (Miles and Huberman 1994, p. 19), have been used to build up a picture of the role of the Attorney General's Office in prosecutions: more particularly, their workload, their powers regarding investigations and their principles and policies on prosecutions. It can be argued that given the strategic position of the Office within the prosecution process, an indirect insight into the whole prosecution system in Cyprus has been also achieved.

Appendix 2
List of Post-Holders Before the Establishment of the Cyprus Republic (1960)

Legal Adviser	
Sir Elliot Charles Bovill	1878–1881
King's Advocates	
William Robert Collyer	1881–1892
Archibald Fitzgerald Law	1892–1893
Frederic Gordon Templer	1893–1898
Alfred George Lascelles	1898–1902
William Rees-Davis	1902–1907
John Alexander Strachey Bucknill	1907–1912
William Alison Russell	1912–1924
John Curtois Howard	1924–1925
Attorney Generals	
John Curtois Howard	1925–1926
Charles Cyril Geraht	1926–1929
Harry Herbert Trusted	1929–1932
Henry William Butler Blackall	1932–1936
Lloyd-Blood	1936–1940
Stafford William Powel Foster Sutton	1940–1944
Stelios Pavlides	1944–1952
Criton Tornaritis	1952–1956
James H. Henry	1956–1960

Source: Loucaides (1974)

Appendix 3
Constitutional and Statutory Provisions

Article 112 of the Constitution

1. The President and the Vice-President of the Republic shall appoint jointly two persons who are qualified for appointment as a judge of the High Court one to be the Attorney General of the Republic and the other to be the Deputy Attorney General of the Republic.
2. The Attorney General of the Republic shall be the head and the Deputy Attorney General of the Republic shall be the deputy head of the Law Office of the Republic which shall be an independent office and shall not be under any Ministry.
3. The Attorney General and the Deputy Attorney General of the Republic shall have the right of audience in, and shall take precedence over any other persons appearing before, any court:
   Provided that the Attorney General of the Republic shall always take precedence over the Deputy Attorney General of the Republic.
4. The Attorney General and the Deputy Attorney General of the Republic shall be members of the permanent legal service of the Republic and shall hold office under the same terms and conditions as a judge of the High Court other than its President and shall not be removed from office except on the like grounds and in the like manner as such judge of the High Court.

Article 113 of the Constitution

1. The Attorney General of the Republic assisted by the Deputy Attorney General of the Republic shall be the legal adviser of the Republic and of the President and of the Vice-President of the Republic and of the Council of Ministers and of the ministers and shall exercise all such other powers and shall perform all such other functions and duties as are conferred or imposed on him by this Constitution or by law.

2. The Attorney General of the Republic shall have power, exercisable at his discretion in the public interest, to institute, conduct, take over, and continue or discontinue any criminal proceedings for an offence against any person in the Republic.

Section 19 of the Police Law (Cap. 285)

Subject to any direction by the Attorney General, it shall be lawful for any police officer to make a complaint or charge against any person before the Courts and to apply for a summons, warrant, search warrant or such other legal process as may by law issue against any person, and to summon before the Courts any person charged with an offence and conduct public prosecutions and preliminary inquiries against such person.

Section 107 of the Criminal Procedure Law (Cap. 155)

No person shall be put upon his trial for any offence not triable summarily, although he may have been committed for trial, except upon an information filed by the Attorney General in the Assize Court in which such person is to be tried.

Section 24 of the Courts of Justice Law (Law 14/1960)

1. Every President, Senior District Judge and District Judge of a District Court has jurisdiction to try summarily all offences punishable with term of imprisonment not exceeding five years and/or a fine not exceeding CY£50,000.
2. Every President, Senior District Judge and District Judge of a District Court has also jurisdiction to try any offence beyond the above limits summarily, provided the consent of the Attorney General is obtained. In such cases, the sentence passed could not exceed the sentence that could be passed by the court trying the case summarily, regardless of what the Criminal Code or any other Law may provide for this offence.

Bibliography

Adler P, Adler P (1994) Observational techniques. In: Denzin N, Lincoln Y (eds) Handbook of Qualitative Research. Sage, Newbury Park, CA

Advisory Committee on Police in Northern Ireland (1969) Report of the Advisory Committee on Police in Northern Ireland, Cmnd. 535. HMSO, Belfast

Aggelides A (2008) Principles of Administrative Law (in Greek). Cyprus Parliament Press, Nicosia

Ambos K (2000) The Status, Role and Accountability of the Prosecutor of the International Criminal Court: A Comparative Overview on the Basis of 33 National Reports. Eur J Crime Crim Law Crim Justice 8(2):89

Arestis G (1993) Arrest and Remand in Custody (in Greek). Cyprus Law Rev 42:6265

Artemis P (1989) An Outline of Criminal Law and the Working of Judicial System in Criminal Cases. Cyprus Law Rev 26:4016

Artemis P (2004) Prerogative Orders: Principles and Cases (in Greek). Cyprus Parliament Press, Nicosia

Ashworth A (1984) The English Criminal Process: A Review of Empirical Research. Oxford University Press, Oxford

Ashworth A (1987) The "Public Interest" Element in Prosecutions. Crim Law Rev 1987:595

Ashworth A (1998) The Criminal Process: An Evaluative Study, 2nd edn. Oxford University Press, Oxford

Ashworth A (2000) Developments in the Public Prosecutor's Office in England and Wales. Eur J Crime Crim Law Crim Justice 2000:257

Ashworth A (2004) Criminal Justice Reform: Principles, Human Rights and Public Protection. Crim Law Rev 2004:516

Ashworth A, Fionda J (1994) The New Code for Crown Prosecutors: Prosecution, Accountability and the Public Interest. Crim Law Rev 1994:894

Ashworth A, Redmayne M (2005) The Criminal Process, 3rd edn. Oxford University Press, Oxford

Auld RE (2001) Review of the Criminal Courts of England and Wales: Report. The Lord Chancellor's Department, London

Baldwin J (1985) Pre-Trial Justice. Basil Blackwell, Oxford

Baldwin J (1992a) Preparing Records of Taped Interview, Royal Commission on Criminal Justice Research Study No 2. HMSO, London

Baldwin J (1992b) The Role of Legal Representatives at the Police Station, Royal Commission on Criminal Justice Research Study No 3. HMSO, London

Baldwin J (1997) Understanding Judge Ordered and Directed Acquittals in the Crown Court. Crim Law Rev 1997:536

Baldwin J (2000) Research on the Criminal Courts. In: King RD and Wincup E (eds) Doing research on crime and justice. Oxford University Press, New York

Baldwin J, Bedward J (1991) Summarising Tape Recordings of Police Interviews. Crim Law Rev 1991:671

Baldwin J, Hunt A (1998) Prosecutors Advising in Police Stations. Crim Law Rev 1998:521

Baldwin J, McConville M (1977) Negotiated Justice: Pressures to Plead Guilty. Martin Robertson, Oxford

Baldwin J, Moloney T (1992) Supervision of Police Investigation in Serious Criminal Cases, Royal Commission on Criminal Justice Research Study No. 4. HMSO, London

Becker H (1970a) Field Work Evidence. In: Becker H (ed) Sociological Work: Method and Substance. Aldine, Chicago

Becker H (1970b) Problems of Inference and Proof in Participant Observation. In: Becker H (ed) Sociological Work: Method and Substance. Aldine, Chicago

Bell RE (1989) The Office of Director of Public Prosecutions for Northern Ireland. Unpublished thesis, Queen's University, Belfast

Belloni F, Hodgson J (2000) Criminal Injustice: An Evaluation of the Criminal Justice Process in Britain. Macmillan, London

Bennion F (1986) The New Prosecution Arrangements (1) The Crown Prosecution Service. Crim Law Rev 1986:3

Biddulft SR (1881) Governor's Annual Report for the Year 1881, KCKMG. C.B, London

Block B, Corbett C, Peay J (1993) Ordered and Directed Acquittals in the Crown Court: A Time of Change? Crim Law Rev 1993:95

Blumberg AS (1967) Criminal Justice. Quadrangle Books, Chicago

Bogdan R, Taylor SJ (1998) Introduction to Qualitative Research Methods (3rd ed.) John Wiley, New York

Bottomley AK (1986) Blueprints for Criminal Justice: Reflections on a Policy Plan for the Netherlands. Howard J 25:199

Bottoms A (2000) The Relationship between Theory and Research in Criminology. In: King RD, Wincup E (eds) Doing Research on crime and justice. Oxford University Press, New York

Brewer J, Hunter A (1989) Multi-method Research: a synthesis of styles. Sage, Newbury Park, CA

Brown AJ, Crisp D (1992) Diverting Cases from Prosecution in the Public Interest. Res Bull 32:7

Brownlee ID (2004) The Statutory Charging Scheme in England and Wales: Towards a Unified Prosecution System. Crim Law Rev 2004:869

Bryett K, Osborne P (2000) Criminal prosecution procedure and practice: international perspectives, Northern Ireland, Criminal Justice Review Group Research Report 16. Stationery Office, Belfast

Bryman A (1984) The Debate about Quantitative and Qualitative Research: A Question of Method or Epistemology? The British Journal of Sociology 35(1): 75–92

Bryman A (1988) Introduction: Inside Accounts and Social Research in Organisations. In: Bryman A (ed) Doing Research in Organisations. Routledge, London

Bryman A (1989) Research Methods and Organisational Studies. Unwin Hyman, London

Bubany CP, Skillern FF (1976) Taming the Dragon: An Administrative Law for Prosecutorial Decision Making. Am Law Rev 13:473

Buchanan D, Boddy D, Calman J (1988) Getting in, getting on, getting out, and getting back. In: Bryman A (ed) Doing Research in Organisations. Routledge, London

Bulmer M (1984) The Chicago School of Sociology. University of Chicago Press, Chicago

Burton M (2001) Reviewing Crown Prosecution Service Decisions not to Prosecute. Crim Law Rev 2001:374

Cappelletti M (1984) The Judicial Process in a Comparative Perspective. Clarendon, Oxford

Casey J (1980) The Office of the Attorney General in Ireland. Institute of Public Administration, Dublin

Casey J (1996) The Irish Law Officers. Round Hall Sweet and Maxwell, Dublin

CCPE (2008) Opinion No 2 of the Consultative Council of European Prosecutors (CCPE) on Alternatives to Prosecution. Adopted by the CCPE at its 3rd plenary meeting, Strasbourg, 15–17 October 2008

CCPE (2008) Opinion No 3 of the Consultative Council of European Prosecutors (CCPE) on the Role of Prosecution Services Outside The Criminal Law Field. Adopted by the CCPE at its 3rd plenary meeting, Strasbourg, 15–17 October 2008
Christodoulou D (1994) A Conceptual Framework for a Political Economy of Twentieth-Century Cyprus. Cyprus Res Centre Rev XX:601
Cicek K (2002) Interpreters of the Court in the Ottoman Empire as seen from the Sharia Court Records of Cyprus. Islamic Law Soc 9(1):1
Clerides F (1984) The Cypriot Criminal Code-developments and Problems. Cyprus Law Rev 5:889
Cole GF (1996) The Decision to Prosecute. In: Sanders A (ed) Prosecution in Common Law Jurisdictions. Dartmouth, Aldershot and Brookfield, USA
Colotas F (1988) Research on State and Legal Institutions of the Ancient Kingdoms of Cyprus. Cyprus Law Rev 21:3267
PA Consulting Group (2003) Charging Suspects: Early Involvement by the CPS: A Pilot Report. http://www.cps.gov.uk
Council of Europe (1996) The Role of the Public Prosecution Office in a Democratic Society. Council of Europe, Strasbourg
Council of Europe (2000) The Role of Public Prosecution in the Criminal Justice System. Recommendation Rec (2000) 19 and explanatory memorandum. Adopted by the Committee of Ministers of the Council of Europe. Council of Europe, Strasbourg
Cretney A, Davis G (1995) Punishing Violence. Routledge, London
Cretney A, Davis G (1996) Prosecuting "Domestic" Assault. Crim Law Rev 1996:162
Cretney A, Davis G (1997) The Significance of Compellability in the Prosecution of Domestic Assault. Br J Criminol 37:75
Crewe I (1974) Introduction: Studying Elites in Britain. In: Crewe I (ed) Elites in Western Democracy. J. Wiley, New York
Criminal Justice Review Group, Northern Ireland (2000) Review of the Criminal Justice System in Northern Ireland. Stationery Office, Belfast
Crisp D, Moxon D (1994) Case Screening by The Crown Prosecution Service: How and Why Cases are Terminated, Research Study no 137. HMSO, London
Crisp D, Whittaker C, Harris J (1995) Public Interest Case Assessment Schemes, Home Office Research Study 138. HMSO, London
Crompton R, Jones G (1988) Researching white collar organisations: why sociologists should not stop doing case studies. In: Bryman A (ed) Doing Research In Organisations. Routledge, London
Crown Office (1992) The Prosecution of Crime in Scotland. Crown Office, Edinburgh
Crown Prosecution Service (1994) Annual Report (1993–1994). The Stationery Office, London
Crown Prosecution Service (1998) The Review of the Crown Prosecution Service: summary of the main report with the conclusions and recommendations. The Stationery Office, London
Crown Prosecution Service (1999) Race and Crown Prosecution Service Decisions. Report Submitted to the Crown Prosecution Service. The Stationery Office, London
Crown Prosecution Service (2004) Annual Report (2003–2004). The Stationery Office, London
Crown Prosecution Service (2005) Annual Report (2004–2005). The Stationery Office, London
Crown Prosecution Service (2006) Annual Report (2005–2006). The Stationery Office, London
Crown Prosecution Service (2007) Annual Report (2006–2007). The Stationery Office, London
Crown Prosecution Service (2008) Annual report (2007–2008). The Stationery Office, London
Crown Prosecution Service Inspectorate (2002) Chief Inspector'S Annual Report (2001–2002). CPS Inspectorate, London
Damaska M (1973) Evidentiary Barriers to Conviction and Two Models of Criminal Procedure: A Comparative Study. U Penn Law Rew 121:506
Damaska M (1975) Structures of Authority and Comparative Criminal Procedure. Yale Law J 84:480
Damaska M (1986) The Faces of Justice and State Authority. A Comparative Approach to the Legal Process. Yale University Press, New Haven
Daskalakis I (1966) Review of the Military Criminal Law (In Greek). Nicosia

Davis KL (1969) Discretionary Justice. Louisiana State University Press, Baton Rouge
Daw KR (1994) The New Code for Crown Prosecutors: A Response. Crim Law Rev 1994:904
Dawe A (1973) The role of research in the construction of social theory: an essay in reflexive sociology. Sociol Rev 21(1):22
De Doelder H (2000) The Public Prosecution Service in the Netherlands. Eur J Crime Crim Law Crim Justice 2000:187
De Smith SA (1964) The New Commonwealth and its Constitutions. Stevens, London
Demetriadou E (1989) Legal Discourse and Social History in Cyprus: an Inductive Inquiry, 1878–1982. Cyprus Law Trib 4:127
Dennis IH (ed) (1987) Criminal Law and Justice. Sweet and Maxwell, London
Denzin N (1978) The Research Act, 2nd edn. Aldine, Chicago
Denzin N (1989) Interpretive Interactionism. Sage, Newbury Park, CA
Denzin N, Lincoln Y (1994) Introduction: Entering the field of Qualitative Research. In: Denzin N, Lincoln Y (eds) Handbook of Qualitative Research. Sage, Newbury Park, CA
Di Federico G (1998) Prosecutorial Independence and the Democratic Requirement of Account-Ability in Italy: Analysis of a Deviant Case in a Comparative Perspective. Br J Criminol 38:371
Dickens BM (1973) Control of Prosecutions in the United Kingdom. Int Comp Law Q 22:1
Dingwall G (1995) Judicial Review and the Director of Public Prosecutions. Crim Law J 1995:265
Dingwall G (2000) Prosecutorial Policy, Double Jeopardy and the Public Interest. Mod Law Rev 2000:268
Dotan Y (1997) Should Prosecutional Discretion Enjoy Special Treatment in Judicial Review? A Comparative Analysis of the Law in England and Israel. Public Law 1997:513
Drakos T (2005) The Need for Reform of the Cyprus Criminal Justice System (in Greek). Politis Newspaper 08/04/05
Duff P (1993) The Prosecutor Fine and Social Control: The Introduction of the Fiscal Fine to Scotland. Br J Criminol 33:481
Duff P (1997) Diversion from Prosecution into Psychiatric Care: Who Controls the Gates? Br J Criminol 37:15
Duff P (1998) Crime Control, Due Process and the Case for the Prosecution. Br J Criminol 38:111
Duff P (1999) The Prosecution Service: Independence and Accountability. In: Duff P, Hutton N (eds) Criminal Justice in Scotland. Ashgate, Aldershot
Duff P, Burman M (1994) Diversion from Prosecution to Psychiatric Care. Scottish Office Central Research Unit, Edinburgh
Duff P, Hutton N (eds) (1999) Criminal Justice in Scotland. Ashgate, Aldershot
Edwards JL (1964) Law Officers of the Crown: A Study of the Offices of Attorney-General and Solicitor-General of England with an account of the Office of the Director of Public Prosecutions of England. Sweet and Maxwell, London
Edwards JL (1989) Walking The Tightrope of Justice: An Examination of the Office of Attorney General in Canada with particular regard to its relationships with the police and prosecutors and the arguments for establishing a statutorily independent director of public prosecutions: a series of opinion papers. Royal Commission on the Donald Marshall, Jr., Prosecution, Halifax
Eliades T (1994) The Law of Evidence: A Practical Approach (in Greek). UP, Nicosia
Eliades T, Nickolaou G (1985) Arrest under Cyprus Law. Cyprus Law Rev 11:1749
Elliman S (1990a) Inadequate Guidance. New Law J 140:14
Elliman S (1990b) Independent Information for the CPS. New Law J 140:812
Elsner B (2005) Police Function Within the Criminal Justice System. Talk at the conference "The Growing Importance of the Public Prosecution Service: Best European Practices in the Face of Heightened Crime Rates", Georg-August University Gottingen, Germany, 6–8 October 2005
Emerson RM, Paley B (1992) Organisational Horizons and Complaint-filing. In: Hawkins K (ed) The Uses of Discretion. Clarendon, Oxford
European Commission (1999) Intermediate Report on the Progress of Negotiations for Cyprus Accession to the European Union, EU

European Committee for the Prevention of Torture and Inhumane or Degrading Treatment or Punishment (2000) Report to the Government of Cyprus on the visit to Cyprus from 22–30 May 2000

Falletti F (2004) The French Prosecution Service. In: Tak JP (ed) Tasks and Powers of the Prosecution Services in the EU Member States, vol I. Wolf, Nijmegen

Feely M (1973) Two Models of the Criminal Justice System: An Organisation Perspective. Law Soc Rev 7:407

Fennel P, Harding C, Jorg N, Sward B (eds) (1995) Criminal Justice in Europe: A Comparative Study. Clarendon, Oxford

Field S (1994) Judicial Supervision and the Pre-Trial Process. J Law Soc 21(1):119

Field S, Alldridge P, Jorg N (1995) Prosecutors, Examining Judges, and Control of Police Investigations. In Fennel P, Harding C, Jorg N, Sward B (eds) Criminal Justice in Europe: A Comparative Study, Oxford: Clarendon Press

Field S, West A (2003) Dialogue and the Inquisitorial Tradition: French Defence Lawyers in the Pre-Trial Criminal Process. Crim Law Forum 14:261

Fijnaut C, Groenhuijsen MS (2002) A European Public Prosecution Service: Comments on the Green Paper. Eur J Crime Crim Law Crim Justice 10(4):321

Fionda J (1994) The Crown Prosecution Service and the Police: a Loveless Marriage. Law Q Rev 110:376

Fionda J (1995) Public Prosecutors and Discretion: A Comparative Study. Clarendon, Oxford

Fisher SH (1977) Report of an Inquiry by the Honourable Sir Henry Fisher into the circumstances leading to the trial of the three persons on charges arising out of the Death of Maxwell Confait and the fire at 27 Doggett Road, London SE6. HMSO, London

Fisher SZ (2000) The Prosecutor's Ethical Duty to Seek Exculpatory Evidence in Police Hands: Lessons from England. Fordham Law Rev 68:1379

Flick U (1992) Triangulation revisited strategy of validation or alternative? J Theory Soc Behav 22 (2):175

Flick U (1998) An Introduction to Qualitative Research. Sage Publications, London

Fontana A, Frey J (1994) Interviewing: The Art of Science. In: Denzin N, Lincoln Y (eds) Handbook of Qualitative Research. Sage, Newbury Park, CA

Galligan DJ (1986) Discretionary Powers. Clarendon, Oxford

Galligan DJ (1987) Regulating Pre-Trial Decisions. In: Dennis IH (ed) Criminal Law and Justice. Sweet and Maxwell, London

Gandy D (1988) The Crown Prosecution Service: its organisation and philosophy. In: Hall Williams JE (ed) The Role of the Prosecutor. Gower, Aldershot

Gebbie GC, Bein D (2002) "Trial within a Trial" in Scotland and Israel. Eur J Crime Crim Law Crim Justice 10(4):253

Gelsthorpe L, Giller H (1990) More Justice for Juveniles: Does More Mean Better? Crim Law Rev 1990:153

Gelsthorpe L, Padfield N (2003) Exercising discretion: decision-making in the criminal justice system and beyond. Willan, Cullompton

Georghallides GS (1979) A political and administrative history of Cyprus, 1918–1926: with a survey of the foundations of British rule. Cyprus Research Centre, Nicosia

Giddens A (1984) The constitution of society: outline of the theory of structuration. Polity, Cambridge

Glasser B, Strauss A (1967) The Discovery of Grounded Theory. Aldine, Chicago

Glidewell I (1998) Review of the Crown Prosecution Service: A Report, Cmnd. 3960. The Stationery Office, London

Glidewell Working Group (2001) An Early Assessment of Co-Located Criminal Justice Units. Home Office, London

Gold RL (1958) Roles in Sociological Fieldwork. Soc Forces 36:217

Goldstein A, Marcus M (1977) The Myth of Judicial Supervision in Three "Inquisitorial" Systems: France, Italy and Germany. Yale Law J 87:240

Gordon P (1980) Policing in Scotland. SCCL, Glasgow
Hall Williams JE (ed) (1988) The Role of the Prosecutor. Gower, Aldershot
Hammersley M (1990) Classroom Ethnography: Empirical and Methodological Essays. Open University Press, Milton Keynes
Hammersley M, Atkinson P (1995) Ethnography Principles in Practice, 2nd edn. Routledge, London
Hans-Jörg A (2000) Criminal Prosecution: Developments, Trends and open Questions in the Federal Republic of Germany. Eur J Crime Crim Law Crim Justice 8(3):245
Hatzidemetriou K (1988) History of Cyprus (in Greek). Nicosia
Hawkins K (ed) (1992) The Uses of Discretion. Oxford University Press, Oxford
Hawkins K (2003a) Order, Rationality and Silence: Some Reflections on Criminal Justice Decision-Making. In: Gelsthorpe L, Padfield N (eds) Exercising discretion: decision-making in the criminal justice system and beyond. Willan, Cullompton
Hawkins K (2003b) Law As Last Resort: Prosecution Decision-Making in a Regulatory aAency. Oxford University Press, Oxford
Hay D (1983) Controlling the English Prosecutor. Osgoode Hall Law J 21(2):175
Herrmann J (1974) The Rule of Compulsory Prosecution and the Scope of Prosecutorial Discretion in Germany. Univ Chic Law Rev 41:468
Hetherington T (1989) Prosecution and the Public Interest. Waterlow, London
Hilson C (1993) Discretion to Prosecute and Judicial Review. Crim Law Rev 1993:739
Hodgson J (2001) The Police, The Prosecutor And The Juge D'Instruction. Judicial Supervision in France, Theory and Practice. Br J Criminol 41:342
Hodgson J (2002) Hierarchy, Bureaucracy and Ideology in French Criminal Justice: some Empirical Observations. J Law and Soc 29(2):227–257
Hodgson J (2004) The Detention and Interrogation of Suspects in Police Custody in France. Eur J Criminol 1(2):163
Hodgson J (2005) French Criminal Justice: A Comparative Account of the Investigation and Prosecution of Crime in France. Hart, Oxford
Home Affairs Committee (2002) The Conduct of Investigations into Past Cases of Abuse in Children's Homes, 4th Report, HC 836
Home Office (1995) Public Interest Case Assessment Schemes, Home Office Research Study 138. HMSO, London
Home Office (2002) Narrowing the Justice Gap. Home Office, London
House of Commons (1989) Crown Prosecution Service, Fourth Report of the Home Affairs Committee. HMSO, London
Hoyano A, Hoyano L, Davis G, Goldie S (1997) A study of the impact of the Revised Code for the Crown Prosecutors. Crim Law Rev 1997:556
Hoyle C (1998) Negotiating domestic violence: police, criminal justice, and victims. Clarendon, Oxford
Hoyle C, Sanders A (2000) Police Response to Domestic Violence: From Victim Choice to Victim Empowerment? Br J Criminol 40:14
Hutter BM (1988) The Reasonable Arm of the Law?: The Law Enforcement Procedures of Environmental Health Officers, Oxford: Clarendon Press
Independent Commission on Policing in Northern Ireland (1999) A New Beginning: Policing in Northern Ireland – The Report of the Independent Commission on Policing in Northern Ireland [Patten Report]. Belfast: Independent Commission on Policing in Northern Ireland
Jackson J (1994) Trial by Jury and Alternative Modes of Trial. In: McConville M, Bridges L (eds) Criminal Justice in Crisis. Brookfield, Aldershot
Jackson J, Doran S (1995) Judge Without Jury: Diplock Trials in the Adversary System. Clarendon, Oxford
Jehle J (2000) Prosecution in Europe: Varying Structures, Convergent Trends. Eur J Crim Policy Res 8:27
Jehle J (2003) Criminal Justice in Germany 2003. Federal Ministry of Justice, Berlin
Jehle J, Wade M (2006) Coping with Overloaded Criminal Justice Systems: The Rise of Prosecutorial Power Across Europe. Springer, Berlin

Johnson DT (2002) The Japanese Way of Justice: Prosecuting Crime in Japan. Oxford University Press, New York

Jones P (1981) Police Powers and Police Accountability: The Royal Commission on Criminal Procedure. Politics and Power, vol 4. Routledge and Kegan Paul, London

Jones T (2003) The governance and accountability of policing. In: Newburn T (ed) Handbook of Policing. Willan, Cullompton

Joutsen M, Kalske J (1984) Prosecutorial Decision-Making in Finland: the Results of a Simulation study. National Research Institute of Legal Policy, Helsinki

Jupp V (1989) Methods of Criminological Research. Unwin Hyman, London

Justice (1970) A Report: The Prosecution Process in England and Wales. Justice, London

Justice (1979) Pre-Trial Criminal Procedure, Police Power and the Prosecution Process. Evidence Submitted to the Royal Commission on Criminal Procedure (mimeo)

Kapardis A (1983) Use and Impact of Imprisonment in Cyprus: a Quasi Experiment. Crim Law Rev 1983(2):374

Kapardis A (2001) Society, crime, and criminal justice in Cyprus, 1878–2000. Ant. N. Sakkoula, Athens-Komotini

Kapardis A (2002) Key issues in sentencing criminal defendants in cyprus. paper presented at the Second International Conference on Sentencing and Society, University of Strathclyde, Glasgow, Scotland, 27–29 June 2002

Kapardis A, Kourakis N, Kranvia-Kapardi M (eds) (2001) Economic Crimes in Cyprus: A Multidisciplinary Approach (in Greek). Ant. N. Sakkoula, Athens-Komotini

Katsiaounis R (1996) Labour, society and politics in cyprus: during the second half of the nineteenth century (in Greek). Cyprus Research Centre, Nicosia

King RD, Wincup E (eds) (2000) Doing research on crime and justice. Oxford University Press, New York

Kirk J, Miller M (1986) Reliability and Validity in Qualitative Research. Sage, London

Kotarba J, Fontana A (1984) The Existential Self in Society. Chicago: Chicago University Press

Krone T (2003) The Limits of Prosecution Authority. Paper Presented at Regulatory Institutions Network (RegNet), Australian National University, 18 November 2003

Kyprianou D (2006) The Role of the Cyprus Attorney General's Office in Prosecutions: Rhetoric, Ideology and Practice. Unpublished PhD thesis, University of London

Kyprianou D (2008a) Comparative Analysis of Prosecution Systems (Part I): Origins, Constitutional Position and Organization of Prosecution Services. Cyprus Eur Law Rev 6:467

Kyprianou D (2008b) Comparative Analysis of Prosecution Systems (Part II): The Role of Prosecution Services in Investigation and Prosecution Principles and Policies. Cyprus Eur Law Rev 7

Kyprianou D (2009a) Adversarial vs. Inquisitorial Prosecution Systems in Europe: Commonalities and Diversities. In: Jaishankar K (ed) International perspectives on crime and justice. Cambridge Scholars, Newcastle upon Tyne, UK

Kyprianou D (2009b) Juvenile Justice Systems in Europe: Report of Cyprus. In: Dünkel F (ed) Juvenile justice systems in Europe: current situation, reform developments and good practices. University of Greifswald, Greifswald

Lacey N (1987) Discretion and Due Process at the Post-Conviction Stage. In: Dennis IH (ed) Criminal Law and Justice: Essays from the W.G. Hart Workshop, 1986. Sweet and Maxwell, London

Lacey N (1992) The Jurisprudence of Discretion: Escaping the Legal Paradigm. In: Hawkins K (ed) The Uses of Discretion. Clarendon, Oxford

Lacey N (1994) Introduction: Making Sense of Criminal Justice. In: Lacey N (ed) A Reader in Criminal Justice, Oxford Readings in Socio-Legal Studies. Oxford University Press, Oxford

Langbein JH (1973) The Origins of Public Prosecution at Common Law. Am J Leg Hist 27:313

Langbein JH (1974) Controlling Prosecutorial Discretion in Germany. Univ Chic Law Rev 41:439

Law Commission (2000) Prosecution Appeals Against Judges' Rulings, Consultation Paper No. 158. The Stationery Office, London

Law Reform Commission of Canada (1990) Controlling Criminal Prosecutions: The Attorney General and the Crown Prosecutor, Working Paper 62. The Commission, Ottowa

Leigh LH, Hall Williams JE (1981) The Management of the Prosecution Process in Denmark, Sweden and the Netherlands. James Hall, Leamington Spa

Leigh L, Zedner L (1992) A Report on the Administration of Justice in the Pre-trial Phase in France and Germany, Royal Commission on Criminal Justice Research Study No. 1. HMSO, London

Leng R (1993) The Right to Silence in Police Interrogation: A Study of the Issues Underlying the Debate, Royal Commission on Criminal Justice Research Study No.10. HMSO, London

Leng R, McConville M, Sanders A (1996) Researching the Discretion to Charge and to Prosecute. In: Sanders A (ed) Prosecution in Common Law Jurisdictions. Aldershot, Dartmouth

Lewis C (2006) The Prosecution Service Function within the English Criminal Justice System. In: Jehle J, Wade M (eds) Coping with overloaded Criminal Justice Systems: The Rise of Prosecutorial Power Across Europe. Springer, Berlin

Lidstone K (1987) The Reformed Prosecution Process in England: A Radical Reform? Crim Law J 11:296

Limbourides L (1983) The Justice System in Cyprus During British rule (in Greek). Nicosia

Little RK (1999) Proportionality as an Ethical Precept for Prosecutors in their Investigative Role. Fordham Law Rev 68:723

Loizou A (1968) The Role of Courts and the Principles of Criminal Justice (Part I). Cyprus Law Trib 1:18

Loizou A (1969) The Role of Courts and the Principles of Criminal Justice (Part II). Cyprus Law Trib 2:11

Loizou A. (1972) Criminal Justice and the Treatment of Offenders (Part II). Cyprus Law Trib 7

Loizou A (1990) Police and Human Rights. Cyprus Law Rev 30:4611

Loizou A, Pikis G (1975) Criminal Procedure in Cyprus. Proodos, Nicosia

Loucaides L (1970) The Police Prosecutor appearing in Court (in Greek). Nicosia

Loucaides L (1974) The Office of the Attorney General of the Republic of Cyprus (in Greek). Nicosia

Loucaides L (1979) Presentation of criminal cases in court by non legally qualified advocates. Cyprus Law Rev 93

Loucaides L (1982) Sources and Methods of Cyprus law. In: Loucaides L (ed) Topics of Cyprus Law. Nicosia

Machlouzarides P (1970) Criminality in Cyprus. Nicosia

Mackie A, Burrows J, Tarling R (1999) Preparing the Prosecution Case. Crim Law Rev 1999:461

Maher G (1994) Reforming the Criminal Process: A Scottish Perspective. In: McConville M, Bridges L (eds) Criminal Justice in Crisis. Brookfield, Aldershot

Malachtou-Pamballi M (2005) Cyprus. In: Tak JP (ed) Tasks and Powers of the Prosecution Services in the EU Member States, vol II. Wolf, Nijmegen

Malleson K (1995) Appeals Against Conviction in the Court of Appeal (Criminal Division). Unpublished thesis, LSE

Mansfield G, Peay J (1987) The Director of Public Prosecutions: Principles and Practices for the Crown Prosecutor. Tavistock, London

Markides A (2000) Introduction. In: Neocleous A, Campbell D (eds) Introduction to Cyprus law. Yorkhill, Albany, NY

Marshall G (1984) Constitutional conventions: the rules and forms of political accountability. Clarendon, Oxford

McBarnet D (1981a) Conviction: law, the state and the construction of justice. Macmillan, London

McBarnet D (1981b) Balance and Clarity: has the Royal Commission Achieved them? Crim Law Rev 1981(2):443

McConville M, Baldwin J (1981) Courts, Prosecutions and Conviction. Clarendon, Oxford

McConville M, Bridges L (eds) (1994) Criminal Justice in Crisis. Edward Elgar, Aldershot
McConville M, Mirsky C (1992) The Skeleton of Plea-Bargaining. New Law J 142:1373
McConville M, Sanders A (1992) Fairness and the CPS. New Law J 142:120
McConville M, Wilson G (eds) (2002) The Handbook of the Criminal Justice Process. Oxford University Press, Oxford
McConville M, Sanders A, Leng R (1991) The Case for the Prosecution. Routledge, London
McConville M, Hodgson J, Bridges L, Pavlovic A (1994) Standing Accused: The Organisation and Practices of Criminal Defence Lawyers in Britain. Clarendon, Oxford
McConville M, Sanders A, Leng R (1997) Descriptive or Critical Sociology: The Choice Is Yours. Br J Criminol 37(3):347
Mental Health Advisory Committee (1993) Diverting Mentally Disturbed Offenders from Prosecution. NACRO, London
Miles MB, Huberman AM (1994) Qualitative Data Analysis, an Expanded Sourcebook. Sage, London
Ministry of Justice and Public Order, Republic of Cyprus (2003) National Report Of The Republic Of Cyprus On The Implementation Of The Conclusions Of The European And World Conferences Against Racism. Government Printing Office, Nicosia
Ministry of Justice and Public Order, Republic of Cyprus (2004) Juvenile Delinquency in Cyprus: an empirical research. Ministry of Justice, Nicosia
Moody SR, Tombs J (1982) Prosecution in the Public Interest. Scottish Academic Press, Edinburgh
Narey M (1997) Review of Delay in the Criminal Justice System: A Report ("the Narey Report"). Home Office, London
National Audit Office (1989) Review of the Crown Prosecution Service, Report by the Controller and the Auditor General, HC 345. HMSO, London
National Audit Office (1997) The Crown Prosecution Service. National Audit Office, London
Neocleous A, Bevir D (2000) Legal History. In: Neocleous A, Campbell D (eds) Introduction to Cyprus Law. Yorkhill, Albany, NY
Neocleous A (ed) (2000) Introduction to Cyprus Law. Yorkhill, Albany, NY
Nickolatos M (1993a) The Judges Rules (in Greek). Cyprus Law Trib 1993(1):17
Nickolatos M (1993b) Structure and Functions of Cyprus Legal System (in Greek). Cyprus Law Trib 1993:349
Office of the Director of Public Prosecutions (2001) Annual Report 2001. http://www.dppireland.ie
Office of the Director of Public Prosecutions (2006) Annual Report 2006. http://www.dppireland.ie
Office of the Director of Public Prosecutions (2007) Annual Report 2007. http://www.dppireland.ie
Osborne, P (1997) The control of the discretion to prosecute in Ireland. Unpublished thesis, Queen's University, Belfast
Padfield N (1995) The Criminal Justice Process: Text and Materials. Butterworths, London
Papaioannou I (1984) Politics in Cyprus between 1960 and 1981. SN, Nicosia
Papaioannou G (1999) The Law Office (in Greek). Unpublished paper given at the Academy of Public Administration, Nicosia
Pashalides (1991) Principles of Criminal Justice (in Greek). Cyprus Law Rev 36:5587
Pawson R, Tilley P (1997) Realistic Evaluation. Thousand Oaks, London
Philips J (1983) The Role of the Director of Public Prosecutions and the Future of the Criminal Justice in Victoria. Law Inst J 57:454
Pikis GM (1981) The English Common Law, the Maxims of Equity and their application in Cyprus. UP, Larnaca
Pikis GM (2003) Fundamentals of Cyprus Law (in Greek). Ant.N. Sakkoulas, Athens-Komotini
Public Prosecution Service for Northern Ireland (2008) Annual Report (2007–2008). http://www.ppsni.gov.uk
Public Prosecution System Study Group (1999) (Chair: Dermot Nally) Report of the Public Prosecution System Study Group. http://www.dppireland.ie/filestore/documents/Report_of_the_Public_Prosecution_System_Study_Group.pdf

Pugh G (1962) The Administration of Criminal Justice in France: An Introductory Analysis. Louisiana Law Rev 23:1

Reiner R (1981) The Politics of Police Powers. Politics and Power, Vol 4. Routledge and Kegan, London

Reiner R (1992) Chief Constables. Oxford University Press, Oxford

Reiner R (2000) Police Research. In: King RD, Wincup E (eds) Doing research on crime and justice. Oxford University Press, New York

Roach LT (2002) Detecting Crime Part II: The Case for a Public Prosecutor. Crim Law Rev 2002:566

Robb L (1988) Note: A Scottish Contribution. In: Hall Williams JE (ed) The Role Of the Prosecutor. Gower, Aldershot

Roberts-Wray SK, Owen SK (1966) Commonwealth and Colonial Law. Stevens, London

Roche D (2003) Accountability in Restorative Justice. Oxford University Press, Oxford

Rock P (1993) The Social World of an English Crown Court. Clarendon, Oxford

Rock P (2004) Victims, Prosecutors and the State in nineteenth century England and Wales. Crim Justice 4(4):331

Rose D (1996) In the Name of the Law. Jonathan Cape, London

Rossidou-Papakyriakou E (2001) Detection of Fraud (in Greek). In: Kapardis A, Kourakis N, Kranvia-Kapardi M (eds) Economic Crimes in Cyprus: A Multidimensional Approach. Ant. N. Sakkoula, Athens-Komotini

Rottman DB, Tormey PF (1984) The System in Criminal Justice. In: Public Social Expenditure-Value for Money? Papers Presented at a Conference 20 November 1984, The Economic and Social Research Institute, Dublin

Royal Commission on Criminal Justice (1993) (Chair: Viscount Runciman) Report, Cmnd. 2263. HMSO, London

Royal Commission on Criminal Procedure (1980) Prosecution by Private Individuals and non-police Agencies, Research Study No. 10. HMSO, London

Royal Commission on Criminal Procedure (1981a) (Chair: Sir Cyril Philips) Report, Cmnd 8092. HMSO, London

Royal Commission on Criminal Procedure (1981b) The Investigation and Prosecution of Criminal Offences in England and Wales: the Law and Procedure, Cmnd 8092-1. HMSO, London

Sanders A (1985) Prosecution Decisions and the Attorney-General's Guidelines. Crim Law Rev 1985:4

Sanders A (1986a) Arrest, Charge and Prosecution. Leg Stud 6(3):257

Sanders A (1986b) Diverting Cases from Prosecution: Can we learn from other countries? Justice Peace 1986:614

Sanders A (1986c) The New Prosecution Arrangements [2] An Independent Crown Prosecution Service? Crim Law Rev 1986:16

Sanders A (1987) Constructing the Case for the Prosecution. J Law Soc 14:229

Sanders A (1988a) Incorporating the "public interest" element in the decision to prosecute. In: Hall Williams JE (ed) The Role of the Prosecutor. Gower, Aldershot

Sanders A (1988b) The Limits to Diversion from Prosecution. Br J Criminol 28:513

Sanders A (1992) Reforming the Prosecution System. Polit Q 63:25

Sanders A (1996) Introduction. In: Sanders A (ed) Prosecution in Common Law Jurisdictions. Dartmouth, Aldershot and Brookfield, USA

Sanders A (2004) Prosecutions in England and Wales. In: Tak JP (ed) Tasks and Powers of the Prosecution Services in the EU Member States, vol I. Wolf, Nijmegen

Sanders A, Cole G (1982) The Prosecution of Weak Cases in England and Wales. Crim Justice Rev 1982:7

Sanders A, Young R (1994) The Rule of Law, Due Process and Pre-Trial Criminal Justice. Curr Leg Probl 47:125

Sanders A, Young R (2000) Criminal Justice. Butterworths, London

Sanders A, Young R (2001) Discontinuances, the Rights of Victims and the Remedy of Freedom. New Law J 151:44
Sanders A, Young R (2002) From Suspect to Trial. In: Maguire M, Morgan R, Reiner R (eds) The Oxford Handbook of Criminology. Oxford University Press, Oxford
Schauer F (2005) Rule-based Decision-making in the Development of Legal Institutions in Political Environments. Guest Lecture Series of the Office of the Prosecutor. ICC-OTP, The Hague
Schwimmer MW (2000) Opening Speech. In: Pan-European Conference: What Public Prosecution Service in Europe in the 21st century? Strasburg, 22–24 May 2000
Smith DJ (1997) Case Construction and the Goals of Criminal Process. Br J Criminol 37:319
Statistical Service (2004) Criminal Statistics 2004, Report No. 31. Printing Office of the Republic of Cyprus, Nicosia
Stebbins R (2001) Exploratory Research in the Social Sciences. Sage, New York
Stedward G, Millar A (1989) Diversion from Prosecution (Central Research Unit Papers). The Stationery Office Books, Edinburgh
Stenning PC (1986) Appearing for the Crown: A legal and historical review of criminal prosecutorial authority in Canada. Brown, Cowansville
Stephan P, Cyrille F, Dirk VD (2000) From Sisyphus to Octopus: towards a modern public prosecutor's office in Belgium. Eur J Crime Crim Law Crim Justice 2000:154
Strauss A, Corbin J (1998) Basics of Qualitative Research, 2nd edn. Sage, New York
Symeonides S (1977) Introduction to Cypriot Law. Univiversity of Thessaloniki Press, Thessaloniki
Symeonides S (2003) The Mixed Legal System of the Republic of Cyprus. Tulane Law Rev 78:441
Tak JP (1986) The Legal Scope of Non-Prosecution in Europe. HEUNI, Helsinki
Tak JP (1999) East Meets West Aspects of Prosecution in Countries in Transition. Eur J Crime Crim Law Crim Justice 7(4):412
Tak JP (2004a) Introduction. In: Tak JP (ed) Tasks and Powers of the Prosecution Services in the EU Member States, vol I. Wolf, Nijmegen
Tak JP (2004b) The Dutch Prosecution Service. In: Tak JP (ed) Tasks and Powers of the Prosecution Services in the EU Member States, vol I. Wolf, Nijmegen
Tak JP (ed) (2005a) Tasks and Powers of the Prosecution Services in the EU Member States, vol II. Wolf, Nijmegen
Tak JP (2005b) The prosecution service in control of police investigation policy? A European comparison. Unpublished talk at the Conference "The Growing Importance of the Public Prosecution Service: Best European Practices in the Face of Heightened Crime Rates". Georg-August University Gottingen, Germany, 6–8 October 2005
Talaridis K (1983) The Constitutional Power of the Attorney General of the Republic to enter a Nolle Prosequi: is it subject to review by the House of Representatives? Cyprus Law Rev 2:225
Taylor SJ, Bogdan R (1998) Introduction to Qualitative Research Methods, 3rd edn. Wiley, New York
Thoma A (2000) Criminal Law and Procedure. In: Neocleous A, Campbell D (eds) Introduction to Cyprus Law. Yorkhill, Albany, NY
Thomas CW, Fitch WA (1976) Prosecutorial Decision Making. Am Law Rev 13:507
Tombs J, Moody S (1993) Alternatives to Prosecution: The Public Interest Redefined. Crim Law Rev 1993:357
Tornaritis C (1969) Constitutional and legal problems in the Republic of Cyprus. Public Information Office, Nicosia
Tornaritis C (1971) The Rights, Duties and Responsibilities of the Attorney General of the Republic in Relation to Legislation. Cyprus Law Trib 2:6
Tornaritis C (1974) Forward. The Office of the Attorney General of the Republic of Cyprus (in Greek). Nicosia
Tornaritis C (1975) The Legal Position of the Attorney General vis a vis the House of Representatives. Cyprus Law Trib 2:3
Tornaritis C (1980) Cyprus and its Constitutional and Other Legal Problems. Nicosia

Tornaritis C (1981) The Legal Advisory State Function in the Republic of Cyprus. UM, Nicosia
Tornaritis C (1982) The Cyprus Constitutional Law. The Cyprus Research Centre, Nicosia
Tornaritis C (1983a) The Constitutional Powers of the Attorney General. UM, Nicosia
Tornaritis C (1983b) The Operation of the European Convention for the Protection of Human Rights in the Republic of Cyprus. Cyprus Law Rev 3:455
Tornaritis C (1983c) The Constitutional Power of the Attorney General to Institute, carry out and discontinue any criminal proceedings. Cyprus Law Rev 2:203
Tornaritis C (1984) The Legal System of the Republic of Cyprus. UM, Nicosia
Tornaritis C (1985) Modern Trends Concerning the Reduction of Prosecutions. Cyprus Law Rev 11(2):1744
Trow M (1957) A Comment on Participant Observation and Interviewing: A Comparison, Human Organisations, Vol. 16, No. 3
Van Daele D (2004) The Belgian Prosecution Service. In: Tak JP (ed) Tasks and Powers of the Prosecution Services in the EU Member States, vol I. Wolf, Nijmegen
Van Den Wyngaert C (1993) Criminal Procedure Systems in the European Community. Butterworths, London
Van Maanen J (1988) Tales of the Field: on Writing Ethnography. University of Chicago Press, Chicago
Van Maanen J, Kolb D (1985) The Professional Apprentice: Observations on Fieldwork Roles in Two Organizational Settings. In: Bacharach SB and Mitchell SM, Research in the sociology of organizations. JAI Press, Greenwich
Vennard J (1985) Decisions to Prosecute: Screening Policies and Practices in the United States. Criminal Law Rev 1985:20
Verrest P (2000) The French Public Prosecution Service. Eur J Crime Crim Law Crim Justice 8 (3):210
Vidmar N (2002) Juries and Lay Assessors in the Commonwealth: A Contemporary Survey. Crim Law Forum 13:385
Vogel M (2007) Coercion to Compromise: Plea Bargaining, the Courts and the Making of Political Authority. Oxford University Press, New York
Wade M (2005) The Changing Role of European Prosecution. Eur Soc Criminol Newsl 4(2):3
Wade M (2008) The Januses of Justice – How Prosecutors Define the Kind of Justice done Across Europe. Eur J Crime Crim Law Crim Justice 16(4):433
Walsh D (2004) Public Prosecutors in Ireland. In: Tak JP (ed) Tasks and Powers of the Prosecution Services in the EU Member States, vol I. Wolf, Nijmegen
Walter VG (2000) Constitutional Conditions for a Public Prosecutor's Office at the European level. Eur J Crime Crim Law Crim Justice 8(3):296
Walther S (2000) The Position and Structure of the Prosecutor's Office in the United States. Eur J Crime Crim Law Crim Justice 2000:283
Weigend T (2004) The Prosecution Service in the German Administration of Criminal Justice. In: Tak JP (ed) Tasks and Powers of the Prosecution Services in the EU Member States, vol I. Wolf, Nijmegen
Whitty N, Murphy T, Livingstone S (2001) Civil liberties Law: the Human Rights Act Era. Butterworths, London
Williams G (1956) Discretion in Prosecuting. Crim Law Rev 1956:22
Williams G (1985) Letting off the guilty and prosecuting the innocent. Crim Law Rev 1985:115
Worboys P (1985) Convincing the Right Person on the Right Evidence. Crim Law Rev 1985:764
Working Party on Public Prosecutions (Northern Ireland) (1971) Report of the Working Party on Public Prosecutions, Cmnd 554. HMSO, Belfast (MacDermott Report)
Young R (1996) Will Widgery do? Court Clerks, Discretion, and the Determination of Legal Applications. In: Young R, Wall D (eds) Access to Criminal Justice: Legal Aid, Lawyers and the Defence of Liberty. Blackstone, London
Zimring NE, Johnson DT (2005) On the Comparative Study of Corruption. The British Journal of Criminology 45(6): 793–809

Index

GPSR Compliance

The European Union's (EU) General Product Safety Regulation (GPSR) is a set of rules that requires consumer products to be safe and our obligations to ensure this.

If you have any concerns about our products, you can contact us on ProductSafety@springernature.com

In case Publisher is established outside the EU, the EU authorized representative is:

Springer Nature Customer Service Center GmbH
Europaplatz 3
69115 Heidelberg, Germany

Batch number: 10755292

Printed by Printforce, the Netherlands